Arrow in the Blue

ARTHUR KOESTLER

Arrow in the Blue

THE FIRST VOLUME
OF AN AUTOBIOGRAPHY: 1905–31

With a new preface by the author

THE DANUBE EDITION

STEIN AND DAY/*Publishers*/New York

FIRST STEIN AND DAY EDITIONS 1984

Arrow in the Blue was published in the United States of America
by Macmillan Publishing Co., Inc., and is reprinted by arrangement.

First American Danube Edition 1969
Originally published in Great Britain in 1952
by Collins with Hamish Hamilton

© 1954 by Arthur Koestler
This edition © 1969 by Arthur Koestler

All rights reserved, Stein and Day, Incorporated
Printed in the United States of America
Stein and Day/*Publishers*
Scarborough House
Briarcliff Manor, N.Y. 10510

Library of Congress Cataloging in Publication Data

Koestler, Arthur, 1905-
    Arrow in the blue.

    Reprint. Previously published: New York: Macmillan,
1969. (The Danube edition)
    1. Koestler, Arthur, 1905-   —Biography—Youth.
2. Authors, English—20th century—Biography. I. Title.
PR6021.04Z463 1984   828'.91209 [B]   83-40349
ISBN 0-8128-2997-2
ISBN 0-8128-6217-1 (pbk.)

'I fled in vain; everywhere I found the Law.
I must give in; Gate, admit the host.
Trembling heart, submit to the master—
To him in me who is more me than myself.'

PAUL CLAUDEL

Passages in this book which appear between quotes without indication of source are quotations from my earlier books. I have adopted this method to avoid the tedium of frequent references to my own work. Where such references are made, I had a special reason for indicating the date or context of the passage quoted.

My warm and sincere thanks are due to Jack and Chris Newsom, of Point Pleasant, Pennsylvania, for working over the manuscript, for their friendship, criticism and encouragement.

A.K.

Contents

Arrow in the Blue

Preface to the Danube Edition

I wrote this autobiographical account when I was forty-six. Now, at sixty-four, I would of course write it differently; but to tamper with it would be cheating. One cannot relive one's life, nor should one rewrite it. Reading through the proofs of this new edition after so many years, I often sweated with embarrassment. But that is a common experience with writers, even if the book is not autobiographical, as one's taste and style are bound to have changed in the course of time. However, in so far as the strictly autobiographical aspect is concerned, I was surprised to discover that although today I would mould the stuff differently, my view of the people and events, including the anti-hero of this tale, has remained essentially unaltered. I am not sure whether this is a comforting or a depressing thought.

A.K.

Alpbach, Tyrol
July, 1969

Part One

AHOR AND BABO

1905 – 1921

*And he went on talking about himself,
not realising that this was not as interesting to the others as it was to him.*

TOLSTOY:
The Cossacks

I. The Horoscope

FROM the beginnings of civilisation man has held the belief that the constellation of heavenly bodies at the moment of his birth had an influence on his fate. It occurred to me that the constellation of earthly events at that moment might also be of some significance and, one day in 1946, I decided to cast my secular horoscope. The idea is not as far-fetched as it might appear. Astrology is founded on the belief that man is formed by his cosmic environment; Marx held that he is the product of his social environment. I believe both propositions to be true : hence the idea of the secular horoscope. The reason why it did not occur to people long ago is, I believe, that until the relatively recent invention of the daily newspaper they had no sure means of finding out what was happening on this earth at the moment of their birth, whereas they did have the means of knowing with considerable accuracy what had happened in the skies. This is obviously due to the greater reliability of heavenly as compared to human bodies; you can calculate to the fraction of a degree where Sirius will be in a million years, but you cannot predict your cook's spatial position within the next five minutes.

The process of casting one's earthly horoscope is simple. All I had to do was to visit *The Times* publishing offices in Printing House Square, London, and ask to be shown the paper's issue of the morning following my birth—which had taken place on September 5, 1905, at approximately half-past three in the afternoon. After a while, a heavy volume, containing copies of the August and September, 1905, issues, was brought to me. I was offered the use of a small reading-room equipped with a desk, a chair, inkpot and blotter; and there, in comfortable seclusion, I installed myself and began turning the slightly yellowed pages of the bulky tome. Into the quiet room, through the window overlooking the Thames, came the faint sound of a tugboat's whistle, wailing in nostalgia for the sea. I felt the mild, mellow excitement of the excavator burrowing into the past, tinged with the more acute thrill of the astrologer calculating the orbits of fate of an important client.

To prolong the pleasure, I started on the periphery, as it were, of the field of force which had existed at the hour of my birth; that is, with the advertisements. The first to catch my eye was, curiously enough, THE LITERARY MACHINE (as supplied to H.M. the King), described as DELICIOUSLY LUXURIOUS, and priced from seventeen shillings and six-pence upward. The machine, however, was a disappoint-ment for it turned out to be nothing more than a contraption 'for holding a book in any position over an easy chair, bed or sofa.'

Turning to ENTERTAINMENTS, I found that in the Crystal Palace a Colonial and Indian Exhibition was taking place, including 'Displays by Native Warriors at 2.30, 4.30, and 6 o'clock,' while a *Café Chantant* was scheduled for 4 and 8 p.m., and a National Fireworks Display was also announced —not, however, to celebrate my birth, but in honour of the French Fleet's visit to Spithead.

The greatest amount of advertising space was devoted to carriages such as broughams, landaus, landaulets, victorias, coaches, and brakes, to harness and saddles, and, above all, to horses of all colours, ages, and temperaments, including a matched pair of fifteen-hand, bay, carriage horses, both warranted sound, 'valuable to a nervous or timid person,' for sale, on fourteen days' approval, for the handsome price of 150 guineas. Motor cars were as yet hardly represented, and their one timid appearance in the 'Miscellaneous' column did not sound encouraging: 'A GENTLEMAN having a 28-36 Daimler Motor Car' announced that he 'would be PLEASED to LET same—with Personal Services—by day, week or month, at home or on the Continent.' Obviously, he must have grown quickly tired of his machine. This seemed excusable in view of the fact that on the same day a Royal Commission on the Motor Car Acts, headed by Viscount Selby, had been appointed to inquire into and report on, among other problems, 'the injury to the Roads alleged to be caused by Motor Cars.'

The gentleman with the Daimler was the only disturbing element in the cavalcade of horses, brakes, and broughams on the advertisement page. The printer's ink had been dry for so many years that it no longer smelt of its substance but of its meaning: of fresh leather and the perspiration on horses' flanks—with a touch of lavender provided by a 'Miss Smallwood of the Leas, Great Malvern,' who was 'anxious to obtain orders for the embroidering of Initials on handker-chiefs—having several Ladies in her Society who earn their living by this kind of work.' I passed on to the Situations-Wanted column where I found a perplexing number of Ladies strongly Recommending their Coachmen, whose Character and Work were mostly described as Excellent. This set me dreaming, but I was brought back to sober reality by the Young German Merchant who, with a Good Knowledge of the Rudiments of the English Language, was seeking a position with a good English firm, as Unsalaried Clerk. Maybe Herr von Ribbentrop, who knows?

So far my horoscope had not taught me much. Turning to the inside pages, I found that while I was in the act of being born, the German Emperor and Empress had attended the autumn Parade of the Guards Brigade at Tempelhof; that King Edward had given a dinner party at the Kursaal at

Marienbad, in Bohemia, for twenty-nine guests, including the Princess Murat, Adeline Duchess of Bedford, and the Marquise of Ganay; that the cholera outbreak in Prussia had claimed twenty-four deaths during the preceding twenty-four hours; that sixteen cases of the Plague had occurred in Zanzibar, and that the Englishman captured by Brigands in Macedonia, Mr. Philip Mills, employé of the Monastir Tobacco Régie, was still alive and still in the hands of his captors. A Violent Gale on Lake Superior had caused the death of twenty sailors; Prince Henry of Prussia had lunched with Rear Admiral Winsloe, commanding the Destroyer Division of the Channel Fleet cruising in the Baltic; the Trade Union Congress had been resumed at Hanley, where the President, Mr. J. Sexton (National Dock Labourers, Liverpool), had urged the necessity of abolishing monopoly in land ownership. Abroad, the Paris *Le Temps,* commenting upon the insurrection in Morocco and the Franco-German complications arising therefrom, was quoted as saying: 'To use an expression which cannot fail to be welcomed in Germany, we shall make the Maghzen feel the weight of our mailed fist until he decides to recognise our rights. . . .'

'Fire, fire!' I said to myself. 'This is becoming significant. Mars enters the Second House.' And, sure enough, the next items struck certain chords whose vibrations were to accompany me for many years:

FIERCE FIGHTING IN THE CAUCASUS

Tiflis, September 5th, 1905

News from Baku is becoming worse hour by hour. The Black Town is in flames and innumerable other incendiary fires have broken out. The troops are acting with the utmost vigour but have not succeeded in restoring order. . . .

The Russian revolution of 1905 was getting into its stride. The events in Baku on my birthday were the prelude to the first general strike in modern history. Revolutionary action by socialist terrorists was being met by the counter-revolutionary action of patriotic terrorists. The latter, known as the Black Hundred, with the connivance of the government and the police, were engaging in anti-Jewish pogroms to side-track popular discontent.

DISTURBANCES AT KISHINEFF

Kishineff, September 5th, 1905

A poor woman who had been killed by hooligans was buried here today, her funeral being attended by Jews and Russian workmen. Shots were suddenly fired and a number of Police and dragoons with drawn swords appeared and charged the procession, wounding many. In the confusion the coffin fell in the street and was removed by sympathisers. The colonel commanding the gendarmerie refused to give any explanation of the affair. . . . The greatest alarm prevails in the town. The total number of killed and wounded cannot be ascertained at present.

It sounded to me like the tuning of the orchestra just before the conductor lifts his wand. My horoscope was taking shape. It did so completely when I began to read the Editorial of the day. It referred to an event that had taken place on September 5th, at 3.47 p.m., the very hour of my birth; and which in the editorialist's opinion represented :

. . . an event of the greatest moment, not merely in the political history of the world, but in the unending moral and intellectual process which we roughly describe as civilisation—a fact of the very highest importance.
To predict with any certainty the consequences of so great a revolution passes the powers of man. We can do

little more than take note of it, and indicate one or two of the directions in which it may perhaps tend to mould thought and character in the world. . . . The great end of all this training has been the subordination of the individual to the family, the tribe, and the State. It teaches that man does not live for himself alone, or even chiefly for himself. His first duty is his collective duty to the different social groups into which he is born. From his boyhood he is hourly and carefully trained to the fulfilment of this duty. He is taught not merely to school his actions and his features, but his very thoughts and feelings and impulses in obedience to it. There is much for the West to learn from this almost monastic discipline of the character, and something also for it to avoid. . . .

The event referred to was the signing of the Treaty of Peace at Portsmouth, New Hampshire, between His Majesty the Autocrat of all the Russias and His Majesty the Emperor of Japan. The rapturous eulogies of *The Times* leader-writer referred to the training of the victorious Japanese for 'the subordination of the individual to the tribe and the State.' That was the lesson which, in his opinion, the West, with its excessive individualism, had to learn from the 'monastic discipline' of the first modern totalitarian state, as it triumphantly emerged from Asiatic obscurity on to the political scene. The clock that struck the hour of my birth also announced the end of the era of liberalism and individualism, of that harshly competitive and yet easy-going civilisation which had succeeded in reconciling, thanks to a unique, kindly-callous compromise, the slogan of 'survival of the fittest' with that of *'laissez faire, laissez aller.'*

If, in the secular horoscope, political events correspond to planetary constellations, then the fixed stars should be represented by the men who, in a slower and more lasting way, shape the features of their age. Thus, to complete the picture, I should mention that in the year and month of my birth the Examiner of Patents at the Patent Office in Berne, Switzerland, published a paper 'On the Electrodynamics of Moving Bodies,' signed Albert Einstein; that in the same year Sigmund Freud published his *Three Lectures on the Theory of Sexuality,* Wells published *Kipps* and *A Modern Utopia,* Thomas Mann published *Koenigliche Hoheit,* Tolstoy published *An Afterword on Chekhov's Story 'Darling';* that *La Grande Revue,* in Paris, called the works of Le Douanier Rousseau, Cézanne, Matisse, and the other Wild Beasts exhibited at the Salon d'Automne 'ridiculous beyond words,' and Picasso sold his drawings to the dealer, Soulier, for twenty francs apiece.

As if to round off the horoscope, there also appeared in my birthday issue of *The Times* a letter by a gentleman writing under the pseudonym of 'Vidi'—though Jeremiah would have been equally fitting—which, *inter alia,* said:

Today it is discouraging to see the lessons of that ordeal [the Boer War] still unlearnt, the warnings in great part unheeded, and all classes of the Nation bent on gratifying an un-English passion for luxury and excitement. Large ideas seem to be tabooed and empty cleverness exalted; responsibilities to be ignored; a hand-to-mouth happy-go-luckiness to be the prevailing mood, and (sorry homage to Carlyle!) the dominant spirit to be visible even in the streets, where women of all classes dress at 10 a.m. as though life was a perpetual garden party. The exaggerations of sport, against which Mr. Kipling pungently protested, are as manifest as ever, and the ravages of various forms of alcoholism unabated....

When I closed the bulky, black tome and left the office in Printing House Square, it seemed to me that my secular horoscope had yielded as much information as the stars ever would on the field of force into which I was born, and on the influences that were to shape my character and fate. Nevertheless, I sometimes feel that to say this is blasphemy, and that the mediæval astrologer, that prophetic clown with his black, pointed hat and ornate silken robe, had a truer inkling of the essence of man's destiny than the politicians and psychiatrists of our day. But this feeling itself may, of course, be determined by my horoscope—by the fact that I was born at the moment when the sun was setting on the Age of Reason.

II. The Koestler Saga

THE family tree of the Koestlers starts with my grand-father Leopold and ends with me.

Leopold X fled during the Crimean War from Russia across the Carpathian mountains to Hungary. I have to call him 'X' because Koestler was not his real name, and he never disclosed his real name to anybody, not even to his children. All that is known about him is that he arrived in the good town of Miskolcz, Hungary, some time in the eighteen-sixties, and that somehow he assumed there the name of Koestler, Köstler, Kestler or Kesztler—all of which figure on various documents.

Why he had fled from Russia is unknown. He may have been a deserter from the army, or he may have been involved in the Social-Revolutionary movement, or again, he may have committed a crime. Naturally, I prefer to believe that he was a Social Revolutionary.

He died in 1911, when I was six. I remember him as a tall and gentle patriarch with a flowing white beard, who was always dressed in a morning coat—this I deduce from the fact that I can still see his characteristic gesture of part-ing and lifting the black tails of his coat before lowering him-self into his rocking-chair.

My only other memory of Leopold X is connected with a ham sandwich. On sunny mornings he used to take me for a walk along one of the pretty, chestnut-shaded avenues of Budapest, called *Városligeti fasor,* which means, literally, 'The row of trees in the town park.' In a small side street off

this avenue there was a delicatessen store, where on each of
our outings the old man bought me a delicious ham sandwich but never one for himself. When one day I asked him
the reason for this, he explained : 'It would be wrong for me
to eat ham but it is not wrong for you. I was brought up
in prejudice.' This pronouncement stuck in my memory
because of its baffling nature in general, and because the
word 'prejudice' in particular was unknown to me at the
time. Its meaning was explained to me later by my mother.
Leopold X had been brought up in strict observance of the
Mosaic law which taboos the eating of pork; and though he
granted his son and grandson full freedom in matters of
worship, he himself stuck to his tradition—referring to it,
with courteous irony, as 'prejudice.' It was an attitude which
combined respect for tradition with enlightened tolerance :
he must have been a Social Revolutionary after all.

Before we part with gentle and obscure Leopold, a brief
mention must be made of his social background and financial status. Indirect evidence suggests that the X family, back
in Russia, belonged to the comfortable middle classes. The
points of evidence are, firstly, certain parcels with foreign
stamps on them, which Leopold received at lengthy intervals. These particular parcels were not brought to our home
by the postman but collected by Leopold himself at the post
office, and opened by him in the privacy of his room; they
were found to contain various gifts of impressive character,
such as silken scarfs, lacework, and the like. Secondly, there
is old Leopold's famous remark made on the one and only
occasion when he talked to my mother about his own family.
This occurred while my mother was showing him a new
evening gown, which probably aroused some distant
memory, for he said wistfully : 'My dear, my own mother
had an evening dress made of silk so heavy, and embroidered with gold thread so rich, that she never had to put it
on a hanger—it stood up by itself, preserving its shape.' But

as the garment in question may have harked back to the days of the crinoline, the evidence is not conclusive. But, thirdly and lastly, his manner of parting and lifting the tails of his morning coat as a preliminary to seating himself betrayed beyond doubt a social background thoroughly conversant with rocking-chairs and other civilised comforts of life.

However that may be, he seems to have prospered for a while after settling down in the town of Miskolcz. He married the daughter of the proprietor of a saw-mill, or the daughter of a judge somehow connected with the saw-mill, I can't remember exactly : at any rate, he directed a saw-mill until it burnt down and he went bankrupt. Bankruptcy, as will be seen, is endemic in my family, and each time it occurs, turns into an unexpected blessing. In this first case, it induced Leopold to migrate with his wife and four small children from provincial Miskolcz to metropolitan Budapest.

In Budapest, during my father's childhood, the family lived on the borderline between the lower-middle and the working class. Leopold never found his feet again. He was unable to give his children anything beyond the education which the Austro-Hungarian monarchy provided for the poor in the eighteen-seventies and eighties. His two daughters, my aunts Jenny and Betty, were married off in a hurry, the one to a bank messenger, the other to a printer's apprentice. His eldest son, my Uncle Jonas, became an accountant's clerk and remained one to the end of his days. His youngest son, Henrik, who in due time was to become my father, started his career as a draper's errand boy.

Thus the Koestlers' fortunes had hit rock bottom and would probably never have risen again had my father not been an infant prodigy—infant prodigies are another endemic trait in my family. He was fourteen when he became an errand boy with the firm of Sommer and Grunwald in Budapest. His working day began at 7.30 a.m., but he got up every morning at four o'clock and spent the next three hours learning German, English, and French—walking up and down in the town park during the warm season, grinding away at his ragged, second-hand grammar-books in the half-dark kitchen during the winter. To learn one foreign language, untutored, at the dawn of a ten-hour working day, would have been a remarkable achievement; to embark on three at the same time was the first of those wildly optimistic and extravagant enterprises which were to succeed each other as long as he lived. As the years wore on, these ventures became more and more fantastic, and ended in plain absurdity; but his youth was a variant of the American success-story of the late nineteenth century, transplanted to the shores of the Danube. He rose within ten years from errand boy to salesman, to general manager, to junior partner. At the age of twenty-nine, when he married my mother, he had travelled in Germany and England, made personal contacts with manufacturers in those countries, and opened a firm of his own.

He was a short man with quick movements charged with energy; his brown, naïve eyes and his dark hair parted in the middle by a straight line as if drawn with a ruler, gave his face a kind of neat and tidy look which sometimes made people mistake him for an American. This flattered him, though he admired England first and foremost, always dressed in English clothes and, in all innocence, made my life hellish by ordering for me, when I was thirteen, an Eton suit—the first ever seen in Budapest—and forcing me to wear it, to the unending hilarity of my schoolmates. He was an incredible mixture of shrewdness and childishness, of ingenuity and ingenuousness. As every spare hour of the hard years of his adolescence was spent over his French, English, and German grammars, he never learnt to read for pleasure; the only book of literature he read during his whole life was *The Three Musketeers,* by Alexandre Dumas. Except for the opera, which he loved, he never went to the theatre, nor the cinema; the Arts did not exist for him. But he devoured newspapers, reading every line, except the stories and fiction serials; and he had a passion for articles on popular science.

I once showed his handwriting to a woman friend, a professional graphologist. 'Do you know this person well?' she asked. 'Fairly well.' 'You do pick up the most extraordinary people,' she said. 'The man who wrote this is completely uneducated, but he has an exuberant, explosive fantasy-life —the kind you find in schizophrenics who paint those marvellous pictures. Come to think of it, maybe he *is* a schizo.' I said: 'He is my father.' We did not pursue the subject.

The inhuman routine of getting up at four, of denying himself the pleasures and indulgences of youth, had resulted in a curiously distorted mental pattern. The emotional satisfaction normally derived from reading a poem or watching a thriller having remained unknown to him, the only outlets he found for his explosive imagination were business ventures of a remarkable nature.

One day—I must have been seven or eight at the time— a truck drawn by six horses rumbled into the courtyard of our apartment house, and half a dozen men, sweating and groaning, carried a monstrous machine up the stairs into our smoking-room. This machine, my father explained with his usual enthusiasm, was the working model of an invention with tremendous possibilities, which he had decided to finance. 'But what does it do?' asked my mother. 'You will see,' he said, beaming. 'The inventor will demonstrate it to us himself. He is a genius, called Professor Nathan.' A few minutes later, the inventor arrived, an astonishingly dirty little man, hunchbacked and bearded, who looked like one of Snow White's seven dwarfs. For a couple of hours he fiddled with the wires, wheels, and levers in the belly of the machine, causing it to emit an occasional frightening spark, for the contraption was operated by electricity. In the end there came a big flash, darkness descended over the flat, accompanied by the smell of burnt rubber and the shrieks of the cook and maid who had joined the family to watch the proceedings. Professor Nathan, unperturbed, declared that there had been a short-circuit, and that he would be back the next day with some wire and other essential ingredients. I was given my supper by romantic candle light and spent most of the night sleepless with excitement, trying to guess what the machine was for. The next morning, after breakfast, Professor Nathan arrived and went to work again. I was only permitted to watch the proceedings through the doorway because, my mother insisted, the machine was dangerous and might explode. After an hour or so the thing really started to work. It rumbled and clattered like an old-fashioned printing press, and its huge body, which occupied half the length of a wall, trembled so violently that all the ash-trays, bronze nymphs, and cuspidors in the smoking-room danced on their bases. My father shook Professor Nathan solemnly by the hand, and now at last proceeded to demonstrate the purpose of the machine to the assembled household. While we watched with bulging eyes, the Professor handed him a briefcase which contained a bundle of tattered envelopes of various sizes. My father took the bundle and pushed the sealed envelopes, one by one, into a slot in the machine while Professor Nathan, standing on tip-toe at the other end, extracted from a second slot the same envelopes after they had passed through the machine— waving each over his head with earnest pride, like a con-jurer displaying a rabbit. The envelopes which had entered the machine sealed were now cut open.

'Isn't it a stupendous invention?' cried my father, happy as a child. 'Stupendous,' 'grandiose,' 'fabulous,' and 'colossal' were his favourite expressions. If business was 'colossal,' it meant, on his scale of semantics, that it was moderately good. If it was merely wonderful, we were on the verge of bankruptcy.

'But what is it for?' asked my mother, displaying the nervous tic which made its appearance whenever she was worried or agitated. The tic consisted of a twitching of her eyebrows and a slight tremor of her chin, accompanied by a faint clucking noise in her throat which was only audible when you knew about it. But my father did know about it; that faint sound was enough to prick the bubble of his happiness instantaneously.

'But can't you see that it is tremendous?' he cried. 'Imagine the millions of working hours it will save those American firms with their colossal number of incoming letters!' He went on talking with an enthusiasm which by now had become artificial; the maid and the cook had slunk back to the kitchen; my mother, without a word but with an audible cluck-cluck, went to her room, and still he continued talking, now only to me, sole disciple of a lonely prophet, ready to betray him before the cock crowed thrice, until I burst into tears.

Soon afterwards the envelope-cutting wonder machine disappeared from the flat, never to be mentioned again, leaving as its only memory a large patch of scorched wallpaper in the smoking-room. The next fabulous adventure that I remember came a few years later, when my father opened the first factory in Europe for the manufacture of radio-active toilet soap.

This was in 1916, during the First World War. We were then living in a boarding-house for, soon after the war started, my mother had decided that running a household was bad for her recurrent migraines; so we gave up our flat and from my ninth year onward we led a gipsy life in hotels, boarding-houses, and furnished rooms, in Budapest or Vienna, moving to new quarters on an average of once every three months, according to the ups and downs of the family fortune. The particular boarding-house at which we were living when the radio-active venture started was called

Pension Moderne, and numbered among its guests a doctor
of philosophy and chemistry by the name of Aladar Bedoe.
He was one of the best-looking men I have ever seen; he had
dark, wavy hair, the high forehead of a scholar, the flashing
eyes of a seducer, a coquettish black moustache, and a quick,
winning, gold-studded smile; in addition to all these assets,
his brother was a *monsignor* and one of the highest digni-
taries of the Roumanian church. In short, he was so much
the opposite of poor Professor Nathan that this time even
my sceptical mother was sold on the radio-active soap.

Thirty-five years ago 'radium' was still a new and magic
word, which the layman associated with Madame Curie, X-
rays, and mysterious healing powers. One day Dr. Bedoe
told my father that he had discovered, a hundred miles from
Budapest, a deposit of clay which contained radium.
'Stupendous!' my father said. 'What are you going to do
with that radium?' Dr. Bedoe's eyes flashed and he broke
into his gilt-edged smile. 'Make soap,' he said.

That is how it started. Dr. Bedoe produced a pound of his
precious clay, and my father sent it to a chemical laboratory.
The analysis showed traces of radio-activity. Any other
sample of clay, rock, or mineral deposit would, of course, also
have shown traces of radio-activity, but this my father did
not know. He did not even look up 'radium' in the encyclopedia. Nor the process of soapmaking. His enthusiasm
carried him along. And what is most amazing, the project
succeeded.

What made it succeed was the wartime shortage of soap
as well as the fatty quality of the clay which, mixed with a
foam-producing agent called Saponin and some scent, made
quite a passable *ersatz* soap. Dr. B. and my father became
partners and opened a small factory in Buda, which went by
the name of Frybourg Chemical Works. When my father
was asked why 'Frybourg,' he gave the same answer my

grandfather Leopold had given when asked why, of all names, he had chosen that of Koestler: 'Because it sounds so nice.' Which in turn reminds one of the answer Gérard de Nerval gave his friends when they asked him why he was walking on the boulevards trailing a lobster at the end of a blue ribbon: *'Parce qu'il est tellement gentil.'*[1]

The Frybourg Chemical Works made radio-active toilet soap and kitchen soap; later it branched out into the production of radio-active brass polish and radio-active cleaning powder. It flourished throughout the war and the Revolution of 1918, and even during the subsequent Hungarian Commune, which nationalised the factory and made my father its managing director.

The truly remarkable thing about all this seems to me that with a mentality as described, my father was, during long stretches, a highly successful businessman. As I grew up I became more and more puzzled by the paradox that a person with such a gullible, and indeed childlike, character could be capable of extracting money from the hard world of commerce. Much later, when I became acquainted with some really big money-makers, the paradox became even more pronounced. The financial heavyweights who have crossed my path—publishers, art-dealers, bankers, movie producers—have been without exception idiosyncratic, eccentric, irrational, and basically naïve individuals; almost the exact opposite of the popular image of the hard, shrewd businessman. Apparently, the shrewd, cold, calculating type is mainly to be found in the light and middle-weight categories of business; while moneymaking on a truly large scale is a special talent, unrelated to intelligence, like playing the trombone or roller skating. And, alas, it is not hereditary.

[1] For the sake of accuracy I ought to mention that my father wrote his name 'Köstler.' So did I; until I bought my first portable typewriter which had no 'ö' on its keyboard. So I had to spell it 'Koestler,' which looks much nicer, and which I have stuck to ever since.

The foregoing data about Leopold X and my father may serve to establish my social background, or rather absence thereof. My formative years resemble a breathless journey on a scenic railway—my father in front, crying 'stupendous,' 'titanic,' and 'colossal,' and my mother swooning, as the little car races upward and downward and swerves wildly around the curves.

My father died in 1939; my mother is, as I write this, a youthful eighty-one, living in yet another boarding-house in London, England. The awareness that she is going to read this passage in print has the same paralysing effect which prevented me as a child from keeping a diary—knowing that wherever I hid it, it would be found and read by her.

In 1947, when she was seventy-seven, my mother came to visit my wife and me on our sheep farm in North Wales. On the day of her arrival she looked over my books in the library.

'*Ach,*' she said in her cosy Viennese, 'so you have the books of that Dr. Freund.'

'Freud, Mama, Freud, not Freund!' I wailed.

'Freud or Freund, who cares? I have never bothered to remember his name.'

'You mean you knew him?' asked my wife, thrilled.

'*Aber natürlich.* He always tried to get on social terms with the family, through your Aunt Lore, but he was never invited. He was *ein ekelhafter Kerl,* a disgusting fellow.'

'But do tell us all about it,' cried my wife. 'How did you come to know him?'

'Through Aunt Lore. Aunt Lore was a very respected person in Viennese society, but she sometimes had strange ideas—she was somewhat *überspannt,* overstrung, you know....'

It transpired that Aunt Lore, in the eighteen nineties, had conducted a finishing school in Vienna, where the daughters of respectable burghers were prepared for matrimony by courses in petit-point, the baking of chocolate cakes, playing the piano, and by acquiring the elements of that peculiar French whose main purpose was to make possible remarks at table which the serving maid was not supposed to understand. ('*La soupe aujourd'hui est brûlée. C'est parce que la femme de la cuisine a de la malaise.*')

Aunt Lore had somehow met young Dr. Freud and had been impressed by him. My mother suffered, as a girl, from violent headaches; so, on Aunt Lore's insistence, it was decided to send her to that doctor. She saw him two or three times, and then refused to see him again. 'But why?' asked my wife. 'What did he do to you?'

'He massaged my neck and asked me silly questions. I told you he was *ein ekelhafter Kerl.*'

With some arithmetic, we worked out that these visits had taken place around 1899, at the time when Freud and Breuer published their *Studies in Hysteria.* Had my mother continued the treatment, she would probably have married someone else, and I would not have been born. My mother, however, shrugged off this hypothesis as 'overstrung'; then remarked with a wistful look : 'In my youth I met much greater celebrities than your Doctor Freud. I can still remember a ball I attended when I was eighteen—you would never guess who asked me for the first waltz. . . .' She paused for a moment, then cried triumphantly :

'Balduin Groller !'

Balduin Groller was a fashionable Viennese humorist of those days, and forgotten long before he died.

My mother came from one of the old Jewish families of Prague, alleged to be descended from the High Rabbi Loeb —the scholar and kabbalist who, according to legend, created the Golem, a Frankenstein monster of clay, to defend the threatened inhabitants of the Prague ghetto. To save embarrassment—political or otherwise—to members of this family who still live in Vienna or Prague, I shall call them 'the Hitzigs.'

My great-grandfather Hitzig was a man of letters who wrote a treatise *Zur Reform der Volks-und Staatswirt-schaftlichen Zustände* in three volumes, and, as my mother never fails to point out when talking about 'the family,' was awarded a Grave of Honour in the Vienna cemetery by the literary club 'Concordia.' A Grave of Honour is certainly no mean distinction; in the mind of every Hitzig it represents, together with Aunt Lore's high-class finishing school, and the fact that a distant Hitzig-in-law had actually been Minister of Finance under Emperor Francis Joseph, an essential part of the glamour of the past, before the Fall.

The Fall came about in the eighteen nineties, when one of the Hitzig girls fell in love with, and married, despite her parents' protests, a villainous adventurer. The villain borrowed money on a promissory note and, in classic villain-ous tradition, induced my mother's father to endorse it. When the note became due my grandfather was ruined, and the other Hitzigs banded together to save the family honour. They hushed up the scandal and arranged everything with the required decorum—and again in the classic tradition, bought Grandfather a passage to America, there to atone for his disgrace. He must have been eager to grasp the oppor-tunity, for he vanished from the scene, never to return. A photograph, dated Washington, Mass., 1907, shows him sitting in a rocking-chair, with a beard, a pipe, and a dog. And that was the last the family ever heard of him.

Thus both my grandfathers broke the sacred ties of the Victorian family. The one entered the scene from nowhere, the other vanished into nowhere; both were restless exiles and runaways. In this respect, at least, I have conformed to the family tradition.

My mother's chronic headaches, irritability, and nervous

tic were probably caused by the sudden Fall of the Hitzigs and the abrupt changes it entailed. She had been a pretty, witty, and much courted girl; almost overnight she became that Cinderella of the Victorian age—the unmarried eldest daughter without a dowry. Worst of all, she had to leave her beloved Vienna and go to live with a married sister in Budapest.

She never ceased to regard the Magyars as a nation of barbarians, and though she lived for nearly half a century in Budapest, refused to learn Hungarian properly. This proved to be a blessing where my own future was concerned, for I was brought up bilingually, talking Hungarian at school and German at home. That I was called 'Arthur,' a name I always loathed and could never pronounce as I can't roll my 'r's,' was due to similar reasons : my mother chose the name because it sounded outlandish and had no Hungarian derivative or equivalent. Her contempt for the Hungarians made her life a kind of exile, without friends or social contacts; in consequence, I grew up without playmates. I was an only child and a lonely child; precocious, neurotic, admired for my brains and detested for my character by teachers and schoolfellows alike.

This report on my ancestry would be incomplete without a brief mention of the later fate of the Hitzigs.

My mother had one brother and one sister. The brother, my favourite uncle, married a sweet German blonde in Berlin, and became a devoted member of the Lutheran church. When the reign of Hitler became intolerable, he drowned himself in the lake adjoining their little suburban home.

The sister was called Rose. During the War old Aunt Rose lived with her daughter and her two grandchildren in a village in Czecho-Slovakia. One day in 1944, the jovial village *gendarme,* an old friend of the family, asked them all to come with him to the police station for a little formality. A few weeks later the formality was completed in the gas chamber of Auschwitz for Aunt Rose, aged seventy-two, Cousin Margit, aged forty-one, and her children Kate, aged seventeen, and Georgy, aged twelve. My mother, who had been invited to stay with them, would have shared their fate but for a quarrel with her sister which made her stay in Budapest. It must have been Providence that prevented Dr. Freud, fifty years earlier, from curing her irritability; but then, miraculous escapes are also endemic in my ancestry.

As I have said before, I am the last of the short line of Koestlers; there is no other male issue on this family tree, and with the present writer's death, which according to a gipsy prediction will be unexpected and violent, the Koestler, or Köstler, or Kestler, or Kesztler saga will come to a fitting end.

III. The Pitfalls of Autobiography

BEFORE we go any farther, it may be useful to clarify the question : Why am I writing this autobiography? This should have been done in a preface, but prefaces are so boring to read, and to write, that I have postponed the issue until the story got moving.

I believe that people write autobiographies for two main reasons. The first may be called the 'Chronicler's urge.' The second may be called the '*Ecce Homo* motive.' Both impulses spring from the same source, which is the source of all literature : the desire to share one's experiences with others, and by means of this intimate communication to transcend the isolation of the self.

The Chronicler's urge expresses the need for the sharing of experience related to external events. The *Ecce Homo* motive expresses the same need with regard to internal events.

The Chronicler is driven by the fear that the events of which he is a witness and which are part of his life, their colour, shape, and emotional impact, will be irretrievably lost to the future unless he preserves them on tablets of wax or clay, on parchment or paper, by means of a stylus or quill, typewriter or fountain pen. The Chronicler's urge dominates the autobiographies of persons who themselves have played a part in shaping the history of their times, or felt that they were better equipped than others to record it—as Defoe must have felt when he wrote his *Journal of the Plague Year*.

The *Ecce Homo* motive, on the other hand, urges men to preserve the uniqueness of their inner experiences, and results in the confessional type of autobiography—St. Augustine, Rousseau, de Quincey. It prompts dying physicians to record with minute precision their thoughts and sensations during the last hours before the curtain falls.

Obviously the Chronicler's urge and the *Ecce Homo* motive are at opposite poles on the same scale of values, like introversion and extroversion, perception and contemplation. And obviously a good autobiography ought to be a synthesis of the two—which it rarely is. The vanity of men in public life detracts from the autobiographical value of their chronicles; the introvert's obsession with himself makes him neglect the historical background against which he moves. The *Ecce Homo* motive may degenerate into sterile exhibitionism.

Thus the business of writing autobiography is full of pitfalls. On the one hand, we have the starchy chronicle of the stuffed shirt; on the other, the embarrassing nakedness of the exhibitionist—embarrassing because nakedness is only appealing in a healthy body; who but a doctor wants to look at a rash-covered skin? Apart from these two extremes there are various other snares which even competent craftsmen are rarely able to avoid. The most common of these is what one might call the 'Nostalgic Fallacy.'

With an aching, loving, bitter-sweet nostalgia, the author bends over his past like a woman over the cradle of her child; he whispers to it and rocks it in his arms, blind to the fact that the smiles, and howls, and wrigglings of his budding ego lack for his readers that unique fascination which they hold for him. Even experienced authors who know that the reader is a cold fish who has to be tickled behind the gills to make him respond, become victims of this fallacy as soon as they embark on the first chapter with the heading: 'Childhood.' The smell of lavender in mother's linen closet is so intimate; the smile on granny's face so comforting; the water in the brook behind the watercress patch by the garden fence so cool and fresh that it still caresses his fingers holding the pen; and on and on he goes about his linen closets, grannies, ponies, and watercress brooks as if they were a collective memory of all mankind and not, alas, his separate and incommunicable own. Never is the isolation of the self so acutely painful as in the frustrated attempt to share memories of those earliest and most vivid days, when out of the still fluid one-ness of the inside and outside world, out of the original mix-up of fact and fantasy, the sharp boundaries of the self were formed. The Nostalgic Fallacy is the result of the craving to melt and undo those boundaries once again.

The sagacious autobiographer will, therefore, with a sigh of regret, put the dry, crumbling, unique sprig of lavender back in the drawer as if it were a packet of common mothballs and restrict himself to relevant facts. But here the trouble starts again, for how is he to know which facts are relevant and which are not? Both the detective and the psycho-analyst affirm that apparently irrelevant facts yield the most important clues. And my experience with sleuths— whether they searched my pockets or my dreams—has convinced me that by and large the affirmation is correct. When one re-reads the entries in one's diary after five years, one is surprised to find that the most significant events are all strangely under-emphasised. Thus the selection of relevant material is a highly problematical affair, and the crux of all autobiography.

Next among the snares is the 'Dull Dog Fallacy.' A great many memoir-writers are so afraid of showing off that they portray themselves as the dullest dogs on earth. The 'Dull Dog Fallacy' requires that the first person singular in an autobiography should always appear as a shy, restrained, reserved, colourless individual; and the reader wonders how he could possibly succeed in making so many friends, in being always in the midst of interesting people, events, and emotional entanglements. But the Dull Dog is, of course, also a paragon of quiet reliability and unobtrusive decency; if he confesses to certain faults, it is merely an added sign of his modesty.

The virtues of understatement and self-restraint make social intercourse civilised and agreeable, but they have a paralysing effect on autobiography. The memoir-writer ought neither to spare himself nor hide his light under a bushel; he must obviously overcome his reluctance to relate painful and humiliating experiences, but he must also have the less obvious courage to include those experiences which show him in a favourable light.

I do not believe that either in life or in literature puritanism is a virtue. Self-castigation, yes. And self-love too—if it is as fierce and humble, exacting and resigned, accepting and rebellious, and as full of awe and wonder as love for other creatures should be. He who does not love himself, does not love well; and he who does not hate himself, does not hate well; and hatred of evil is as necessary as love if the world is not to come to a standstill. Tolerance is an acquired virtue; indifference is a native vice. 'When I have forgiven a fellow everything, I am through with him,' said Freud. And even Christ hated the moneylenders.

In 1937, during the war in Spain, when I found myself in prison with the prospect of facing a firing squad, I made a vow: if ever I got out of there alive I would write an autobiography so frank and unsparing of myself that it would make Rousseau's *Confessions* and the *Memoirs* of Cellini appear as sheer cant.

That was fifteen years ago; since then I have tried several times to fulfil that vow. I never got farther than the first few pages. The process of self-immolation is certainly painful, but that isn't the real trouble. The trouble is that it is also morbidly pleasant, like the analyst's couch. It leads to the Nostalgic Fallacy in reverse: the scent of the lavender-bag in the drawer is replaced by the sewer smells so dear to our little ids. Moreover, it offers that wrong form of catharsis which the artist learns to avoid like the plague. And whatever is bad art is also bad autobiography. I forced myself to go on because I suspected that my loathing for the job, my revulsion against turning an autobiography into a clinical case-history was due to moral cowardice; and it took me a long time to discover that in this domain the artless truth is obsessional and strident. In short, all art contains a portion of exhibitionism—but exhibitionism is not art.

There is still another aspect to this tricky problem of selecting the relevant material. There is the question: relevant to whom? To the reader, obviously. But what type of reader does the author have in mind? This question, at least, I can answer without ambiguity. The Chronicler's urge is always directed toward the unborn, future reader. This may sound presumptuous, but it is merely the expression of a natural bent. I have no idea whether fifty years from now anybody will want to read a book of mine, but I have a fairly precise idea of what makes me, as a writer, tick. It is the wish to trade a hundred contemporary readers against ten readers in ten years' time and one reader in a hundred years' time. This has always seemed to me what a writer's ambition should be. It is the point where the Chronicler's urge merges with the *Ecce Homo* motive.

IV. The Tree of Guilt—Ahor and Babo

I WAS born in the eighth year of my parents' marriage, their first and only child, when my mother was thirty-five. Everything seems to have gone wrong with my birth: I weighed over ten pounds; my mother's labour lasted two days and almost killed her. The whole unsavoury Freudian Olympus, from Oedipus Rex to Orestes, stood watch at my cradle.

As might well be expected in the case of an only child born to a woman on the threshold of middle age and frustrated by a self-imposed exile, my mother's love was excessive, possessive, and capricious. Plagued by her recurrent migraines, she was subject to abrupt changes of mood, from effusive tenderness to violent outbursts of temper, so that in my earliest years I was constantly tossed about from the emotional climate of the tropics to the arctic and back again.

From my third year onward I was given into the charge of a long succession of foreign governesses—*Fräuleins, Mademoiselles,* and Misses, who succeeded each other at intervals of various lengths until I was twelve. None of them stayed longer than a year. One pretty *Fräulein* vanished under mysterious circumstances because, as I learned later, a distant cousin of mine, one of the villain's sons, got her in the family way. An English Miss was sent packing after a fortnight when my mother found out from a photograph in her room that she had been a horseback rider in a circus. Another must have been a sadist, for my memories of her consist only of the series of elaborate punishments she inflicted on me. All these foreign governesses of the pre-1914 era had apparently come to far-away Hungary because of some freak event or catastrophe in their lives : they were the type who, had they been born men, would have joined the Foreign Legion. I still own a photograph, dated 1910, which shows a group of these weird and forbidding females assembled with their unhappy charges in the Budapest Zoo. They looked like a group of convicts in a women's prison, uniformed in bustles, cheap fur-trimmed coats, muffs, feather boas, and feathered hats.

Second in importance, both in our household and as a neurosis-forming factor, was Bertha, the parlourmaid. Her full name was Miss Bertha Búbala. She had a son called Béla Búbala who was approximately my age, born out of wedlock, and boarded out in the country. Bertha was a bony, horse-faced woman with a grudge against life which had bitten into her character and turned it acid; she was devoted to and tyrannised by my mother, and tyrannised me in turn.

I was in her care during the intervals between governesses. These periods sometimes lasted several weeks or months and, as my mother was frequently bedridden, Bertha was the one stable factor in the flux of events, and held unrestricted sway over me. The guiding rule of her reign was that the accused is guilty unless proved innocent. The memory of my early years seems to consist of a continuous series of crimes which brought in their wake an equally monotonous succession of punishments and disgraces. Though it was impossible to know beforehand whether an action constituted a crime or not, there never was any doubt in my mind about my guilt. One acquired guilt automatically, in the same way one's hands grew dirty as the day wore on : and to be in disgrace was the natural outcome of this process.

Thus the first major fact that took root in my mind was the consciousness of guilt. These roots grew quickly, silently, and greedily, like a eucalyptus tree, under the driftsand of early experience.

My mother not only tolerated but encouraged Bertha's despotism, for she saw in it the Spartan touch which would prevent me from being 'spoilt.' That children should not be spoilt, and that they must be ruled with an 'iron rod', was a basic tenet of Victorian education in general, and of the Hitzigs in particular. This conviction led to another reversal of the legal code. In the normal walks of life everything is permitted that is not forbidden by law. In my childhood everything was forbidden that was not expressly permitted.

The home which is the stage of my early memories was a typical middle middle-class flat of the turn of the century, stuffed with plush curtains, antimacassars, tassels, fringes, lace covers, bronze nymphs, cuspidors, and Meissen stags at bay; and the inevitable polar-bear skin between the piano and the potted palm. All these objects were NOT TO BE TOUCHED; outside the nursery the flat was a forest of forbidden trees and poison-ivy.

The list of major offences included : to be noisy; to answer back; to offend Bertha; to speak in the presence of strangers without being spoken to; to omit saying 'please' and 'thank you very much'; to ask for a second helping without waiting for it to be offered. But these were all explicit, identifiable offences; the dark menace of life consisted in acquiring guilt without noticing it.

I was rarely chastised by my parents; punishment mostly took the form of Being In Disgrace. Disgrace started by being made to stand 'in the corner,' face to the wall; this was followed by 'not being spoken to' for several hours and sometimes for a day or two, until the ceremony of formal forgiveness took place. It consisted in the recital of a formula of contrition and the solemn promise never to be bad again followed by the formal statement of forgiveness. There was also an intermediary state between complete disgrace and absolution. In this state one was spoken to and permitted to speak, but only about matters of strict necessity; it was, in diplomatic parlance, a condition of being recognised *de facto* but not *de jure*.

I only remember a single occasion on which I was acquitted of a charge by Bertha. This event was so exceptional that its recall, after some thirty years, is still accompanied by emotion. Noticing one day that I was in disgrace again, I asked Bertha what I had done. For there were two kinds of disgrace : one which began with an official declaration, based on a specific charge; and another, undeclared one, of which one only became aware by noticing that one was 'not being spoken to.' In the latter case inquiry into the nature of the crime was expected and in order. When I made my inquiry, Bertha compressed her lips and observed a few seconds of bitter silence as she usually did when spoken to by me. Then she issued the formal statement, which was both accusation and verdict : I had moved a china figurine several inches from its appointed and consecrated place on the mantelpiece. At that moment my mother chanced to enter the room and, having overheard part of Bertha's indictment, remarked offhandedly that it was she who had moved the object to its new location. The unparalleled event of her having taken my side against Bertha, and of Bertha letting me off with a grudging 'watch out in the future,' caused such a surge of relief and gratitude within me that I recognised its echo many years later on those blessed and rare occasions when a drill sergeant or a prison guard suddenly revealed himself in a humane light. The fact that this unexpected reprieve made so deep an impression seems to reveal an early acceptance of guilt, and of the deservedness of any punishment that might be meted out.

In all this, my father hardly enters the picture. He was too absorbed in his chimerical world of envelope-cutting machines and radio-active soap to interfere with my education. Besides, he was painfully aware of his own ignorance in matters of learning, and it must have been agony for him to cope with a precocious bookworm of a child whose questions he was unable to answer. He loved me tenderly and shyly from a distance, and later on took a naïve pride in seeing my name in print.

Our shyness was mutual; from my earliest schooldays to the end of his life we never established any intellectual contact, and never had a single conversation of an intimate nature. Nor did we ever quarrel; we liked and respected each other with the guarded reserve of strangers thrown together on a train journey. Though he was half mad in one way and I in another, we instinctively turned toward each other our saner aspects. On the whole it was a more courteous and civilised relationship than I have ever had with anybody over so long a period of time.

All my earliest memories seem to group themselves about three dominant themes : guilt, fear, and loneliness.

Of the three, fear stands out most vividly and persistently. My formative experiences seem to consist of a series of shocks.

The first that I remember occurred when I was between four and five years old. My mother dressed me with special care, and we went for an outing with my father. This in itself was unusual; but even more peculiar was the strange and apologetic manner of my parents as they led me down Andrássy Street, holding on firmly to both my hands. We were to visit Dr. Neubauer, they said; he was going to take a look at my throat and give me a cough medicine. Afterwards, as a reward, I was to have some ice-cream.

I had already been taken to Dr. Neubauer the week before. He had examined me, and had then whispered with my parents in a manner which had aroused my apprehensions. This time we were not kept waiting; the doctor and his woman assistant were expecting us. Their manner was oily in a sinister way. I was made to sit in a kind of dentist's chair; then, without warning or explanation, my arms and legs were tied with leather straps to the frame of the chair. This was done with quick, deft movements by the doctor and his assistant, whose breathing was audible in the silence. Half senseless with fear, I craned my neck to look into my parents' faces, and when I saw that they, too, were frightened the bottom fell out of the world. The doctor hustled them both out of the room, fastened a metal tray beneath my chin, prised my chattering teeth apart, and forced a rubber gag between my jaws.

There followed several indelible minutes of steel instruments being thrust into the back of my mouth, of choking and vomiting blood into the tray beneath my chin; then two more attacks with the steel instruments, and more choking and blood and vomit. That is how tonsillectomies were performed, without anæsthesia, A.D. 1910, in Budapest. I don't know how other children reacted to that kind of thing. In all probability I must have been sensitivised by some earlier, forgotten traumatic experience for I reacted with a shock that was to have a lasting effect.

Those moments of utter loneliness, abandoned by my parents, in the clutches of a hostile and malign power, filled me with a kind of cosmic terror. It was as if I had fallen through a manhole, into a dark underground world of archaic brutality. Thenceforth I never lost my awareness of the existence of that second universe into which one might be transported, without warning, from one moment to the other. The world had become ambiguous, invested with a double meaning; events moved on two different planes at the same time—a visible and an invisible one—like a ship which carries its passengers on its sunny decks, while its keel ploughs through the dark phantom world beneath.

It is not unlikely that my subsequent preoccupation with

physical violence, terror, and torture derives partly from this experience, and that Dr. Neubauer paved the way for my becoming a chronicler of the more repulsive aspects of our time. This was my first meeting with 'Ahor'—the irrational, Archaic Horror—which subsequently played such an important part in the world around me that I designed this handy abbreviation for it. When, years later, I fell into the hands of the régime which I dreaded and detested most, and was led in handcuffs through a hostile crowd, I had the feeling that this was but a repetition of a situation I had already lived through—that of being tied, gagged, and delivered to a malign power. And when my friends perished in the clutches of Europe's various dictators, I could, in writing about them, without much effort put myself in their place.

It may seem that I am exaggerating the effects of an experience which consisted, after all, in one of the most trivial surgical interventions carried out in a somewhat clumsy and brutal manner. More precisely, it may be thought that the study of psychiatry has equipped the author with a kind of dramatic hindsight. No one can guarantee the correctness of his memory; but the fact is that for more than a year after that experience I lived in a strange fantasy world of my own, playing hide-and-seek with an evil power which persecuted me. This power was personified by our gentle family physician, Dr. Szilagyi.

Shortly after the tonsil operation, I was in bed with an upset stomach. Dr. Szilagyi examined me, and after the usual consultation with my mother behind closed doors, he remarked with a jovial pat on my cheek: 'Well, well! The best thing to do seems to be to cut your tummy open with a knife.' With that he contentedly departed in his morning coat and striped trousers, carrying his black leather bag—and in it, no doubt, lay the knife.

I was old enough to understand that Dr. S.'s remark was

meant to be a joke. But with the precocious child's uncanny ear for nuances, I caught an undertone which was not jocular. In fact, Dr. Szilagyi had discussed with my mother the advisability of getting rid of my appendix.

For a long time thereafter, my days became divided into dangerous and secure halves. The dangerous half was the morning, when the doctor made the rounds of his patients. The safe half was the afternoon when he received them in his consulting room. The situation was complicated by my father's habit of taking me on some mornings for rides in a hired horse-cab; while he was visiting his business acquaintances, I was left waiting in the cab. Before Dr. Szilagyi's threat had got hold of me, I used to enjoy those morning rides. Now I dreaded them because, while alone in the cab, I felt particularly vulnerable and exposed; if Dr. S. happened to pass by, he might remember his threat, snatch me out of the cab and take me with him. So on every outing I pestered my father to take a closed carriage instead of an open one. The closed carriages had little curtains which you could pull across the windows. As soon as my father got out of the cab, I pulled the curtains tight.

My obsession took even more extravagant forms. Once a fortnight I had to accompany my father to the barber's shop to have my hair cut. The shop had an ill-lit back room which was reflected in the mirror in front of the barber's chair. When the door was opened I could catch a glimpse of the back room and vaguely distinguished several strange instruments which hung from hooks. The instruments became somehow associated with the knife that was to cut my tummy open, and the barber's shop became another place of terror.

It never occurred to me to confess my fears to my parents nor to ask for their protection; and I had no playmates to confide in. Since they had sided with Dr. Neubauer and trapped and betrayed me, they could no longer be trusted; the very mention of the matter might remind them of the temporarily shelved and forgotten project and hasten its execution. I must have had at that period a greater capacity for dissimulation than in later years, for my parents never guessed what went on in my private underworld. But then, most children are like that : while unable to keep a secret referring to the world of facts, they are perfect conspirators in defence of the world of their fantasies.

I cannot recall how long this attack of mild paranoia lasted; but it must have persisted for some months because in the meantime the seasons changed, and the weather became too warm for closed and curtained cabs. I was sent to school just after my sixth birthday, and by that time this particular obsession had dissolved.

A second series of upheavals, which would have affected even a normal child, occurred between my ninth and tenth year. I set fire to our home, underwent two operations, and witnessed a disastrous conflict between my parents. The last mentioned of these shocks was the worst, but for evident reasons cannot be discussed; it involved a succession of lurid and harrowing scenes which, apart from their frightening nature *per se,* taught me the anguish of split loyalties. All my experiences of that critical year were silhouetted against this background—which, for the time being, must remain a blank.

The year was 1914-15. The outbreak of the First World War had ruined my father's business in Budapest; we had given up our flat and moved to Vienna. From then on we never again had a permanent home.

The first station in our nomadic wanderings was a boarding-house called Pension Exquisite; it was, and probably still is, on the fifth floor of an old building in the heart of Vienna, facing St. Stephen's Cathedral. One afternoon, at a time when the conflict between my parents was at its height, I was left alone in our rooms in the Pension. I was depressed, and thought that the glow of some coloured candles which my mother had bought would create a pleasant change of atmosphere. I lit them, put them on the window sill and, becoming absorbed in my reading, forgot all about them—until one of the candles fell into a waste-paper basket and set it alight. I tried to extinguish the flames by waving the basket in the air; and when the flames grew too hot, hurled it against the gauze curtains. The room, like every self-respecting boarding-house room of the period, was richly draped with velvet and plush, and the fire spread rapidly. I was too frightened of being punished to call for help, and tore in a frenzy at the burning curtains in the thickening smoke. The next thing I remember is waking up on the bed of Fräulein Schlesinger, a teacher of French who lived in the boarding-house and with whom I was very much in love. My parents' return coincided with the arrival of the fire brigade; some three or four rooms facing the Cathedral were gutted before the fire was brought under control. I was not punished, not even in disgrace; the heroic dimensions of my misdeed had evidently transcended the limits of any possible retribution.

Not long after this event, I was again reading in my room one lonely afternoon when suddenly there was a loud report, and a hard object hit me on the back of the head, knocking me momentarily unconscious. A big can of tinned beans which had been standing on the radiator cover had exploded, presumably under the effect of fermentation. The elaborately far-fetched nature of this further catastrophe made the inmates of the Pension Exquisite regard me as a boy endowed with somewhat awe-inspiring potentialities, and I was much sought after for table-lifting seances, a popular pastime in those days.

Next, Dr. Szilagyi's long-standing threat materialised: an abscess on the appendix got me on the danger list. Feigning sleep, I overheard a conversation from which I gathered that

I was to be operated on the next day. I was taken to the hospital in an ambulance. It was a bright, clear, winter morning; as we crossed the lovely courtyard of Vienna's Imperial Palace, small flakes of snow began to whirl down from the sunny sky. Through the window next to my pillow in the ambulance, I watched hungrily the dance of the white crystals in the air, and while I did so a curious change of mood came over me. I believe that in those moments I became for the first time aware of the gentle but overwhelming impact of beauty, and of the feeling of one's own self peacefully dissolving in nature as a grain of salt dissolves in the ocean. At the beginning of the journey I had watched the faces of passers-by in the street with impotent envy; they laughed and talked, their morrow would be like yesterday; only I was set apart. Under the snowflakes in the courtyard of the palace, I no longer minded; I felt reconciled and at peace.

That journey in the ambulance was a turning-point. A few moments of terror were still to come : being wheeled into the operating theatre; and the panic of suffocation under the ether. But the phantoms of the nether-world had been made to retreat by some other power of even more mysterious origin. As it turned out, they were not routed, but merely forced to fall back to prepared positions.

I was told that the appendectomy, which had failed the first time, had to be repeated. I was now treated as a brave boy who is never afraid of the big bad wolf; but in fact I was in mortal fear of the ether mask, of a repetition of the choking agony before going under. The old enemy, Ahor, had appeared in a new guise. Then, one day, while reading the *Tales of Munchausen,* I had an inspiration. The chapter I was reading was the delightful story of the boastful Baron falling into a bog and sinking deeper and deeper. When he has sunk down to his chin, and his remaining minutes seem to be counted, he saves himself by the simple expedient of grabbing his own hair and pulling himself out.

I was so delighted with the Baron's escape that I laughed aloud—and in that same instant found the solution to the problem which had been haunting me. I was going to pull myself out of the bog of my fears by holding the ether mask myself over my face until I passed out. In this way I would feel that I was in control of the situation, and that the terrible moment of helplessness would not recur.

I mentioned the idea to my mother who understood instinctively, and induced the surgeon to satisfy my whim. Although the operation was too long delayed and I again had to be rushed to hospital in the same ambulance, along the same road, I felt no fear when I put the mask on my face under the encouraging grin of the anæsthetist.

Since that episode I have learned to outwit my obsessions and anxieties—or at least to come to a kind of *modus vivendi* with them. To arrive at an amicable arrangement with one's neuroses sounds like a contradiction in terms—yet I believe that it can be achieved, provided one accepts one's complexes and treats them with respectful courtesy, as it were, instead of fighting them and denying their existence. It is my profound belief that man has the power to pull himself by his own hair out of the mire. The Baron in the Bog, abbreviated 'Babo,' conqueror of 'Ahor,' has become for me both a symbol and a profession of faith.

The closing episode of this education by shock occurred when I was thirteen. I had become an addict of the science-fantasies of Jules Verne. While reading a scene from *A Tour of the Moon*, a long forgotten memory of my earliest days suddenly emerged with extraordinary vividness in my mind; and this was followed by an equally extraordinary sense of quietude and relief.

The content of the chapter I was reading is as follows: As the cannon-ball carrying the explorers towards the moon travels through space, one of the animals aboard, a little fox-terrier, dies. After some hesitation the explorers decide to throw the corpse out through the air-tight hatch. This is done; and then the passengers, looking through the thick glass window, realise to their horror that the body of the dog is flying on a course parallel to their own through space. They thought it would drop away, but the carcass shares the momentum of the cannon-ball, just as an object thrown from the window of a moving railway carriage shares the momentum of the train; and outside the earth's atmosphere there is no friction to act as a brake. Gradually the carcass increases its distance from the window, impelled by the per-sistence of the gentle thrust which had sent it through the hatch; but though slowly receding, it maintains its parallel speed and keeps abreast of the window. The dead fox-terrier has become a planet or a meteor which will continue to travel in its dark elliptic orbit round the earth through eternity.

Reading this scene, it occurred to me that perhaps one day criminals, instead of being hanged or electrocuted, might be pushed out into space from rocket-ships. The cosmic tem-perature of absolute zero would for ever preserve their bodies from decay. To have these astral corpses floating around the earth as permanent satellites might be inconvenient and give rise to various superstitions, but for this there was an easy remedy : at the moment of the expulsion, one had only to steer the rocket in the open orbit of a parabola instead of the closed orbit of an ellipse. The corpse would then follow the course not of planets but of comets : perform one semi-circular sweep round the sun and then recede deeper and deeper into interstellar space, past the fixed stars and the spiral nebulae, into infinity.

I considered this method quite practicable not only for executions but for disposing of the dead in general. After all, it had become a practice to cremate them and strew their ashes to the winds. To release the dead from their bondage to the earth and send them off on their eternal journey through space, transformed into silent comets with hands folded on their breasts, was a thought full of peace and consolation, and my nearest approach to the idea of immortality; it made of death an enviable adventure. The comfort was not so much in the idea of conserving the body, afloat in the cosmic refrigerator, but in the fact that, however many eons of light-years they travelled along their parabola, they could never *fall out* of this world.

It was during this reverie that the long-buried memory slipped into my consciousness as unobtrusively as if it had always been there. It was the memory of a scene that had taken place—though this may seem hard to believe—when I was a little over two years old. I had been locked up in the unlighted bathroom in punishment for some offence. I was in the throes of a wild panicky fear that I would have to stay for ever in the dark and would never see my mother again, nor the light of day, nor anything else. Then there was a blank in my memory, or rather a black patch, like the sudden darkness on the screen when the film breaks in the projecting room. Next I remembered crashing head-foremost against the iron support under the washbasin; this was followed by a sudden flood of light as my mother flung open the door and rushed to the rescue, while I howled in an ecstasy of relief, self-pity, and love. I also remembered having registered with satisfaction her worried and self-reproachful antics; and the dim, nascent cloud of a thought, which in coherent language would amount to: 'That will teach her!'

That was the scene which came back to me so unexpectedly when, while dreaming of space-ships and comets, I discovered that, alive or dead, one cannot fall out of this world. The memory had lost its poisoned sting, the primeval horror of the dark prison. It seems to me that since then I have been more or less free of the fear of death—though not of the fear of the act of dying, with its painful and degrading paraphernalia. As I grow older, this latter fear increases, like the apprehension of a painful operation to which one submits only reluctantly—though one knows that it is for one's good.

V. The Hour Glass

NEXT to guilt and to fear, loneliness played a dominant part in my childhood.

Until I went to school I had no playmates. Owing to my mother's settled conviction that she was an exile from glamorous Vienna in barbaric Budapest, we had no friendly ties with other families. I only had a chance to play with other children on the rare occasions when my mother was obliged to invite the family of some business relation of my father's to a *jour*—which, in Viennese French, means a ceremonial afternoon party complete with coffee, whipped cream, and cakes—or when we, in turn, had to attend a *jour* given by a family with a child of my own age. These events occurred perhaps once or twice a year. They were discussed for days in advance and, at my persistent nagging, my mother always did her best to describe the little boy or girl I was going to meet. But her descriptions were never detailed enough to satisfy my feverish curiosity and excitement; so I built up for myself fantasy portraits of my future playmates, made plans to squeeze the last drop of pleasure out of the short span of time vouchsafed me, deliberated which of my toys to parade, and which of the games to play that I had thought up and never had a partner to try with. As the hour of the visit approached I became almost sick with apprehension. Then came the agony of waiting—either for the door bell to signal the visitors' arrival or, if we were going out, for my mother to finish dressing, or put the last touches to her hair, and give her ultimate orders to the servants about polishing the silver or cleaning the polar-bear rug during our absence.

The first minute or so after meeting the other child, I felt petrified with timidity. The worst moment was the formal pumping of hands under the encouragement of the grown-ups with their grotesquely honeyed, piping voices. The other child was always startlingly different from what I had imagined, and this caused me both to be disappointed and to fall in love at once with the unexpected apparition, so real and so alive. For the other child, even if stupid and ugly, was in my eyes always a happy prince, bathed in the glory of having brothers or sisters, or regular playmates; it lived in that fairy-tale world where children played together day and night, and into which I was only admitted for a short and irretrievable hour.

However, as soon as the adults had settled down at the *jour* table and we children were left alone in the nursery, my timidity wore off and I changed into a frenzied little maniac. The ingenious games I had devised in my daydreams all had to be tried out during those infinitely precious moments, after the manner of lovers who, meeting between periods of long separation, put into hurried practice their erotic reveries. The other child, whether younger or older, would usually be swept off its feet by this torrent of new games and ideas, and within a quarter of an hour I would become transformed from a tongue-tied puppet into a fierce bully who had to have it all his own way. Then, in the midst of this revelry, I would suddenly be struck by the thought that the afternoon would soon be over, that it might in fact be broken up at any minute by the grown-ups; and this dread would further increase my fever and give it a morbid taste. Thus I taught myself early the art of poisoning my pleasures by reminding myself of their ephemeral nature. After the guests had left or we were home again, I became depressed or intractable, and there would follow renewed disgrace, culminating in Bertha's promise that I would never, never be allowed to play with other children again.

The pattern was repeated on the equally rare occasions when I was taken by my parents to the circus or the theatre. If the play had three acts, I would tell myself at the end of the first : now one third of the pleasure is already gone; and from the middle of the second act on I felt with growing melancholy that I was gliding down a slope towards the inescapable end. Later, when I became a soccer enthusiast, I would keep glancing at my watch during an exciting game to find out how many of the ninety minutes of playing time were left.

This obsession with the hour-glass character of pleasure never left me. As I grew up, it gradually changed its object from self-pity to pity for others who were engrossed in the pursuit of pleasure without being aware of its treacherous nature. I read with a scorching pity Gogol's story of the little clerk who buys, at the price of a lifetime of privations, a magnificent, warm overcoat, goes to a party to celebrate its purchase, and is robbed of it on his way home, having only worn it once. A few days later he dies of pneumonia and a broken heart; but his ghost goes on robbing other people of their coats at night in the snow-covered, deserted squares of Moscow.

When I was about fifteen, and the misery of the post-war inflation years in Vienna was at its peak, I saw one day an elderly man standing in front of Gerstner's luxurious tea-room. He had the fine intellectual head of the dying race of Viennese patricians, and was dressed with meticulous care in what was obviously his one remaining good suit, freshened up with a damp brush. He tried to act as if he had just paused casually in front of Gerstner's sparkling window, but his gaze was riveted on the colourful pastries and chocolates behind the polished pane, and there was a desperate, childish greed in his eyes. For several minutes I watched him standing there, and although I had outgrown my taste for sweets, my mouth filled with a vicarious flow of saliva. After a while he became restless, then seemed to waver and finally to reach a decision. I was standing a few steps away, on the edge of the pavement, and I read the various phases of his pathetic inner struggle from the almost imperceptible shifts of his shoulders and his back. When his resolution was made, his shoulders straightened in a youthful, almost jaunty manner, and an instant later he entered the shop through the narrow, elegant door with its gilt rococo ornaments.

I followed behind. The air inside Gerstner's was hot, perfumed, and sweet; the sounds were muffled to a low murmur by the thick, soft carpets on the floor, the silk tapestry covering the walls, and the velvet curtains on the doors; it was like the padded interior of a chocolate box. The people who sat chatting and smiling at the small, polished tea-tables all looked wealthy and well-groomed and happy. They were mostly *nouveaux riches,* speculators and profiteers, for the old bourgeoisie of Vienna had been destroyed by the inflation as finally and completely as if it had been buried by a landslide; nevertheless, this new clientele of Gerstner's looked perfectly civilised and did not even try to assume blasé manners. The people of Vienna had never learned that an air of boredom is an essential part of *savoir faire*; and so warmly saturated with tradition was the atmosphere of their city, that the parvenus had already acquired the unique Viennese art of being not only rich but actually enjoying it. They had that courteous gaiety and amused self-mockery and warm malice and flickering erotic spark, which had prevailed at Gerstner's in the past Imperial days. So that elderly man, hesitantly entering the tearoom, could not even comfort himself with the thought that the new patrons were lacking in appreciation of the pleasures which for him had become unobtainable and part of a lost paradise.

Once inside, he would probably have preferred to get out

again; but it was too late. It was folly on his part to go to Gerstner's, where at that time a cup of tea or chocolate with *petits fours* cost two or three thousand Kronen, or as much as his monthly salary amounted to. Blindly, he chose a table in a quiet corner and picked up the gilded menu card with its astronomical prices printed in small, graceful italics. Then, with a pathetic show of assurance he gave the waitress his order and sat back, bracing himself for the desperate task of enjoying every minute of his ruinous escapade.

I bought a packet of peppermints at the counter and left; I could not bear watching him any longer. The wrench of pity which I felt was not caused by his poverty, but by the transitoriness of his enjoyment, the knowledge that the golden *petits fours* would turn to dust on his palate. I have often wondered why this little scene left such a deep, aching impression in my memory—so deep indeed that I had to include it in this text though I am unable to define its relevance. Apparently I must have identified myself with that lonely figure, whom I only saw for a few minutes, by virtue of a kind of Cinderella Complex. He was a solitary outcast like myself, a man with a spiritual face and an abject craving for sweets, victim of the same hour-glass which counted my pleasures and made them run out as the sand runs through its hole. But that, of course, isn't much of an explanation.

As in the struggle against Ahor, the obsessive fears which haunted my childhood, it was again the Baron in the Bog who came to my rescue in the fight against loneliness.

When I was thirteen, we stayed for a while with my mother's sister. One afternoon the whole family went to the movies; even the servants had the day off. I was accustomed to being alone in the succession of hotel and boarding-house rooms which were our temporary homes; but this was a strange flat, huge and deserted, and I bitterly resented being left alone for a whole afternoon without my books and building kit, when I was, so to speak, a guest. To vent my resentment, I lay down in my boots on the silk counterpane on my aunt's bed. This criminal act put me at once in a better mood; I lay on my back, hands folded behind my head, staring at the ceiling, and gradually an infinite well-being descended upon me—I became aware that *I enjoyed being alone*. It was a tremendous discovery, and in a way the direct opposite of the hour-glass process: the desert sands of my solitude had suddenly turned to gold. There were an infinite number of things to think about, to occupy and amuse me, things about which the others in their humdrum life knew nothing; they were walking in their sleep and I, alone, was awake. Twenty years later this moment of exultation suddenly popped up in my memory when, after weeks in solitary confinement, I was given de Maestre's *Journey Around My Chamber,* and read this soliloquy:

> They have forbidden me to walk in the streets and to move about freely, but they have left the entire universe at my disposal: its boundless, infinite space and infinite time are at my service. . . .

It was a true Babo-rescue, which closed another chapter of my childhood. Loneliness, too, retreated to prepared positions. Like fear, it was never completely defeated, but I had found a means of living with it. A *modus vivendi* is not necessarily a compromise; it may be merely a precarious state of balance between unreconciled opponents. As the years wore on, my life gradually fell into a pattern, oscillating, like a pendulum, between periods of complete isolation and short bursts of hectic gregariousness. I would live in the country for several months without seeing anybody and without desire for company; then go to town with a provincial's eagerness for entertainment—an echo of the trembling excitement which came over me when I was taken to a *jour*. The lack of playmates during my childhood has left me with a passion for playing games, from chess to cards to pin-tables; with a chronic inability to terminate an evening once it is properly started; with a tendency, on the rare occasions when I go to a party, to get drunk and make a fool of myself —followed by another long stretch of complete seclusion. I admire people who lead a well-adjusted social life and have achieved the golden mean of sociability, but would not relinquish my own pattern even if this were in my power. The path of excess does not always lead to the palace of wisdom, as Blake held; but there can be as much harmony and rhythm in the oscillations of a pendulum from one extreme to the other as in the turning of a wheel on smooth bearings.

VI. Arrow in the Blue

I HAVE spoken of guilt, and fear, and loneliness; so much for the emotions. And now for the intellect.

Looking back on my intellectual development, I find a curious contradiction. I was a precocious child, far in advance of my age. But as an adolescent, and even during my twenties, I was less mature than others of my years, and not only looked younger, but was also markedly childish, both mentally and emotionally. In psychiatric terms, there was a strong trend towards infantilism with pronounced fixations. In plainer language, I acquired cleverness rapidly, but wisdom very slowly. At ten I was an infant prodigy; at twenty-five still an adolescent.

Concerning infant prodigies, it is reported that John Stuart Mill wrote Latin verse at the age of three, and that the first utterance of Lord Macaulay, instead of the usual 'Dada' or 'booboo,' was a formal statement in answer to an inquiry whether he had hurt himself : 'Thank you, Madam, the agony has abated.'

I can offer no equally impressive feat. Still, my first words in French, pronounced at the age of three, are reliably reported. They were addressed to a new governess and con-sisted in the laconic statement : *'Mademoiselle, pantalons mouillés.'* The statement referred to the fact that I had wet my pants.

I learnt avidly, read greedily, developed an early passion for mathematics, physics, and the construction of mechanical toys, and in my early teens spoke Hungarian, German, French and English with tolerable fluency. When, around ten, I became an expert in changing fuses and repairing electric lamps, and shortly after built a submarine which navigated successfully in our bathtub, it was decided in concurrence with my own wishes that I should study engineering and physics. Accordingly, when I finished elementary school, I was sent to the *Realschule,* which I attended for the next seven years, first in Hungary, then in Austria.

The educational system of the Austro-Hungarian Monarchy provided three types of secondary schools for pupils from the age of ten to eighteen : the *Gymnasium,* which prepared for a career in the humanities, with emphasis on Latin and Greek; the *Realschule,* which specialised in science and modern languages; and the *Real-Gymnasium,* a mixture of the two. I went to the *Realschule,* which suited me perfectly.

From my childhood to my university days, mathematics and science remained my almost exclusive interests, and chess my main hobby. I was particularly fascinated by geometry, algebra, and physics because I was convinced—much as the Pythagoreans and the alchemists had been—that these disciplines contained the clue to the mystery of existence. I believed that the problems of the universe were hidden in some well-defined secret, like the combination-lock of a safe, the philosopher's stone, or the elixir of life. To devote oneself to the solution of this secret seemed the only purpose worth living for, and every step of the quest full of excitement and delight.

For people who regard mathematics as dry and the sciences as boring, this kind of mentality is difficult to understand. It is a peculiarity of our present civilisation that the average educated person will be ashamed to admit that a work of art is beyond his comprehension although, in the same breath, he will proclaim not without pride his com-

c

plete ignorance of the laws which make his electric switch work, or govern the heredity of his offspring. He uses his radio set and the countless gadgets surrounding him with no more comprehension of what makes them function than a savage. He lives in an artificial world of cheap, mass-produced mysteries which he is too lazy to penetrate, without any understanding of the objects which he manipulates and is, in consequence, mentally isolated from his immediate environment. Our whole higher educational system is designed to foster this lopsided mentality, to create indifference toward the laws of nature, a deficiency comparable to myopia or colour-blindness.

Given these circumstances, and the ways in which science is taught in our schools, it is difficult to convey a child's delight and excitement in penetrating the mysteries of the Pythagorean triangle, or of Kepler's laws of planetary movement, or of Planck's theory of quanta. It is the excitement of the explorer who, even though his goal is limited and specialised, is always driven by an unconscious, childlike hope of stumbling upon the ultimate mystery. The Phoenician galleys journeyed over uncharted seas to find the Pillars of Hercules, and even Captain Scott may have been unknowingly tempted by the hope that perhaps there really was a hole at the South Pole in which the earth's axis turned on bearings of ice. From the star-gazers of Babylon down to the great artist-scientists of the Renaissance, the urge to explore was one of man's vital drives, and even in Goethe's day it would have been as shocking for an educated person to say that he took no interest in science as to declare that he was bored with art. The increasing volume of facts and the specialisation of research have made this interest gradually dry up and become a monopoly of technicians and specialists. From the middle of the nineteenth century onward, physics, chemistry, biology, and astrophysics began to fade out as ingredients of a rounded education. However, in pre-

Relativistic days it was still just possible for the non-specialist to keep abreast of general developments in science. I grew up during the closing years of that era, before science became so formalised and abstract that it was removed from the layman's grasp. Atoms still moved in three-dimensional space and could be represented to the senses by models—little glass spheres revolving around a nucleus like planets around the sun. Space was still non-curved, the world infinite, the mind a rational clockwork. There was no fourth dimension, and there was no subconscious id—that fourth dimension of the mind which transforms straight lines into crooked lines, and the deductions of reason into a web of self-delusions.

The heroes of my youth were Darwin and Spencer, Kepler, Newton and Mach; Edison, Herz and Marconi—the Buffalo Bills of the frontiers of discovery. And my Bible was Haeckel's *Die Weltraetsel*. In this popular classic of the turn of the century, seven 'riddles of the universe' were listed; of these, six appeared 'definitely solved' (including the Nature of Matter and the Origin of Life); while the seventh, the question of the Freedom of the Will, was declared to be 'a pure dogma, based on an illusion, and having no real existence.'

It was very reassuring to know, at the age of fourteen, that the riddles of the universe had all been solved. Nevertheless, there remained a doubt in my mind, for the paradox of infinity and eternity had by some oversight not been included in the list.

Infinity and eternity—aye, there was the rub. One day during the summer holidays, in 1919, I was lying on my back under a blue sky on a hill slope in Buda. My eyes were filled with the unbroken, unending, transparent, complacent, saturated blue above me, and I felt a mystic elation—one of those states of spontaneous illumination which are so frequent in childhood and become rarer and rarer as the years wear on. In the middle of this beatitude, the paradox of spatial infinity suddenly pierced my brain as if it had been stung by a wasp. You could shoot a super-arrow into the blue with a super-force which could carry it beyond the pull of the earth's gravity, past the moon, past the sun's attraction—and what then? It would traverse inter-stellar space, pass other suns, other galaxies, Milky Ways, Honeyed Ways, Acid Ways—and what then? It would go on and on, past the spiral nebulæ, and more galaxies and more spiral nebulæ, and there would be nothing to stop it, no limit and no end, in space or in time—and the worst of it was that all this was not fantasy but literally true. Such an arrow could be made real; in fact the comets which moved in open parabolic orbits were such natural arrows, rising in space to infinity—or falling into infinity; it came to the same thing, and it was sheer torture to the brain. The sky had no business to look so blue and smug if its smile hid the most awful secret which it was unwilling to yield, just as adults drove one crazy with their smiles when they were determined to withhold a secret, cruelly and lawlessly denying one's most sacred right—the right to know. The right to know was self-evident and inalienable—otherwise one's being here with eyes to see with and a mind to think with made no sense.

The idea that infinity would remain an unsolved riddle was unbearable. The more so as I had learned that a finite quantity like the earth—or like myself reclining on it—shrank to zero when divided by an infinite quantity. So, mathematically, if space was infinity, the earth was zero and I was zero and one's life-span was zero, and a year and a century were zero. It made no sense, there was a miscalculation somewhere, and the answer to the riddle was obviously to be found by reading more books about gravity, electricity, astronomy, and higher mathematics. Had not Haeckel promised that the last riddle would be solved within a few years? Maybe I had been chosen and elected to solve it. This seemed all the more likely to me as nobody else appeared to be as excited about space and the arrow as I was.

In retrospect it seems probable that this early infatuation with infinity was the product of environmental pressures and frustrations. Innate disposition may have played a part; but without environmental pressure it could hardly have gained so much power over me. The thirst for the absolute is a stigma which marks those unable to find satisfaction in the relative world of the now and here. My obsession with the arrow was merely the first phase of the quest. When it proved sterile, the Infinite as a target was replaced by Utopias of one kind or another. It was the same quest and the same all-or-nothing mentality which drove me to the Promised Land and into the Communist Party. In other ages aspirations of this kind found their natural fulfilment in God. Since the end of the eighteenth century the place of God has been vacant in our civilisation; but during the ensuing century and a half so many exciting things were happening that people were not aware of it. Now, however, after the shattering catastrophes which have brought the Age of Reason and Progress to a close, the void has made itself felt. The epoch in which I grew up was an age of disillusions and an age of longing.

When I was three or four I comfortably knew all about God. It was explained to me that God sees all our actions, hears all our words, knows all our thoughts; and that He dwelt 'up there.' This 'up there,' which was always indicated by a pointing finger, I took literally. The white ceiling over my cot was decorated with a fringe of dancing figures silhouetted in black, representing the Seven Muses. I became convinced that those figures 'up there' were God; and for what seems a long time I addressed my evening prayers to them. I have since found out from various people that, 'come to remember it' they were able to recall similar experiences of animism or totem worship in their own childhood.

I don't remember how long I worshipped the Seven Muses. Apparently, it is easier to remember the acquisition of a belief than its loss. To become converted or convinced is a more or less sharply defined act; to lose a conviction is a long process of wear and tear. The dancing figures on the ceiling faded, and were replaced by a benevolent old gentleman with a white beard, suspiciously like Grandfather Leopold X, reclining somewhere among the clouds. That image, too, became less and less real until it faded away like an old photograph, and its place was occupied by the arrow, travelling through infinite space in search of its secret and its boundaries. That quest was the legitimate successor of the black figures on the ceiling and the bearded God in the clouds, just as Kepler's search for the planetary laws succeeded earlier visions of celestial topography.

For the pursuit of science in itself is never materialistic. It is a search for the principles of law and order in the universe, and as such an essentially religious endeavour. If the inferences drawn from it are at times materialistic, this merely means that those who draw them happen to be partisans of a materialist philosophy.

To say that the personal God of my childhood became completely absorbed in the spirit of science would, however, be an over-simplification. Some unresolved portion of that personal God was to reappear, for many years to come, in various disguises. The Hungarian language has a curious word for scholars : the word *tudós,* whose nearest equivalent is the French *savant*—the 'knowing one.' The English 'scholar' and the German *Gelehrter* merely convey academic erudition. The mysterious sound of the word *tudós* evoked in my mind, hungry for the answer to the great enigma, the idea that it designated a kind of all-knowing person—a medicine man or shaman. This belief, at first naïve and overt, lingered on unconsciously in my mind long after puberty and adolescence.

The first *tudós* I met in the flesh was a Professor Gergely who, I believe, had written a book on English literature. He was a man of perhaps thirty, with a pronounced stoop, and precisely that sharp, bespectacled intellectual face which I imagined befitting the 'one who knows.' I was about thirteen, and had just read *Hamlet* and *Othello*. Professor Gergely was courting an older cousin of mine and one day, after a *jour* in her parents' house, I was presented to him. I was inwardly quivering and full of feverish expectation of the revelations to come—boys of the Zuni tribe, I imagine, must feel like that before undergoing the mysteries of initiation. Professor Gergely beamed at me with great kindness, and inquired what sort of books I was reading. I told him that I had just finished *Othello*; and the conversation continued something like this:

Professor G.: 'But isn't it too early for a boy of thirteen to read Shakespeare?'

I: (embarrassed shrug).

My Cousin: 'Can't you answer the Professor's question?'

I: (blush, shrug).

Professor G.: 'Are you sure you understand the meaning of what you are reading?'

I (exploding): 'No! That's just the point.'

Professor G. (smiling): 'If you understand that there are things which you don't understand, that is already something.'

I: 'But I understand the action and all that is said, only . . .'

Professor G.: 'Only?'

I: 'But what I don't understand is the hidden meaning.'

Professor G.: 'The hidden meaning?'

I: 'Well, *you* know—the hidden meaning. The secret behind it.'

Professor G.: 'And what kind of a secret do you think it is?'

I: 'Well, *you* know that there is only one kind of secret. The meaning behind it all.'

Professor Gergely became embarrassed. The one kind of secret I was talking about could only be sex. He blushed and squinted at my cousin, who sent me in disgrace from the room. I realised that a dreadful misunderstanding had arisen, but I didn't know what it was. I had as yet no notion of sex—about which more later. But I had an absolute, unshakable conviction that there was a basic central mystery, related to eternity and the infinite, and that some fraction of the secret was contained in all great works of literature—that in fact their greatness and fame was due to their containing part of the mystery. And 'knowing ones' were those who had the key to the secret or at least to some portion thereof.

The professor was only the first of a long series of 'knowing ones' to whom I felt drawn as the years went by. Some were men of letters, some scientists, some politicians. Not all were as disappointing as Professor G., and I learned from them in varying degrees. But though I no longer believed in their omniscience, my attitude toward them remained basically the same. Unconsciously I continued to believe that they were guardians of the holy grail, of the one and indivisible secret. Some I deserted in bitter resentment when I discovered that they did not come up to my expectations; to two of them I remained devoted unto their death. One of them was Vladimir Jabotinsky, the spiritual father of the Palestine terrorists; the other, Willy Muenzenberg, the Communist leader.

Still later on, when a book of mine had some success, readers would confront me with their problems, asking for guidance and help. Whenever this happened, and I in turn had to play the part of the 'knowing one,' I remembered Professor G. and was made aware of my woeful inadequacy for the task. As these experiences became more frequent, they made me understand why in our emotionally immature and confused times so many are attracted by movements offering the benefit of a rigidly organised hierarchy of shamans—such as the Communist Party and the Catholic Church.

History, politics, social and ethical problems played hardly any part in my mental development until my university years. My preferred poets were Ady, a Hungarian modern, Rilke, Goethe, Heine, and Byron, in that order. And, of course, I devoured all novels I could lay hands on. But I regarded the reading of fiction as a guilty pastime with no real bearing on the problem that alone mattered : the ultimate mystery which could only be approached through science and natural philosophy. For those among my classmates who took an interest in history and social science I had only contempt; they were on the wrong track. Man as a social and moral being was without interest, a speck in the universe, and his history a dance of dust stirred up by the vacuum cleaner. The fascinating thing about man, and his only aspect worthy of study, was the chemistry of his tissues, the algebra of his heredity, his descent from the monkeys, and the switch-board mechanism of his brain.

This whole mental world collapsed and was swept away around my seventeenth year. Before that I had been, though born in 1905, a true child of the nineteenth century—the century of crude philosophies and arrogant oversimplifications which lingered on into the twentieth, until the First World War brought it to a close with a bang.

VII. And so to Sex . . .

WHEN I was five, I was sent for a few months to an experimental *avant-garde* kindergarten in Budapest. It was run by a young lady belonging to a very erudite family, whose members now occupy some half a dozen chairs at various English and American universities. Mrs. Lolly (which isn't her real name) had committed an intellectual mésalliance by marrying a successful businessman and, feeling frustrated, had opened the kindergarten for five-and-six-year olds, where she put into practice some extremely advanced and, I suspect, somewhat confused, pedagogical ideas. Had my mother known what she was letting herself in for I would never have gone to Mrs. Lolly's school; when she did find out after a few weeks, she hastily took me out.

We were thirteen at Mrs. Lolly's, nine boys and four girls; I have counted the number on an old photograph. We attended class, all dressed in bathing suits, around a long, rustic table beneath a sunny pergola in Mrs. Lolly's garden. The lessons were extremely stimulating. One day we heard stories about 'primitive man'—a near-gorilla who lived in caves, wore animal skins, and hunted wild beasts with clubs; the next, we were given coloured crayons and told to express our feelings by drawing anything that came into our heads while a gramophone played 'Santa Lucia' and the Barcarole from 'The Tales of Hoffman.' On still another memorable day, Mrs. Lolly startled us all by explaining that her two children (both of whom attended the class) had come out of her own tummy, where she was now hatching a third, and that this was the way all children were born. This, indeed, was food for thought. It led me to ask my mother for more explicit information during a family *jour*—and to my abrupt withdrawal from the school.

During this brief period I fell in love with a little girl called Vera, the daughter of one of the leaders of the Hungarian Socialist Party. It was not the first time I had been in love; before that I used to think and dream of another little girl by the name of Sarah Berger—a fairylike apparition with whom I had been allowed to play on one of those rare, unforgettable afternoons when we went visiting, and had never seen again. Vera, however, was my first true and real love; I saw her not once, and that once in a daze, but every day under the pergola, in a bathing suit, in street attire, and in the nude—for one of Mrs. Lolly's advanced ideas was that we should all dress and undress together before and after class. Oddly enough, in spite of this enlightening practice, I remained in ignorance of the anatomical difference between the sexes until I was fourteen. How I managed to remain blind to the obvious is rather a mystery. According to a psycho-analyst friend, it is an outstanding example of early repression—a kind of sexual colour-blindness, apparently. This may be so, for the taboo surrounding the region of the groins was very effective during my childhood—owing to my mother's earnest warning that any manipulation of objects within that region would inevitably be followed by lingering illness and death. The nimble-witted analytical reader may discover here a connection with my fear of Dr. Szilagyi's knife; but let sleeping dogs lie in peace.

To come back to my love, Vera. My feelings for her had not, of course, escaped our teacher's observant eye, so one day she asked me why I always stared at Vera in the dressing-room, and whether I thought she was prettier than the other little girls. Having elicited an affirmative answer, she further inquired which of Vera's features, or part of her countenance, I found so particularly attractive. This I was able to answer without hesitation, and I truthfully said:

'Her vaccination marks.'

I was indeed fascinated by the delicate and symmetrical tattoo patterns which vaccination against smallpox had left on Vera's arm, and, to a lesser degree, by the scars exhibited by the other children. To the best of my knowledge, this is the only case of vaccination-mark fetishism known in psychiatric literature. I still have a certain weakness for such well-designed marks, preferring a triangular to a circular arrangement; as for pentagons, they are a rarity and a delight to the connoisseur. In my dotage I shall probably collect photographs of vaccination marks, classified according to size, texture and design.

I attended Mrs. Lolly's school in 1910. Only once did I meet Vera again, in 1948. I had to make a speech at Carnegie Hall, and was feeling rather jittery for this was my first visit to the United States, and my first public appearance in that country. A quarter of an hour before the meeting was due to start, I was strolling up Broadway to relax and think over once more what I was going to say, as the speech was to be ex tempore. At the corner of 57th Street I was accosted by a lady in a raincoat who, as the reader has guessed by now, was none other than Vera. She had recognised me from a photograph in the papers, and at once proceeded to tell me all that had happened to her, her parents, her husband, her children and one grandchild, during the intervening thirty-eight years. The minutes were slipping away, and I had to get that speech right, but discreet hints were of no avail. The speech was a fiasco, mainly because of Vera's vaccination marks, though a breakdown of the microphone also helped. Nearly all my encounters with erstwhile schoolmates and paramours have followed a similarly sad pattern; so nowadays when I get a letter beginning 'I don't know whether you still remember me,' I pretend that I don't, and let the friends of my youth rest in my memory like well-preserved, smiling mummies under glass, knowing that if you try to touch them they will fall to dust.

From Mrs. Lolly's school until I reached the age of fourteen there is a suspicious blank in my sex life. The usual homosexual experiences of puberty, which play such an important part in English life and letters, are missing.

At fourteen, my classmates explained the facts of life to me in an incomplete and distorted manner—which puzzled me considerably until I got hold of a medical text book.

At fifteen, I was initiated into auto-erotic practices, which I found delightful and to which I reverted, as most people do but few admit, in periods of sexual frustration.

At sixteen, I had my first sexual experience with the maid at the boarding-school I was attending in Baden, near Vienna. After the initial mishaps, this proved even more delightful.

From seventeen to twenty, as an undergraduate, I shared the uninhibited and wildly promiscuous life of a students' *Burschenschaft* in the Vienna of the inflation years. In part it was very enjoyable, in part mildly disgusting. In our taboo-ridden civilisation the male's yearning for floozies, trollops, and pin-up models is endemic and incurable, but it can at least be confined within reasonable limits. The total effect of those three years of licence was to take the edge off the highbrow's traditional *nostalgie de la boue*.

VIII. The Dawn of Politics

O<small>N</small> July 28th, 1914, the Austro-Hungarian Monarchy marched against Serbia, and thereby started World War I. This event, translated into the personal experiences of a nine-year-old, left only two traces :

(*a*) I had to fetch a glass of water with bicarbonate of soda for my father, who was lying on a sofa with nervous indigestion and explaining to my mother that he would have to go into some new business as no more English textiles would be available for import.

(*b*) During the usual afternoon walk with my governess, we met a joyous demonstration marching down the street and singing the national anthem : '*God bless the Magyar / With good humour and a good harvest / Shield him with thy protecting arm / On the field of battle.*' It was the first mass-demonstration I ever saw, and its effect was so irresistible that I tore myself away from the unhappy *Fräulein* and joined the marching crowd, alternately yelling 'Death to the Serbian dogs,' and 'God bless the Magyar.'

Six months later Serbia, the hereditary foe, was defeated. This event provided the inspiration for my first poem, which I sent to a boys' magazine. I still remember the opening lines :

> *In the month of December Belgrade capitulated*
> *And the Magyar stood on its citadel, elated.*

This sounds considerably more beautiful in the Hungarian original; nevertheless, the poem was rejected.

Against general expectations, the war was not over by Christmas, so I lost interest in it—though I continued to stick little flags on coloured maps of the battlefront, which was considered both as a sport and a patriotic ritual. My father was over the age limit for military service; we spent the four war years partly in Budapest, partly in Vienna, moving from one boarding-house to another. The next political event which made a personal impression on me was the Hungarian revolution in November, 1918, because it was again associated with a mass-demonstration, and because it started just next door to my father's office in Kossuth Lajos Street.

This occasion, which signalled the collapse of the Austro-Hungarian Monarchy, and the reshaping of the map of Europe, is preserved in my memory as if it were an old and often-seen documentary film. A few houses down the street from my father's office, a balcony is decorated with draperies and flags. A huge, milling, cheering crowd blocks the street for half a mile. A tall, dark, stooping man, with awkward gestures, addresses the crowd from the balcony. He is Count Michael Károlyi, who has just proclaimed Hungary's secession from the Austrian Empire and its rebirth as a free, independent, democratic republic—of which he is soon to be elected President. His voice sounds artificial, his diction is laboured : he wears a silver plate in his palate, as the consequence of a throat operation. The crowd cheers in a frenzy and sings the national anthem : *God bless the Magyar*. My father and I march with the crowd and get home very elated; we are both fervent Hungarian patriots. My mother disapproves, being Viennese and a devoted reader of the Austrian Court news.

Four months later Károlyi's liberal government resigned and handed its powers over to Béla Kún's Communist dictatorship. I was then in my fourteenth year, and my memories of these events are more articulated.

My first contact with Communism is forever associated with Chopin's Funeral March.

A few days before its ascent to power, the Communist Party staged a demonstration in Budapest in the course of which a few of its members were killed. The Party, as a test of strength, appealed for a gigantic funeral procession. Some fifty thousand workers from the factory-belt surrounding Budapest followed the hearse, which was adorned with green wreaths and red draperies. They marched slowly, with discipline and dignity. Hungary was a country emerging from a semi-feudal state; never before had the citizens of Budapest seen a crowd of sturdy proletarians parading through their elegant shopping streets; many of them had probably never seen a factory worker before. Chopin's *Marche Funèbre,* played over and over again by the band of the railroad workers as the procession slowly traversed the town, sounded for them the death-knell of an era.

To my ears it was more moving than any music I had ever heard. It was perhaps my first experience of musical ecstasy. This emotion became fused with the sight of the martyrs' coffins at the head of the procession of hard-boned men with their strong and simple faces and open, confident glances. Chopin's March made a romantic Communist of me long before I knew what that word meant. But its meaning soon became clearer, and what I understood of it met with the full approval of my budding scientific mind.

The Communist revolution was achieved without bloodshed. Count Károlyi had hoped that his régime would be supported by the Western democracies whom he regarded as his political allies, and for whom he had risked his neck by proclaiming his sympathy at a time when Hungary was still at war. His hopes were disappointed; without outside help and support, he was forced to abdicate in favour of the only organised power in the country which seemed able to prevent chaos. Only some twenty years later, when I became friends with Károlyi during our common exile, did I fully grasp the tragic significance of those days—the blindness and unimaginative blundering of the Western democracies who turned their back on their Liberal allies and acted as unwitting midwives for the power which was set to destroy them. The Hungarian Commune of 1919 was the direct result of Western policy—the first example of a pattern which during the next quarter-century was to be repeated over and over again.

Of all this, of course, I knew nothing at the time. Chopin's March was succeeded by the rousing tunes of the *Marseillaise* and of the *Internationale* which, during the hundred days of the Commune, drowned the music-loving town on the Danube in a fiery, melodious flood. As Vienna had danced to the fiddle of Johann Strauss, so the people of Budapest now marched to the tune of the *Marseillaise*.

The people in this case comprised not only the working class, the farmhands and the poor peasantry, but also the progressive-minded urban middle classes and the leading intelligentsia. Communism was a new word in 1919, and it had the sound of a good, just, and hopeful word. One of the first articles I read in the *Red Gazette* explained that more than thirty per cent of all the arable land in Hungary was the property of feudal landowners, who numbered around two per cent of the total population. This was news to me. The article asked whether it was just and healthy for a nation that out of every thousand people one should be very rich and all the others very poor; or whether it would be better to distribute wealth equally among all. The latter alternative seemed the more logical. I had not before that time been in the habit of reading newspapers; now I read the *Red Gazette* with almost as much interest as Jules Verne. Why had nobody talked about these matters before?

No doubt the Hungarian Social-Democratic Party had

been saying most of these things for years, but what they said had not reached the ears of the unpolitically minded. European Social Democracy had signed its own death warrant in 1914 when in every belligerent country it had supported the war—the same Imperialist War which two years earlier, at the Congress of Basle, it had foreseen and unconditionally condemned. The chauvinistic pro-war attitude of the various sections of the International was on a par with the policy of the churches whose priests and ministers, in every nation, prayed for the victory of mutually hostile armies. After this tragedy, European Social Democracy remained a factor in politics, but its revolutionary *élan* was gone for ever. The new revelation from Russia had a fresh, unusual ring. To many, on a continent in shambles, it sounded like the voice from Sinai.

The Hungarian version of the *Internationale* had a verse which ran :

> *To wipe out the past for ever,*
> *O army of slaves, follow us.*
> *We shall lift the globe from its axle,*
> *We are nothing, we shall be all.*

During those hundred days of spring it looked indeed as if the globe were to be lifted from its axis—a feat, I remembered, Archimedes had already dreamed of. Even at school strange and exciting events were taking place. New teachers appeared who spoke to us in a new voice, and treated us as if we were adults, with an earnest, friendly seriousness. One of them was Dezsö Szabó, author of a celebrated novel about the Hungarian peasantry. He was a shy, rather tongue-tied and absent-minded person who talked to us in a gentle voice about a subject more remote than the moon : the life of a farm-hand in a village. Other new teachers were young members of the intelligentsia who had never taught in a school before. They gave courses about the elements of economics and constitutional government—subjects which were not included in the curriculum, which opened sudden new vistas and offered a new contact with reality.

The first poem we had learnt at school had been the National Anthem; next had come a patriotic song which exhorted us to remain unflinchingly faithful to the Fatherland 'from cradle to grave.' Third in popularity had been a poem by Petöffi which stated that : 'If the earth is the cap of God, Hungary is the feather in the cap.' The Hungarians, a small ethnic enclave in Europe, oppressed for centuries by the Germans and Slavs surrounding them, had developed a particularly fervent brand of chauvinism, but with minor local variations the same type of stuff was taught in French, German, Italian, or Russian schools in pre-1918 Europe. To hear our new masters gently deride the sacred feather in God's cap and address us as citizens of a new world, was a shattering revolutionary experience in the true and full meaning of that word.

On May Day, a celebration was held at our school. One of the boys from the top form, a charming and gifted youngster of seventeen who had already published several poems in a literary magazine, extolled the memory of Danton and St. Just. The speech was enthusiastically received by the boys and the new masters; the old teachers listened in acid silence. After the collapse of the Commune the young man was thrown out of school and, according to rumour, killed by the White Guardists. It was my first experience of this nature; it gave the words 'counter-revolutionary terror' a personal and frightening meaning.

That May Day celebration of 1919 was the apotheosis of the short-lived Hungarian Commune. The whole town seemed to have been turned upside down. The public squares of Budapest suffer from an abundance of oversized statues of worthies in bronze, charging the enemy on prancing horses, or orating with one arm upraised, a scroll under the other. On May Day all these statues were concealed by spherical wood frames covered with red cloth on which were painted the continents and seas of the world. These gigantic globes—some over fifty feet high because the bronze hero inside was sitting on a particularly tall horse—had a curiously fascinating effect. They looked like balloons anchored to the public squares, ready to lift the whole town into the air; they were symbols of the new cosmopolitan spirit, and of the determination of the new régime 'to lift the globe from its axis.' Even more moving and beautiful were the posters which covered every wall and transformed the streets into colourful picture galleries. They had been designed by the élite of modern Hungarian painters who later on swarmed out over Europe and America and became prominent as artists, cartoonists and magazine-cover designers. Some of the posters were cubistic, some futuristic; all celebrated anonymous workers, peasants, and soldiers; not a single one was a portrait of a leader. It is a historical curiosity, known only to experts, that the posters of the Hungarian Commune of 1919 represented one of the peaks of commercial art.

Another curiosity of the hundred days was that the people of Budapest seemed to live mainly on ice-cream. There was a near-famine, caused by the refusal of the peasants to sell their produce against paper money; all food was rationed and had vanished from the shops. The only things ration cards and the paper money issued by the red régime could buy were cabbages, frozen turnips—and ice-cream. I suppose an imaginative food commissar must have stumbled upon a consignment of vanilla in a government storehouse and decided to turn it into ice-cream in some requisitioned refrigeration plant.

The whole country lived on a barter system; the peasants came to town with their chickens, eggs, milk, and butter, and went home laden with grandfather clocks, bronze statuettes, antimacassars, second-hand shirts and suits. During the Soviet famine in 1932, I had occasion to watch exactly the opposite process : Ukrainian peasants and Kulaks, driven from the land by enforced collectivisation, were bartering in the streets of Kharkov their beautiful embroidered table-cloths, lace bedspreads, silken handkerchiefs, and golden ikons against loaves of black bread or sacks of potatoes. The peasantry has been the stumbling block of all socialist revolutions; it is the unsolved problem of Marxist theory. For the problem of dealing with the peasant is primarily one of psychology; and the psychological factor is absent from Marx's schematic abstractions. Lenin succeeded in temporarily allaying the hostility of the peasants mainly because he departed from the gospel of orthodoxy. The Hungarian Communist Party had no genius of Lenin's calibre; they postponed the distribution of the land for fear that too hasty action would lead to chaos. This was probably the biggest mistake of the short-lived régime.

I have no doubt that Communism in Hungary would in due course have degenerated into a totalitarian police state, forcibly following the example of its Russian model. No Communist Party in Europe has been able to hold out against the corruption imposed on it from Moscow by direct authority and indirect contamination. But this later knowledge does not invalidate the hopeful and exuberant mood of the early days of the Revolution in Hungary, in Bavaria or the Ruhr, and in Russia itself.

To return to the ice-cream. It may be suspected that my sympathies for the Commune were influenced by the fantastic amount of it we ate, for breakfast, lunch, and dinner, during the hundred days. This suspicion would be the more unjust as there was only the one kind, vanilla, which I dislike. I mention this curiosity, due to the imaginative commissar, because it was typical of the happy-go-lucky dilettantic, and even surrealistic ways in which the Commune was run. It was all rather endearing—at least when compared to all the lunacy and savagery which was to descend upon Europe in years to come. There was no terror. There were small outbursts of violence in the provinces and some beatings-up at police headquarters, but these merely conformed to Hungarian tradition. The total number of people executed during the Commune was under five hundred.

Although we were a family of confirmed bourgeois and my father, as a factory owner, fell into the official category of capitalist exploiters, we never felt unsafe. The factory for radio-active soap was duly nationalised and my father was appointed managing director, with a salary about equal to his former profits. We kept two hens on the balcony of the boarding-house where we lived; these were pointed out by the Communist warden of the block as an example worthy of imitation in the common effort to make the red metropolis self-supporting.

One day at the crack of dawn we were awakened by two men in uniform with slung rifles and bayonets pointing to the ceiling. They were soldiers of the Red Army in charge of requisitioning flats and rooms—a housing shortage is another chronic accompaniment of all revolutions. We occupied two rooms in the boarding-house—one for my parents, one for me. The soldiers looked around with large, naïve eyes, obviously embarrassed by their task. My father was out—I believe he had slept the night at the factory. But my mother, sensing the soldiers' lack of self-confidence, was a sufficient match for them. One of them tried to argue that a single room might be enough for us. 'How do you expect three people to live in one room?' my mother asked indignantly. 'Well, well,' the soldier said with an uneasy grin, 'I have seen worse than that.' He was obviously from the country, and Hungarian peasants often slept seven in a room. The other soldier never opened his mouth; he just kept goggling at his surroundings, trying not to look at my mother in her dressing-gown. Then they both clumped out, with muttered apologies for the disturbance.

It was like that all over. I have said before that the average burgher in the better residential districts of the town had probably never seen a member of the industrial working class. He had had dealings with the plumber, and the electrician, and the man who came to hang the curtains—all of whom belonged to that hybrid stratum of small artisans in a big town, corrupted by tips and used to the servants' entrance. But the large mass of factory workers and railwaymen, of miners, day labourers, and farm-hands are an alien race to the average, middle-class town-dweller. One of the exciting things about the Commune was that these strange creatures could now be seen everywhere and turned out to be, to everyone's surprise, quite different from the plumber, the charwoman, and the taxi-driver who until then had represented 'the people' in the bourgeois' limited world. They were awkward, and they had a strange self-confidence and dignity. They were quite a discovery to the people in the cafés and on the elegant Corso—and to myself.

One day my cousin Margit took me along to a metal works in suburban Ujpest, where she was giving a course in political economy. She was a rather plain girl of twenty, and a member of the Galileo Circle—the rallying centre of the radical intelligentsia, Budapest's Fabian Society and Jacobin Club, all in one. A sentry who knew my cousin, and seemed to like her, led us into a workshop where some twenty men of all ages were sitting on benches. When my cousin entered, with me in tow, they all got up like schoolboys when the teacher enters the classroom, then sat down amidst much shuffling of feet. My cousin—the same who later on, together with her two children, was gassed at Auschwitz—spoke for about ten minutes on the meaning and history of money, explaining how some natives used shells for money, others tobacco or salt, to simplify the operations of barter, which, she said, was what money really was for. No sooner had she started than one or two of the men went to sleep with the amazing promptitude of hens cooped up for the night; a few listened with half-closed, squinting eyes in which no spark of comprehension would ever gleam; but the remainder of the men drank her words in avidly, with a puzzled and rapt expression. The pathetic thirst for knowledge written on their faces made me suddenly feel close to them. I had already taken a liking to these members of a strange race who had invaded our streets; I had liked the soldiers who had tried to requisition my room, and the posters on which they were represented in a beautifully stylised way, all cubes and triangles and angular surfaces. Now, by seeing them transformed into wide-eyed schoolboys, I understood that they had the same feelings, and frustrations, and aspirations as I. Then the thought struck me that I was undeservedly lucky to go to school and have books to read while these hulking, grimy, sweaty characters obviously regarded my cousin's lecture as a rare and special treat. At fourteen, the idea that it was a privilege to go to school seemed quite fantastic, and I regarded it as a very original and important discovery. But then, I have always found that the emotionally deepest experiences are those in which one suddenly grasps the full meaning of some very commonplace proposition. From that day on the slogan about 'equal educational facilities for all' has retained a private meaning for me; that the parents' financial status should determine the amount of mental development accorded to a child still appears to me as one of the most nauseating injustices of our civilisation.

My cousin's lecture was followed by questions from the men—some stupid, some shrewd, but all proffered with a puzzled hungry look, with the visible urge to make the most of that short and exceptional occasion. When my cousin broke up the meeting, because she had to address two more that afternoon, they were as disappointed as children and begged her to come back. I don't suppose she ever did, for the hundred days ended soon afterwards; and I suppose that those in her audience who had asked the most intelligent questions became the first targets for the avengers' rifle-butts.

Several years later I witnessed a continuation of sorts of that memorable meeting. In 1932 and 1933 I was travelling through Soviet Russia and attended a number of educational lectures in factories. The average political lecture in a Soviet factory lasted two to three hours—following upon a working day of eight hours or more. Whatever the actual subject of the lecture, it had to cover all the 'theses' and slogans enumerated in Stalin's last speech or in the last Party resolution. To omit a single one—say, 'the strengthening of the production-offensive for the over-fulfilment of the light metal industry's revised counter-plan,' or 'the intensification of the struggle for unmasking the German Social-Fascist traitors to the working class as allies of the Trotskyite agents of the Hitlerite bandits and of the imperialist warmongers in general'—to omit, I say, a single one of the tongue-twisting ritual formulæ would have laid the lecturer open to the accusation 'that he deliberately neglected an important point of the Party programme and has thereby become guilty of counter-revolutionary agitation.' Each meeting ended in unanimous resolutions expressing 'flaming greetings' or 'indignant protests'; the deadly, infinitely involved Byzantine ritual had to be played out from the first letter to the last. In the 1930s mass-education, like every other aspect of Communist life, had become a cruel parody of its original intention.

This is true even of such apparently personal matters as the psychological attitude of intellectuals towards the working class. In 1919, the intelligentsia suddenly discovered the suburban proletarian as he really was in flesh and blood and sweat; and this discovery opened a flood of generous impulses and new vistas of human fraternity. By the 1930s this spontaneous feeling had become petrified into the 'Prolet-Cult' prescribed by the Party line. The feeling of fraternal warmth towards fellow beings handicapped by their social background became transformed into a self-degrading worship of the primitive, the uncouth, the humourless; of the blockheaded, 'class-conscious' proletarian —the cult of the lowest common denominator.

Not the least remarkable thing about the Hungarian Commune was that rare quality in a revolution, a sense of humour. Budapest was buzzing with funny stories told in the cafés and on the stage of its famed cabarets. Later, in Hitler's Germany and Stalin's Russia, telling a 'counter-revolutionary' joke or even listening to one became sufficient grounds for being sent to a concentration camp. In the idyllic days of 1919, Budapest's most popular humorist could still permit himself to appear every night on the stage and produce his celebrated 'it goes on and on' act.

During the first days of the Commune the burghers of Budapest were all convinced that this strange régime would only last a week or less; the consensus was that 'it can't go on.' The humorist in question, whose name I forget, appeared before his audience wearing a hang-dog expression and carrying an accordion. He planted himself in the middle of the stage and, without a word, started pulling out the accordion. The battered instrument kept expanding to an inordinate length amidst the giggles of the audience, until the comedian remarked with a puzzled look, '*It just goes on and on.*' The people of Budapest have a peculiar shaggy-dog kind of humour; this phrase 'it goes on and on' became somehow the most popular slogan of the Commune. It was rumoured that one night the Communist dictator, Béla

Kún, had attended the performance; and that, after the comedian's act, he had stood up in his orchestra seat and remarked amiably to the audience : 'You will be surprised— it *will* go on.'

I cannot vouch for the veracity of the last part of the story; but the fact that people believed it to be true is in itself characteristic of the atmosphere of the hundred days.

In July, 1919, the Hungarian Commune was overrun by the Czech and Roumanian armies. Those among its leaders, including Kún, who succeeded in escaping to Russia were liquidated during the Purges in the late thirties. After a short occupation of the capital by the Roumanian Army, Admiral Horthy took power and established the first semi-Fascist terror régime in post-war Europe. By the late twenties, Horthy's régime had become gradually liberalised; but during its first few years it gave, with its organised pogroms, with its bombs thrown into synagogues, its torture chambers and man-hunts, a nasty foretaste of things to come.

It was during the Roumanian occupation that my parents and I said definitely farewell to Hungary and took up residence in Austria. The excitement over the entry of the Roumanian troops, our somewhat adventurous crossing of the Austrian frontier without an exit permit, the change of scenery and intense work for the entrance examinations to an Austrian school, made me rapidly forget the hundred days.

Their impact on me had been deep, but mostly on an unconscious level. The emotional effects of the majestic funeral procession and of Chopin's March, of the giant red globes, the May Day celebration in school, and the lecture at Ujpest, remained latent for a long time. They did not quicken my interest in politics and social questions; I even lost the habit of reading newspapers and went back whole-heartedly to science, mathematics, and chess. My political libido had been aroused and had then gone back to sleep again; it entered, in the terminology of Freud, upon a 'period of latency,' which lasted several years.

IX. Portrait of the Author at Sixteen

I EMERGED from childhood an exasperating and pathetic figure. Almost the whole of my adolescence is painful to remember. For a period of two or three years, Cyril Connolly's remark about his youth was equally true of mine: 'I have always disliked myself at any given moment; the sum of these moments is my life.'

I was short, slim, wore my hair parted on the side and plastered down with water and brilliantine, had a rather handsome face with unformed, infantile features and a constant smirk which looked impudent and masked my boundless timidity and insecurity.

Some twenty years later a shrewd Comintern agent said to me: 'We all have inferiority complexes of various sizes, but yours isn't a complex—it's a cathedral.'

The elements which shaped that structure have already been discussed or hinted at. The conviction that whatever I did was wrong, a pain to others and a disgrace to myself, had laid a permanent foundation of anxiety and guilt. The long periods of solitude, and the hectic excitement which came over me when I was allowed to see other children, transmitted their tensions to my later friendships and social contacts. In addition, there was a circumstance which for some time tortured me more than anything else: at sixteen I was the shortest boy but one in class, and that one happened to be a dwarf.

As I said before, I was slow in maturing both physically and mentally. I kept growing until around twenty-two, when

I reached my present height of five feet seven. Even today I feel ill at ease if at a cocktail party I have to talk, standing, to a woman taller than I; and, as every author knows, the type of woman who rushes at you at parties to gush about your books is usually over forty-five, and over six feet tall. But what, today, is an occasional moment of mild discomfort was downright torture at sixteen. I refused to go to dancing-classes for fear that I would be forced to dance with taller partners. If friends asked me to a party, I inquired with infinite cunning about the intellectual faculties, colour of hair and eyes, and, incidentally of course, the stature of the young ladies expected to be present. The announcement that a beautiful, tall, blonde girl would be there was enough for me to plead indisposition. The examples of Napoleon, Beethoven, and other undersized great men comforted me, but not much. Nor did they serve as a warning against the short man's traditional vanity, aggressiveness, and lust for power.

Much of this pain and distress was caused by a conversation I overheard between the parents of two of my classmates outside a bathing-cabin where, unknown to them, I was changing my clothes. One said: 'Isn't it terrible how quickly my boy is growing?' And the other answered: *'That's* no reason to worry. The terrible thing would be if he were as short as that Koestler boy.' But, of course, this unpleasant experience could not have produced such a strong effect without a neurotic disposition, ready to feed on any nourishment offered by careless hands.

At seventeen I entered the university. In the *Burschenschaft* which I joined, every freshman was given a fraternity nickname. This name was conferred during an impressive ceremony; and until that solemn moment it was kept secret. The name which was sprung on me, and which I had to carry for years was 'Perqueo'—taken from an old German students' song:

Es war der Zwerg Perqueo, im Heidelberger Schloss
An Gestalt kleinwinzig, am Durste riesengross.
Man schalt' ihn einen Narren; er sprach: 'Ihr lieben Leut'
Währt Ihr, wie ich, doch alle
Feuchtfröhlich und gescheit....[1]

The end of the poem was in a way a redeeming factor.

Next to shortness, my inferiority complex fastened on my preposterously juvenile appearance. At sixteen I looked like fourteen, at twenty like sixteen, at thirty like twenty-one. Today, when appearance has caught up with age, I would no longer object to having ten years wiped off my face and my rump. Once the agonies of the past have been safely embalmed in memory they appear silly beyond belief. Yet agonies they were—such, for instance, as that awkward misunderstanding with the adjutant of King Feisal of Iraq. . . .

This occurred during a visit to Bagdad in 1928. I was at that time Middle East correspondent of the Ullstein papers and had been sent out to cover one of the recurrent government crises in Iraq. On my arrival I applied for an interview with King Feisal Ibn Hussein. I was received by Tahsin Bey, the King's adjutant, in a resplendent white uniform; he had been advised of my arrival which, as befitting the representative of the biggest Continental newspaper chain, had also been announced in the local press. Tahsin Bey received me kindly; but whenever I broached the subject of politics, or the audience with His Majesty, he side-tracked the conversation and with a friendly smile inquired what young boys were taught in European schools. After the ritual number of cups of sweet and bitter coffee, and a painfully dragging conversation, he rose and concluded the talk with the question :

'And when can we now expect the visit of your papa?'

---

[1] There was a dwarf, Perqueo, in the castle of Heidelberg;
His stature was short, his thirst gigantic.
They called him a fool; he said : 'Ye good people
If only you were like me : a tippler, serene and wise.'

He obviously thought the representative of Ullstein's must be a middle-aged worthy who had sent his son ahead on a courtesy visit. For once, however, I proved equal to the occasion by declaring with a courteous bow :

'*Mon père, c'est moi.*'

We are not only disloyal to others, but also to our own past. The *gauche* adolescent, the foolish young man that one has been, appears so grotesque in retrospect and so detached from one's own identity that one automatically treats him with amused derision. It is a callous betrayal, yet one cannot help being a traitor to one's past.

Worse than this betrayal is the distortion of truth which accompanies it. The agonies of youth are not funny, but distance and perspective make them appear funny, and one inadvertently falls into a patronising, anecdotical style. I am trying to fight this impulse as I write this story, yet it is hard to recapture any sympathy for, and even less a feeling of identity with, the boy who was mortified when his classmates called him 'Awtuah Koestla' because he could not roll the r's in his name; who unconsciously rose on tiptoe, like a fighting cock, when talking to taller boys; and who, at sixteen, when for the first time invited to a formal luncheon, could for an hour or more only squeeze out of himself an occasional 'Yes, Madame,' or 'No, Madame,' while growing alternately purple and pale, and being desperately aware of a condition aptly described by the French as '*suer entre les fesses.*'

Timidity was the worst curse, unrelieved by the fact that it came in intermittent attacks. The timid youngster may be compared to a high-tension cable surrounded by thick layers of insulation, which protect him but also cut him off from contact with the outside world. There are several types among the timid. With some, the tension gradually relaxes as time marches on, the insulating layer becomes more flexible, shyness becomes transformed into courteous restraint—an attitude so well suited to the Anglo-Saxon temperament that it is even cultivated as a mannerism. With others, the opposite happens : the protective layer becomes a rigid, impenetrable veneer which chokes its wearer and frightens all passers-by away. Then there is a third type, the one to which I belong, which may be called the 'intermittent timid.' In the case of the intermittent timid, phases of tongue-tiedness and cramp alternate with others of extreme garrulousness and uninhibited behaviour. Which of the two will come to the fore on a given occasion depends on circumstances beyond the subject's control. If the circumstances are such that contact is established between the live core of the cable and the environment, the current will flow freely, and the chances are that a short-circuit will occur, with a display of sparks and the blowing of fuses. Other occasions will merely produce a rubbing and grating of the environment against the insulating layer in which the timid person remains encased, swathed, stifled, deaf and dumb.

Alcohol helps, but only within limits. Mostly it soaks through the insulation and makes it promiscuously conductive. If, during the initial phase, the subject is in a cramp, liquor may have the effect of intensifying the cramp until a kind of *rigor mortis* ensues. It is one of the most unpleasant social experiences.

The type of the intermittent timid should not be confused with the manic-depressive character, though the two often go together. If the manic-depressive also happens to suffer from intermittent timidity, the manic phases will facilitate the breakdown of inhibition, and *vice versa*.

Such, then, was the anatomy of the accursed shyness which I carried throughout my youth as a leper carries his bell : laughter ceases when he enters the room and the street grows empty at the sound of his footfall. My contacts with others were either non-existent or headlong plunges into

D

intimacy. But the latter were rare; and most of the time I felt that I was living in a portable prison of my own devising, surrounded by cold stares of bewilderment and rejection.

In this particular predicament even the Baron in the Bog's miracle cure is of little avail. Or rather, it acts only gradually; you have to keep pulling at your hair to keep your face out of the mire until slowly, very slowly, you again find your *modus vivendi*.

The first Babo-method which I tried, the flight from timidity into cocky aggressiveness, proved a failure. It led through a series of painful beatings, both physical and moral, which were even more humiliating than the condition which they were meant to cure. The worst of these batterings lasted through my fifteenth and sixteenth years, which were spent in a small *pensionnat* for boys at Baden, near Vienna. There were about a dozen boarders in the *pensionnat*; and of these only four were over fifteen. The smaller boys lived downstairs; the four of us senior boys on the first floor. As a logical result of my character, so lovingly described above, the seniors were divided into two camps : one was known as 'The Triumvirate,' consisting of the other three; the other was I. This situation lasted until the end of my stay; everybody who, in his youth, has gone through the purgatory of a boarding-school can appreciate the nature of this experience.

The aggressive phase was followed by its opposite : the pose of the lonely, sensitive, starry-eyed poet, somewhere between Hamlet and Werther, doomed to early death by consumption. But this was definitely not in my line. I tried various other attitudes and poses to mask my extreme insecurity and lack of self-confidence. They were like suits bought off the peg—too tight at the waist or with sleeves inches too long. Underneath, there was no definite personality, no solid core, only fluid emotions, contradictory impulses, an amorphous bundle of tensions.

At some time during my sixteenth year I developed a new obsession; I called it the 'Paradox of the Ego Spiral.' The underlying problem was as old as the paradox of Achilles and the tortoise; but that did not prevent it from becoming an obsession. It went something like this:

A dog eats his supper. The dog is enjoying himself. But does the dog know that he is enjoying himself? Doubtful. . . . A man reads a thriller. He is enjoying himself. He knows that he is enjoying himself. But does he know that he knows he is enjoying himself? If he is an average person, he probably doesn't. Now let's try it ourselves, with our superior powers of introspection. I am thinking of this problem. I know that I am thinking of this problem. I know that I know that I am thinking of this problem. I know that I know that I know . . . and so on. Who, or what, is this elusive, receding 'I' that is always one step removed from the process, and how can one catch up with it? As I had acquired the habit of thinking in terms of diagrams and geometrical figures, I saw the quest of that slippery, fugitive ego represented as an angular spiral (see page 100).

Now, it can be mathematically shown that a spiral of this kind will draw closer and closer to its centre without ever quite reaching it—just as a series of the form $1, \frac{1}{2}, \frac{1}{4}, \frac{1}{8}, \frac{1}{16}, \ldots$ etcetera, will generate smaller and smaller fractions, but never quite reach zero. Thus the effort to 'catch the I,' to achieve identity between the subject who knows and the object of its knowing, could be represented as a converging spiral which will only reach its own centre after an infinite number of involutions. Here, then, was the exact counterpoint to the arrow. The arrow went off at a tangent on its quest for the infinitely remote; the ego spiral curled inward, toward the infinitely close, which was yet as unattainable as the other.

So far so good. But what about the ego of the flatworm which could be sliced into two or more parts and regenerated

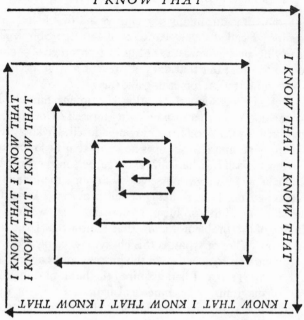

into as many complete individuals? Could you cut an Ego into an 'E' and a 'go'? And did a two-headed calf have egos in duplicate? I found that the worm and the calf agreed quite well with my spiral. For you can't cut the centre of a spiral which is a geometrical point into parts, but the ego spiral did not contain a centre; that spiral was not a locale, it was a function or process which could be duplicated as often as you liked. To have this point settled took a load off my chest and gave me a great feeling of satisfaction.

The more so, as convergent series have quite beautiful qualities. If you continue the series: $1, \frac{1}{2}, \frac{1}{4}, \frac{1}{8}, \frac{1}{16}, \ldots$ *ad infinitum,* and then add together all its numbers, the total sum will be exactly 2. Though we can never complete the series, we know precisely 'what it is up to,' as it were. Similarly, though you can never reach the core of the ego spiral, you can predict with fair precision how it will function and behave.

More than twenty-five years later, when I took up the study of psychology and neurology, I remembered my naïve speculations about the arrow and the spiral, and it occurred to me that they could be regarded as archetypal symbols of two opposite trance-like states of heightened consciousness. In the 'arrow state' consciousness expands towards mystic union with the All-One while the ego is felt to dissolve in the infinite. In the opposite 'spiral state' consciousness contracts, is focused on the self, strives to establish identity between subject and object, to permeate the self with awareness of itself. The ecstasies described by most Christian mystics seem to belong to the former category, whereas certain yoga exercises, aiming at the conscious control of all functions of body and mind, seem to belong to the spiral state.

That there are two opposite types of heightened consciousness or contemplative trance, is a hypothesis which I am trying to substantiate in a work now in progress. The purpose of this digression was merely to give another example of the early origin and the obsessional character of certain *leitmotifs* which keep recurring in one's development. I have always felt that *'on revient toujours'* should be altered to *'ça revient toujours.'*

The lack of a clear-cut personality, of a solid centre of gravity in the flux of emotions, was in later years compensated by a greater adaptability to people and situations. Quick progress in my career as a journalist gave me a minimum of professional, though not of personal, self-confidence, and the great variety of social contacts which my job required forced me to develop a superficial technique in coping with them. For many years my relations with people, even with chance acquaintances on trains or at parties, remained emotionally as unbalanced as before, but the *façade* became smoother and more urbane. I became what is called a good mixer; from a hedgehog I gradually changed into a chameleon. I no longer displayed an artificial pose or mask, but a complete false personality, produced by outside conditioning and the inner need to find some *modus vivendi* with society.

Such organically grown false personalities—as distinct from consciously adopted poses—function automatically and without effort. Our society abounds in false personalities, which were developed in self-defence and later have become so ingrown that they even alter the features of the face and make it incongruent with the true personality of its owner. That may be the reason why the majority of outstanding painters, musicians, writers, and scholars, look so entirely different from what one expects. One of our most famous orchestra conductors looks like a head waiter; our best-known painter like a wizened clown; a group photograph of the Nobel Prize winning poets and writers would look like a meeting of chartered accountants and insurance salesmen. Perhaps Gide alone among them looked truly himself—partly because he wore a Basque beret and partly because he was an exhibitionist. On the other hand, if you meet a person with a striking intellectual head and spiritually noble expression, he is sure to be either a treasury official, or an artistic dilettante and a second-rater.

There are various types of false personalities; the one to which I belong is recognisable, among other things, by the fact that he feels sure of himself when addressing a meeting or holding forth at a crowded party, but becomes the more insecure the smaller the audience, and reveals his basic timidity when alone with one other person. Genuine people are mostly the other way around.

Shyness and insecurity have remained my silent companions to this day. I have never outgrown, merely over-grown, them by a chatty, sociable, synthetic personality which I despise—as some women despise the bouncy rubber falsies which, nevertheless, they are obliged to wear to com-pensate for a natural defect.

Adolescence is a kind of emotional seasickness. Both are funny, but only in retrospect. The youth of sixteen that I was, with the plastered-down hair, and the fatuous smirk, at once arrogant and sheepish, was emotionally seasick: greedy for pleasure, haunted by guilt, torn between feelings of in-feriority and superiority, between the need for contemplative solitude and the frustrated urge for gregariousness and play; still obsessed by the arrow's flight into the Absolute, though hope of catching up with it had begun to fade; still in search of the knowing shaman, but equally worried about the possible withdrawal of the favours of Mathilda, the generous boarding-school maid. The archaic horrors of early child-hood had receded but had not disappeared; they were latent, lying in wait, ready to pounce when provoked. Early in-timacy with Ahor had achieved a lasting awareness of the other world, the tragic plane which existed parallel to the trivial routine of existence, even when the manholes through which the two communicated were tightly closed and bolted under one's feet.

This latent apprehension, the awareness of guilt and impending punishment, seemed to be always present, like the rhythmic beat of the surf at night along the shore. While there are voices under the open window and laughter on the pier, one is able to forget it. But when the laughter dies away and the voices are stilled, the muffled thunder swells up again, and one realises that it has always been present; and that the waves will never stop beating their heads against the stones of the pier.

Part Two

THE ARROW SPLITS

1922–1926

Tout comprendre, ne rien se pardonner

X. A Bunch of Cosy Cannibals

THE *Technische Hochschule* in Vienna enjoys, like other Polytechnic colleges on the European Continent and unlike those in Anglo-Saxon countries, the status of a university. Its graduates—Engineers and Doctors of Engineering —occupy, again in contrast to Anglo-Saxon practice, approximately the same rank in the social hierarchy as lawyers, physicians, and other professional men. Accordingly, students at the Vienna Polytechnic displayed the same snobbery and *esprit de corps* as undergraduates at other universities. They were regarded as inferior beings by students of medicine and philosophy, and reciprocated these feelings according to the traditions of inter-faculty rivalry. The real alignment of the various student groups was, however, not by faculties or colleges, but according to racial and political principles.

About half of the university students in Vienna 'wore colours,' that is, they belonged to duelling fraternities, called *Korps* or *Burschenschaften*. These were patterned upon the example set by the German universities and were a relic of mediæval days. The German *Schüler*—scholar—of those days was a proverbially wild and lawless swashbuckler whose only preoccupations, according to legend and folk-song, were gambling, drinking, transpiercing rivals with his sword, and seducing rustic Gretchens who were either the innkeeper's or the miller's daughter—see the ribald Auerbach cellar scene in *Faust,* and Mephisto's disguise as a wandering scholar.

These rakes and rowdies banded together in fraternities

according to their land of origin—the various German Principalities—and were the ancestors of the *Korps* or *Burschenschaften,* which survived through the centuries—some of them for almost five hundred years—until the National Socialist régime, distrusting their spirit of independence, dissolved them. The names of the different *Korps*—Teutonia, Saxonia, Swabia, Thuringia, Bavaria, Gothia, Vandalia, and so on—were still the same as in mediæval times; and so were the ceremonial uniforms in which, every Saturday morning, they solemnly paraded around the 'Aula'—the great entrance hall of Vienna University. Their uniforms displayed the heraldic colours of the original German Principalities on caps, smocks, trouser seams, and shoulder sashes. About a hundred generations of *Fuechse* (foxes—freshmen) had become *Burschen* (seniors) and then *Alte Herren* (old boys); yet the *Korps* had retained their identity, their customs and traditions. They had played a leading part in politics during the German *risorgimento* after the Napoleonic Wars; then had gradually turned into colourful petrefacts of chauvinism, snobbery, and of the black reactionary spirit in German academic life. Before the First World War, the *Herr Professor,* with his duelling scars, cropped hair, and arrogantly imbecile expression, was the favourite target of cartoonists. Nevertheless, these strange fossils retained enough pride and independence to make them incompatible with the structure of the Fascist state; and during my time, in the middle twenties, they still dominated the scene at the University of Vienna.

Having been a Communist at fourteen, I became a member of a duelling fraternity at seventeen. And what is more, mine was a Zionist *Burschenschaft.*

Three main categories of *Burschenschaften* existed at that time in Vienna: the Pan-Germanists, the Liberals, and the Zionists. There were also some Catholic *Korps*, composed of students of the Theological Faculty, but they did not go in for duelling, so they were not taken seriously. As for the Socialists, they had no *Burschenschaften,* merely clubs, and were altogether beneath contempt.

The Pan-Germanist fraternities were Austrian branches of Saxonia, Gothia, Vandalia, and the other original German *Korps.* They had adopted a racist doctrine long before the name of Hitler was known, and only admitted pure-bred Aryans to their ranks.

The Liberal *Korps* were anti-Pan-Germanists, more progressive in outlook, and accepted Czechs, Hungarians, Jews, and members of other inferior races.

The first of the Zionist *Burschenschaften*—there were twelve of them at the University of Vienna—had been founded in the 1890s by Dr. Theodor Herzl, prophet of the New Zion. Their aim was to show the world that Jews could hold their own in duelling, bawling, drinking, and singing just like other people. According to the laws of inferiority and over-compensation, they were soon out-Heroding Herod once more. The founders of the first Zionist *Burschenschaft,* Kadimah (which means 'forward' in Hebrew), spent eight hours a day for six months learning the art of duelling with cavalry sabres before their first public appearance, complete with 'colours' and trappings, in the Great Hall of Vienna University. The 'Teutons,' 'Saxons,' 'Goths,' and 'Vandals,' were so flabbergasted that they started a riot. The riot led to a series of duels, in which the Kadimites made mincemeat of their opponents. After 'Kadimah' my own *Burschenschaft,* the 'Unitas,' was founded; after that the 'Ivriah,' 'Lebanonia,' 'Robus,' 'Jordania,' and the others. Overcompensation is a mighty spur; just as Demosthenes, the stammerer, became the foremost orator of Greece by forcing himself to speak with pebbles in his mouth, so the determined Lebanonians and Jordanites became the most feared and aggressive swordsmen at the university.

In 1920 the Pan-German *Burschenschaften* held a

National Convention in the town of Weidhofen. The Convention adopted a Resolution which became binding on members of all Pan-German *Korps*. It ran : 'Any son of a Jewish mother is to be regarded as devoid of honour and satisfaction by arms is therefore to be refused him.' Whether or not the famous 'Weidhofen Resolution' was a direct consequence of the Zionists' fencing prowess, as the Jews alleged, or the outcome of independent developments, remains a moot question; at any rate, it puts the Zionists into a difficult position. Unable to fight their opponents with the chivalrous sword, they now had to prove their mettle with fists and clubs. The result was that the University of Vienna became the scene of a series of bloody and undignified riots.

These usually occurred on Saturday mornings, during the traditional parade of the *Burschenschaften* under the arcades of the Aula. The Pan-Germans and the Liberals would march slowly in pairs around the arcade, the Zionists would stand and stare, each *Burschenschaft* clustered at the base of its appointed column. The Pan-Germans and the Liberals wore their caps and sashes and carried stout walking sticks; the Zionists carried equally stout sticks, and wore sashes and bowler hats. This state of affairs had originated in a Rectorial decree forbidding Zionist Fraternities to wear caps because they bore 'alien colours'; but, as a typical Austrian compromise, we were allowed to wear our sashes, which displayed the same colours. Our standing at the foot of the columns instead of marching round the arcade had originally been an act of protest, and had by now become an established custom. However, the prohibition of caps had its advantages, for we could stuff more newspaper into our bowlers than our enemies into their caps; and that stuffing was excellent protection when you were hit over the head with a club masquerading as a walking stick.

The fighting started almost invariably through the same type of incident. A Lebanonian or Jordanite would feel 'provoked' by some real or imaginary offence such as a stare or a brush of the elbow from a Teuton or Vandal. He would then walk up to the man, click his heels, and declare :

'*Herr Kollege*, you have provoked me. I invite you to follow me to the ramp.'

This the other could not refuse, for the rules required that all Affairs of Honour should be settled on the ramp, outside the territory and jurisdiction of the Alma Mater.

So the two would walk out to the ramp, discreetly followed by the members of their fraternity and their allied and associated forces. Once outside, the injured party would again click his heels and bawl out his name; the other would do the same. The injured party would then hand over his visiting card and ask the ritual question :

'At what hour and place shall my seconds wait on you ?'

At this point one of two things would happen. If the offender's fraternity did not abide by the Weidhofen Resolution (the Liberals and a minority of the Pan-German *Korps* did not), he would accept the challenge; and the next day the seconds would meet in a café, and the matter would be settled either by Honourable Apologies or by a duel. If, however, he was a 'Weidhofenite,' the offender would solemnly ask :

'*Herr Kollege,* are you an Aryan?'

The rules of the Zionist Fraternities required that this question be answered either by hitting the man over the head with one's stick or by slapping him in the face; in other words, by a symbolic bodily insult. Failure to react in this way entailed immediate 'dishonourable discharge' from the fraternity. The first time I witnessed a scene of this kind, its hero was a member of my own *Korps* who, a Hungarian like myself, went by the nickname of Attila. He was short; his opponent a blond Teutonic giant. Attila tried dutifully to hit him over the head but the other, grinning, parried the blow and sent my friend's stick whirling through the air.

Almost simultaneously Attila reached out with his left, and actually managed to brush the other's cheek with the back of his hand. Now that the ceremonial part was over, it became a free-for-all, and the next thing I remember is finding myself sitting on the ground with my bowler bashed in (more exactly my father's bowler which I always borrowed for these Saturday occasions), and blood dribbling down from a cut over one eye. From this comfortable position I watched the remainder of the fight and the arrival of the police; then our fraternity marched in good order to our favourite chemist's shop to get patched up, and thence to our favourite Bierstube.

Through the irony of fate, it was my over-cautious mother who got me involved in all this. One of her friends was a striped-trousered worthy, Herr Finanz-Rath Dr. Benedikt. (In Austria all self-respecting people had titles such as Government-, Court-, or Finance-Councillor, just as in France they were Officers or Knights of the Legion of Honour.) Finance-Councillor Benedikt was an Old Boy of 'Unitas.' 'Unitas' was as always on the lookout for new recruits. Finance-Councillor Benedikt had hardly set eyes on me at a family *jour* when he started to explain to my mother that joining his *Burschenschaft* was the surest way to keep a young man just entering upon University life from getting into trouble, bad company and dubious temptations. 'Unitas,' he explained, only accepted young men of the best society, for the purpose of joint visits to the opera, mutual education and enlightenment. There was not a word about duelling, broken heads, Zionism, or any such shocking subjects. Incidentally, neither my parents nor I had ever heard of Zionism.

The residence of 'Unitas' had for the past thirty years been located in the basement of an apartment-house in Vienna's respectable Josefstadt quarter. This *Bude* (digs, or quarters) consisted of a large fencing hall, a Convention room where matters official were discussed, and another room where guests were entertained. During the next three years this curious establishment was to be my second, and in fact real, home. My first visit had decisive consequences; it involved me in the struggle for a Jewish State; an involvement which was to last for over twenty-five years, four of which were spent in Palestine. So that occasion ought to be described in some detail.

The time was September, 1922; I had just completed my seventeenth year and had matriculated at the Polytechnic. When I inquired at the caretaker's lodge after the 'Academic Fraternity Unitas,' the caretaker's wife gave me a curious and searching glance, which I correctly interpreted as meaning 'you look too young for that sort of thing.' This woman, Frau Dvorzak, was, as I soon discovered, an important pillar of the Fraternity; when a duel was fought in the digs, she stood sentry to warn us of police raids, while on the kitchen range in her lodge, the surgical needle and yards of surgical thread required for stitching up the contestants were being sterilised in a saucepan. With a maternal gesture she directed me to a dark staircase which led down to the basement. At the foot of the staircase a door, adorned with the colours and armorial bearings of the Fraternity, opened straight into the fencing hall, where Dr. Otto Hahn, who later was to become a close friend, was engaged in drilling two young 'Foxes.' They all wore huge fencing-masks, padded on the back and shoulders, which gave them a martial and knightly appearance. As I came in, they lifted their masks with a certain *grandezza*, clicked their heels, and bellowed their names in the Continental way of introduction. I was early, the other members of the Fraternity had not yet arrived; so Hahn, who during that semester was 'Major of Foxes' (fencing master and drill sergeant), invited me to get myself a mask and a sword and join in the fun. I asked for nothing better.

For the next delightful quarter-hour the two Foxes and I kept hitting the air, practising quarts, reverse quarts, and tierces. The swords used were the medium-heavy sabres of the Austrian cavalry and, according to the 'German high style' which all *Burschenschaften* used, the sword-arm was held rigidly extended, never dropping below shoulder-height, and the weapon was wielded with a twist of the fore-arm and a flick of the wrist—which in view of the weight of the sabre was rather difficult to master. A quart received full on the mask made your head reel and stars dance before your eyes, while you smelt the pleasant burnt smell of the sparks which the sword drew when it hit the iron grill. I wondered what it would be like to take one of those thunder-ing quarts without a mask, but Hahn, reading my thoughts, explained, grinning across his pleasantly scarred face, that the worst thing that could happen to you would be to lose a chip or two of your cheek-bone; and even that, he added, was a rarity. He also said that I had the makings of an excel-lent swordsman which, as events proved, was a barefaced lie.

More members of the Fraternity arrived, and two seniors gave an exhibition—a mock duel with seconds and all the solemn paraphernalia—which was very impressive. When it was over, Hahn came up to me and said :

'Of course, you agree that duelling is a most idiotic sort of custom?'

I blushed and hemmed and hawed; whereupon Hahn explained with friendly seriousness that they all despised this barbarous institution but, by force of circumstance, had to cultivate it, because it was the only way to disprove the legend of Jewish cowardice; you had to fight your opponent with his own arms. But if I thought they took this mummery seriously, I was mistaken.

These astute dialectics impressed me even more than the romantic atmosphere—which I had been quite prepared to take at face value. But romantics combined with cleverness and a superior tongue-in-cheek attitude suited me even better. What pleased me most was that everybody called me *Herr Kollege,* the formal address in academic circles, that they all seemed to take me seriously as an honoured guest, and went out of their way to be nice. I was looking forward with excitement to the beginning of the real show, which was the occasion to which I had been invited—the 'Kneipe.'

The 'Kneipe' was, next to duelling, the most outstanding institution of the *Burschenschaften.* It was a strictly regulated, ritual drinking orgy. The word 'Kneipe' meant in mediæval German an inn or public house, and is still used as a slang expression for a bull session or else to designate a low tavern. The obsolete verb form, 'kneipen,' means tippling.

With trestles and boards, kept in readiness for these occasions in the huge armoury chests, two Foxes expertly put together a very long and narrow table, and covered it with white cloth. Two other Foxes, assisted by jovial Mr. Dvorzak, rolled a barrel of new wine, Vienna's famed *Heuriger,* down the staircase. At the word of command we all sat down in prescribed order. The table was divided into an Upper House for the Seniors and a Lower House for the Foxes. At the head of the Upper House sat the *Præses*; the Lower House was presided over by the Major of Foxes seated at the opposite end of the long table called the *Contrarium.* Both *Præsidium* and *Contrarium* had swords lying before them on the table; the other members of the Fraternity merely wore their sashes—violet, white, and gold— across the chest. The guests—myself and another hopeful young man, who later on got very drunk, had to be carted away in a taxi, and was never seen again—sat with the Foxes. It was a solemn assembly, surrounded by the trophies and emblems on the walls of the vast fencing hall.

The programme of a 'Kneipe' is divided into three parts :

the official part, the unofficial part, and the 'pigsty.' If lady guests are present, which happens once or twice a year, the 'pigsty' is omitted.

The *Præses*—a dark, good-looking young man from Croatia named Hans Kolban, who was deported and killed during World War II—rose and struck the table three times with his sword and after a few words of greeting to the 'distinguished guests,' declared the 'Kneipe' open. The official part consisted in the singing of songs and the drinking of toasts. Strict ceremony ruled, as on state occasions; the commands for intoning a song and offering toasts were given in Latin. The order of the songs was immutably fixed. It ran as follows :

1. *Gaudeamus Igitur*—in Latin.
2. *Hatikvah*, the Zionist Anthem—in Hebrew.
3. *O Alte Burschen-Herrlichkeit*—in German.
4. *Ergo Bibamus*—in Latin.
5. *Vivat Academia*—in Latin.
6. The Unitas Fraternity Song—in German, sung to a Hebrew melody :
    '*Arise, my people, to noble deeds,*
    Be ready for the battle,' and so on and so forth.

All songs were sung standing at attention. All toasts (to the *Præsidium,* the *Contrarium,* and to various old boys, dead or alive) were drunk at attention, with clicking of heels. The lifting of the full and the putting down of the empty glass was done with the precision of shouldering arms in a Guards regiment. The slightest misconduct of a Fox, such as fidgeting during a song or spilling wine, was solemnly reported by the *Contrarium* to the *Præsidium.* The *Præsidium* inflicted punishment by ordering the offender to 'dive into his glass' either *ad diagonalem* (until the level of the liquid in the tilted glass touched the upper end of its base), or *ex,* to the last drop. In the latter case the offender had, on request, to furnish the 'nail-proof'—tip his glass over his thumb-nail to show that not a drop was left. No drinking was permitted during the ceremonial part except by command; but it was lawful, and even meritorious, to share another offender's punishment by jumping up, clicking one's heels, bawling out the words 'in sympathy,' and drinking *ex* or *ad diagonalem* according to the case. The glasses were tumblers, the wine strong, and the only nourishment provided was salted pretzels. Towards the end of the official part two of the Foxes asked permission, in Latin, *per Contrarium ad Præsidium,* to go to the bathroom to be sick. This they did, white in the face, but with great discipline and dignity, and came back looking much better, their hair plastered down after having been dipped in cold water. They were greeted with cheers, like soldiers wounded in battle rejoining their regiment.

During the unofficial part things became more cosy. One could now talk freely to one's neighbours and across the table, or apply for permission, *per Contrarium ad Præsidium,* to make a speech. There were solos and choir songs, now rendered while sitting—standing at attention would have been by this time difficult even for seasoned veterans. There was, however, still no drunkenness; high spirits reigned, but were kept in check by courtesy and decorum. This was made possible by the Roman expedient of absenting oneself from time to time and putting a finger down one's throat. The highlight of the unofficial part was the 'wine yarn.' This was a humorous speech about cabbages and kings, studded with allusions to public and private events, delivered by one of the seniors. According to the rules, the yarn had to proceed 'in loops'—it had to jump from one subject to another by means of alliteration, assonance and free association. With my judgment mellowed by the wine, the speech seemed the wittiest I had ever heard.

Strangely enough, I did not get drunk. This was partly

due to Hahn's keeping an eye on me, and partly to the fact that under the influence of strong intellectual stimulation or emotional excitement, I have always burned up alcohol at a quick rate; whereas when bored or depressed I often got unpleasantly drunk on amounts of liquor the multiple of which had no ill effects under happier circumstances. On this particular occasion I was both stimulated and excited by the strange surroundings, the exotic rites, but above all by the novel experience of being accepted into a friendly and fraternal community. I had always been lonely—as a child, as a schoolboy, and lonelier than ever in the *pensionnat* that I had just left with the persecutions of the Triumvirate still fresh and bitter in my memory. At that long table in the festive hall, surrounded by jolliness, laughter and songs, with the pleasant glow of a litre or two of new wine inside me, I felt as if I were emerging from a dark tunnel into a new dazzling light. For the first time I experienced that strongest of all social emotions: the feeling of comradeship, the feeling of belonging.

I was recruited by the Fraternity the same evening. At some point during the unofficial part of the proceedings, Hahn and Attila, both of whom were to become my intimate friends, involved me in a political conversation. Attila started by asking what I thought of Zionism. I answered truthfully that I had never thought about it and hardly knew what the word meant. It meant, in substance, explained Attila, that the Jews had been persecuted during some twenty centuries and that there was no reason to expect they would not be persecuted in the twenty-first. To argue with anti-Semites was all the more hopeless as the Jews were in fact a sick race. They were a nation without a country, which was like being a man without a shadow; and they were socially top-heavy, with a disproportionately great number of lawyers, merchants, intellectuals, and with no farmers or peasants—which was like a pyramid standing on its top. The only cure was : return to the earth. If Jews wanted to be like other people, they must have a country like other people and a social structure like other people. That was all there was to it, and there was no other way.

This seemed so simple and obvious that I wondered why I had not thought of it myself. But then, I had never been personally victimised or bothered by anti-Semitism, and had always regarded the so-called 'Jewish Question' as the same kind of boring and remote subject as Municipal Autonomy or the War of the Spanish Succession. It struck me as particularly funny that both Attila and Hahn, who were so preoccupied with the Jewish Question, did not look Jewish at all. Attila, whose real name was Jacob Teller—he later became a dentist in Tiberias, where he died a few years ago —had a typically Mongolian face, with high cheek-bones and the twinkling, humorous eyes of a Tartar; hence his nickname. As for Hahn, alias 'Gockl,' the cock—now a surgeon in Tel Aviv—he is, with his blond hair, snub nose, and duelling scars, the prototype of Hitler's Aryan hero.

I asked Hahn for argument's sake how he knew that he was a Jew.

'How do I know that I am Otto Hahn?' he said. 'They call me by that name, so I must accept it.' He went on to explain with the scientific precision of a medical student that all theories of race were nonsense, that most of the so-called racial characteristics were not hereditary but acquired by environmental pressure, and that there was no way of defining a Jew except by looking at what was written on his birth certificate. But all this, he said, had nothing to do with the problem. It was not a matter of definition, but of courage and dignity.

This was slightly confusing, but it did not matter. Emotionally, I had already taken the plunge. By the time the 'pigsty' stage of the proceedings was reached, I considered it a self-evident truth that the most enviable situation in life was to be a Senior of 'Unitas,' and a fighter with sword and pen for the New Jerusalem.

The 'pigsty' itself, this time-honoured institution of the *Burschenschaften*, was less shocking than might be expected. Its name, if I am not mistaken, is derived from the Students' Song in *Faust* : 'We're a bunch of cosy cannibals/A herd of ten thousand pigs.' Its programme consisted in the singing of the old bawdy songs of the *Schülers*, some of which were of mediæval origin and had a strange folk quality of poetry blended with straight obscenity. Pornography thrives on the veiled allusion; in these songs a spade was called a spade. Compared to the atmosphere of some American 'smokers' this pigsty had a healthy, earthy smell; there were outbursts of laughter, but no suppressed giggles. One of the old boys, 'Puttl', a giant of Falstaffian dimensions who had been the terror of the Pan-Germans at the Aula, was an expert at reciting the famous ballad of 'The Innkeeper's Wife.' This ballad, or saga, was begun in the early nineteenth century; since then, generations of students have added new stanzas, but only those which were really witty survived by word of mouth and in rare, privately printed editions. Altogether it was said to consist of about two hundred and fifty stanzas, of which P. was alleged to know a hundred and seven by heart. The verses were Limericks of the kind which starts 'There was a young lady of Trent.' The highlight of a 'pigsty' came when somebody recited a new strophe of his own composition; but it was a risky business, for if it did not find acclaim, the author had to take severe punishment by diving repeatedly into his glass.

The notorious bawdiness of the Viennese student fraternities was an expression of the vitality and exuberance proper to that age, not of frustrated yearnings. The average Austrian student needed neither a high income nor a particularly attractive appearance to find a little friend among that bygone type of femininity known as '*das süsse Wiener Mädl*.'

The 'sweet Vienna girl' was a shopgirl or typist or a dress-maker's employee. Unlike her French equivalent, the *midin-ette,* who became extinct early in the century, the sweet Vienna girl was still a most comforting reality in the 1920s. Her tastes were modest; she loved for love's sake; to be occasionally taken to the movies or to a *Weinstube* for dinner was regarded by her as the peak of generosity. She was pretty, flirtatious and extremely well behaved; and she was treated by her student friends with great consideration and courtesy. Thanks to her existence, the Viennese fraternities were free of homosexuality and of the neurotic quarrels and entanglements so frequent in other youth clubs.

If I seem to romanticise my memories of that intellectually absurd, emotionally very satisfactory association, it must be due to an echo of its warm *camaraderie.* It is certainly a paradox that these extremely conservative, fossilised, brag-ging and duelling *Burschenschaften* were psychologically healthier than any closed community or clique that I have come across since. Looking back today, as a veteran of count-less feuds and factional battles fought in the ghettos of Com-munist cells, of editorial offices, writers' congresses and progressive committees, it seems almost incredible that I spent three years, as a very neurotic young man, in daily intimate contact with a small group of budding intellectuals, and Jewish intellectuals to boot, without becoming involved in, or being witness of, a single serious quarrel or feud. Per-haps this was only possible in that unique Viennese atmo-sphere of *laisser-faire* and erotic tolerance, combined with the restraining influence of tradition-grown discipline and ceremonious decorum. For the same harmony prevailed within most of the other fraternities, whether they were Pan-German, Liberal or Zionist, whether they wore the colours of Teutonia or Jordania. Internal quarrels were frequent, however, among the Socialist student clubs who treated us as 'colour monkeys,' barbarians and blockheads.

XI. I Become Almost Normal

THUS my first political awakening had been caused by Chopin's Funeral March, the second by the tune of *Gaudeamus Igitur*. In both cases the emotional commitment came first, and the arguments came later.

This may seem a humiliating confession for a political writer to make. How can anybody value the judgment and trust the critical faculties of a person whose political allegiances were derived, by his own admission, from such absurd sentimental experiences?

The subject is worth a digression; for it seems to me that the story I have told is a fairly typical one. It certainly must sound grotesque to those who take it for granted that political attitudes are primarily formed by rational considerations. In contrast to this naïve belief, all evidence tends to show that the political libido is basically as irrational as the sexual drive, and patterned, like the latter, by early, partly unconscious experiences—by traumatic shocks, complexes, identifications, repressions, and the rest. Early emotional conditioning plays a decisive part; the arguments which justify and rationalise the credo come afterwards. 'There is nothing, Sir,' said Dr. Johnson, 'that you may not muster up some plausible arguments for.'

All this does not imply an abdication of political judgment. Recognition of the irrational sources of impulses does not invalidate the necessity for their control by reason. But diagnosis must precede therapy; and the diagnosis of the causes of any political attitude ought to penetrate through the layers of rationalisations and phraseology, down to the psychological roots—which will often be found to consist of such logically absurd, emotionally powerful, experiences as the *Gaudeamus* and the Funeral March.

Judgments on the rational and ethical value of a political attitude are only possible if a clear distinction is made between primary and secondary developments of the political libido. The first phase must of necessity be irrational; it may be dominated by some overwhelming emotional experience such as the hanging of Lenin's brother, or by steady conditioning like that of an English public school. The majority of people never seem to outgrow this primitive emotive phase—their political loyalties remain in the state of infantile fixations. The votes they cast at elections are about as rational as the neurotic's choice of a mate.

The second phase, if it occurs, is one of doubt : critical reasoning asserts itself over emotive belief. It corresponds, in Freudian terms, to the ascendancy of the reality-principle over the pleasure-principle. This phase should end—and so rarely does end—with the emergence of a new, mature faith, in which reason and emotion are harmoniously blended.

Political maturity does not, alas, coincide with age. Many conversions at an adult age, whether religious or political, are the result of an immature psychological make-up, and differ only little from the primary infantile process of acquiring faith.

My juvenile infatuation with the Hundred Days had passed like measles, without leaving much conscious trace. When I joined the Communist Party twelve years later the reasons which prompted me to do so were of an entirely different quality and order. But whether half-remembered images of cubist posters and red globes exerted a subconscious influence, I am unable to decide. But if they did, they now had to pass through the filter of reasoning. Maybe some lingering after-taste of ice-cream sweetened the acid texts of Marx; maybe a shadow of the friendly, grimy characters listening to my cousin Margit's lecture superimposed itself on my concept of the international working class. May he, whose opinions and convictions are entirely free of unconscious bias, cast the first stone.

My attitude to Zionism also evolved through several stages. To take the plunge was easy; the struggle for clarity that followed was not. It took the best part of twenty-five years. On that first evening with 'Unitas,' the whole problem had looked so simple—merely a matter of courage and dignity, as Hahn had said. It must have looked equally simple to Pharaoh's slaves, when they set out for their promised land, happily ignorant of the desert that lay ahead.

There is a span of three years between that evening, and my running away from home to embark for Palestine, at the age of twenty.

Several independent threads run through this period. The first was a greedy pursuit of the pleasures of *Wein, Weib und Gesang*. I did my best to live up to my nickname and become 'a tippler, serene and wise.' What I lacked in serenity and wisdom, was compensated by nervous exuberance, the explosive backstroke of a childhood famished for play. I still suffered from shyness and cramp in the presence of people who, for one reason or another, provoked my sense of inferiority, but among my comrades I felt completely at ease; and as I spent most of my time with them, their influence was rather similar in its effects to occupational group therapy in psychiatric treatment. The intermittent attacks of timidity became less frequent, and although I have never got rid of them entirely, the outward change in social behaviour effected by this fraternal environment was swift and conspicuous. So much so, that even my bad swordsmanship failed to give me an inferiority complex. I fought a single duel, against an opponent from a Liberal *Korps,* who fortunately was as bad as I. He gave me a cut on the chin which, to my deep regret at the time, left no conspicuous scar—and an even smaller one over the eye; and though I did not succeed in drawing blood, he had to give up, because of heart trouble, after half an hour or so (duels between evenly matched opponents, lasting two or three hours, with both men bleeding like stuck pigs, were no rarity).

In short, I had neither distinguished myself nor made a fool of myself, which gave me a reassuring feeling of normality. Luckily for me, duelling opportunities were becoming infrequent as our enemies, the Pan-Germans, could only be fought with sticks and fists, while there was no point in picking quarrels with the Liberals, who on the whole were on our side. Altogether I watched about a dozen duels, some of which were nasty sights, including one in which a friend of mine lost all his back teeth on the left upper jaw through a deep quart; yet Ahor did not come into the picture. Ahor was only roused by the irrational and the unknown, whereas sword-fights and the scuffles at the University were gentlemanly and ritualistic affairs.

Having served my time as a Fox, I became, in my fourth semester, *Præses* of 'Unitas,' and at the same time chairman of the Convention of all twelve Zionist *Burschenschaften* in Austria—the youngest who had ever exercised that illustrious function, which flattered my vanity to no small extent. The climax of all this glamour was my presiding, at nineteen, over a banquet of some three hundred colour-wearing students and old boys in a hall of the former Imperial Palace of Vienna, which the Austrian Republic had nationalised and rented out for festive occasions—in this case the thirty years' Jubilee of our *Burschenschaft.* The banquet was followed by a dance which I had to open by waltzing with Hans Kolban's sister, down a lane between two rows of martial and colourful stalwarts holding their swords above our heads, as in a period film of the Congress of Vienna. After this orgy of satisfied vainglory, my vanity gradually began to subside—or rather it became diverted into less obvious channels. By the time I became moderately known as a writer, the coarser forms of vanity, such as the enjoyment of public appearances, receptions and the like, had burnt themselves out. There is much to be said for satisfying, even to excess, one's more imbecile yearnings in youth, before they go sour on one. It is not in the artist's power to cast off entirely his vanity, which is probably a vital ingredient of his creative gifts; but he ought at least to be able to knead and mould the trembling clay of his self-conceit into a slightly less silly pattern than appearances on the television screen or the autographing of books at charity bazaars.

Looking back upon the pleasurable aspects of those three years spent in Vienna, I am glad that I discussed the Nostalgic Fallacy at the beginning of this book as a warning to myself. I was not much tempted to dwell on the scent of the lavender bag in the linen closet, nor on the wrinkled smiles of uncles and grannies; but it is difficult to resist a tête-à-tête with the charming ghosts of Vienna, difficult not to indulge in memories of summer nights in the vineyards of Grinzing, of picnics on the Danube, of sitting with a book in the sunbathed public parks, of nocturnal processions with lighted candles along the 'Ring,' of Richard Strauss first nights at the Opera or Alexander Moissi's performance in *Hamlet*; and above all, to pass in silence the gallery of smiling portraits of sweet Vienna girls, Friedls and Hansls and Christls and Bertls, who seem to curtsy with tender and mocking glances, as in a ballet scene by Degas. There was a song in Vienna at that time : 'Why cry when we part?/ We say au revoir/And think with a smile :/Praised be the Lord/ Who ties and unties our hearts.'

That Vienna is as distant from us today as the lost continent of Atlantis. The stars which shone in its firmament are extinct without having been properly charted on the maps; who in the West knows, and who in the East remembers Karl Kraus, the most brilliant satirist in the German language; Peter Altenberg, the Dr. Johnson of Vienna's cafés; the early Werfel; Anton Kuh; Egon Erwin Kisch; von Hofmannsthal's books for the operas of Richard Strauss? The opera and the ballet, and the repertory of classics in the Burg Theatre; the concerts, and the Philharmonic Orchestra were a permanent festival, the last display of fireworks before the clock struck twelve and it was closing-time for Europe. To revive that period, without the sugar-icing of the movie industry's idea of Vienna, is one of my cherished projects for those hypothetical later years when I shall permit myself to indulge in the Nostalgic Fallacy.

I have little hope that that time will materialise. As far as this present undertaking is concerned, all that needs to be recorded is that during those three years, from seventeen to twenty, and only during those three years, I was able to enjoy myself without a feeling of guilt. Ahor was dormant; it was the one period of my life in which the sum total of pleasurable moments outweighed the others. In short, during these three years I was as happy as it has been given to me to be; and, when all is said, three years of happiness out of forty-six is not such a bad ratio in our time.

XII. The Arrow Splits

THE second main development of my undergraduate years is more difficult to summarise.

I have a vivid image of the arrow, whose timeless flight through space was, in one way or another, always present in my mind, splitting lengthwise into two. The two halves have a repellent effect on each other, their orbits become deflected; they continue their flight in opposite directions, one symbolising Action, the other Contemplation. The juvenile quest for the secret of infinity, split into two simultaneous and in all respects contradictory pursuits.

I can remember fairly clearly the moment when the arrow split and the two halves began to lead their independent existence. It was on a spring morning in 1924. I was sitting on a bench in the *Volksgarten,* one of Vienna's enchanted parks, with a pile of books beside me. On top lay a pamphlet about the latest Arab riots in Palestine, with appalling details of children put to the sword as in the days of Herod, of Jewish pioneers being killed after having been blinded and castrated, of the passivity of the Mandatory Administration and their refusal to allow the Jews to arm in self-defence.

While I was reading the pamphlet, I felt myself choke and seethe with impotent anger. Moral indignation did and still does affect me in a direct physical manner. Like most people who suffer from Chronic Indignation—as others do from chronic indigestion—I can feel, during an attack, the infusion of adrenalin into the bloodstream, the craving of the muscles, flooded with blood-sugar, for violent action. As the case may be, you begin to tremble, or throw a choleric fit, or write a revolutionary tract, or start growing an ulcer. When I had finished reading the pamphlet and had calmed down a little, I fell into one of my habitual reveries about devoting my life to the cause of the persecuted as a fighter and writer of books which would shake the conscience of the world. I must have used up since then tons of adrenalin on that job.

While still in the grip of that dream, and all geared for action, I opened the next book in the pile at its marked page. It was Weyl's introduction to Einstein's theory of Relativity. A phrase suddenly struck me and has remained in my memory ever since. It said that the theory of General Relativity led the human imagination 'across the peaks of glaciers never before explored by any human being.' This cliché had an unexpectedly strong effect. I saw Einstein's world-shaking formula—Energy equals Mass multiplied by the square of the velocity of light—hovering in a kind of rarefied haze over the glaciers, and this image carried a sensation of infinite tranquillity and peace. The martyred infants and castrated pioneers of the Holy Land shrank to microscopic insignificance. Beast had fed on beast in sea and jungle since the beginnings of organic life; it was a law of Nature and of history; there was nothing to get excited about. The fate of these unfortunates had to be viewed with the same serene, detached, meditative eye as that of stars bursting into novæ, of sunspots erupting, of rocks decaying into swamps, and primeval forests being transformed into coal. This change in perspective was accompanied by an equally pronounced physiological change. The sensation of choking with indignation was succeeded by the relaxed quietude and self-dissolving stillness of the 'oceanic feeling.'[1]

I have often since experienced both of these opposite states of mind, but never in such close proximity as on that occasion. They are opposites in every respect—in their physio-

[1] The term used by Freud to denote mystic or religious experience.

E

logical mechanism, emotional tone, intellectual outlook, and in the social attitudes which they produce. Moral indignation may be compared to a sudden, or continuous implosion which provides the heat and pressure required for action. The effect of the 'oceanic feeling,' on the other hand, is an expansion of consciousness, its liberation from any pressure and itch, its temporary dissolution in Nirvana.

Though the two states are mutually exclusive at any given moment, they may alternate in time. They may succeed each other in quick oscillations of mood and outlook within a single day, or there may be periods of several years in an individual's life when one or the other is dominant. The institution of the 'retreat' known in various forms to all civilisations, was obviously developed under the influence of this duality. The retreats were in my case provided by periods of confinement in prisons and concentration camps, each of which turned into a spiritual blessing; and later on by the more moderate habit of living in rather inaccessible places in the country—the present is written on an island in the Delaware River—in nearly complete solitude.

In the following sections the contemplative trend will play a quantitatively smaller part than the active trend. This is unavoidable because the 'oceanic experience' to a large extent eludes verbal communication, and attempts to convey it (unless one has the gift of poetic expression, which I have not) tend to fall flat or take a maudlin turn. The balance between the two antagonistic forces will thus necessarily be distorted. But although not much explicit mention will be made of it, it was always the 'oceanic' type of experience which dictated the really important decisions of my life, and determined its abrupt zig-zag course.

All this sounds rather a mouthful, for to talk about one's own split personality is a special form of vanity—particularly in the case of Central Europeans fed on Goethe's 'Two souls, alas, inhabit my bosom.' But if I am to remain truthful, the separate existence of those two souls in my bosom must be emphasised, for the split has remained with me, and the resulting tug-of-war is one of the recurring *leit-motifs* of this report. It is reflected in the antithetical titles of my books: *The Yogi and the Commissar, Insight and Outlook, Darkness at Noon, Le Zéro et l'Infini, Arrival and Departure*, and so on. The choice of these titles was more or less unconscious, and the underlying pattern only dawned on me much later.

Like Professor Pavlov's laboratory dogs when exposed to two simultaneous and contradictory stimuli, I stumbled along my zig-zag path, pulled in opposite directions by political fanaticism and contemplative detachment, by simultaneous urges to become an apprentice-Yogi and a pocket Commissar. Our time has created a field of force rather similar to the conditions in Pavlov's laboratory. The poor dog, when exposed to them, reacts with a behaviour called 'experimental neurosis'; the author, instead of barking, responds to the contradictory stimuli by verbalising them into books. What I have written may be regarded as the chart of an experimental neurosis produced in the laboratory of our time.

More specifically, the laboratory in question was Central Europe in the second quarter of this century; and the stimuli to which I reacted were first the financial, then the physical destruction of the cultural stratum from which I came. At a conservative estimate, three out of every four people whom I knew before I was thirty were subsequently killed in Spain, or hounded to death at Dachau, or gassed at Belsen, or deported to Russia, or liquidated in Russia; some jumped from windows in Vienna or Budapest, others were wrecked by the misery and aimlessness of permanent exile. My reaction to these stimuli was, on the other hand, the state I have described as Chronic Indignation; each new shock made detachment appear a crime, restraint a shameful escape. On the other hand, I knew that detachment and restraint are essential values in art. Thus the conflict between action and contemplation logically led into the conflict between art and propaganda. I have spoilt most of my novels out of a sense of duty to some 'cause'; I knew that the artist should not exhort or preach, and I kept on exhorting and preaching. The temptations of the devil are easier to resist than those in which the tempter appears in the guise of a crusader full of righteous indignation, with the unanswerable accusations of 'escapism' and 'fiddling while Rome burns' on his fanatical lips. Besides, he did not say 'while Rome burns,' but 'while your cousins were gassed at Auschwitz,' and 'while your friend confessed that he was a Nazi spy before the People's Court.' So, naturally, I had to plead guilty to the charge of Criminal Artistic Detachment, and get back into crusader's armour. But that solution was not a lasting one either, for in the long run you cannot write with a mailed glove on your hand. Again you plead guilty, and the whole cycle starts afresh.

The disturbing fact is that both pleas of guilt are valid. 'You cannot rule guiltlessly,' St. Just said. There exist conditions under which one cannot act, or write, or even live guiltlessly. Train a dog to run after bicycles but not to run after motor cars, and then ride past him on a motor cycle; he will react with an experimental neurosis. Train a nation to believe that tolerance is good, persecution is bad, and ask them whether or not to persecute people who want to abolish tolerance; they will react in much the same way. In peaceful times such paradoxa are merely amusing logical puzzles; in times of crisis they may become fatal to an individual or a civilisation.

The farthest I got, after some thirty years of unsuccessful attempts to bridge these contradictions and reunite the split halves of the arrow, is a tentative approach, formulated by one of the characters in *The Age of Longing*:

'Art is a contemplative business. It is also a ruthless business. One should either write ruthlessly what one believes to be the truth, or shut up. Now I happen to believe that Europe is doomed, a chapter in history which is drawing to its finish. This is so to speak my contemplative truth. Looking at the world with detachment, under the sign of eternity, I find it not even disturbing. But I also happen to believe in the ethical imperative of fighting evil, even if the fight is hopeless. And on this plane my contemplative truth becomes defeatist propaganda, and hence an immoral influence. You can't get out of the dilemma between contemplation and action. There were idyllic periods in history when the two went together. In times like ours, they are incompatible. And I am not an isolated case. European art is dying out, because it can't live without truth, and its truth has become arsenic. . . .'

'If the pessimism of the philosopher is a valid attitude, the duty of the militant humanist to go on hoping against hope is no less valid. The reproach of morbid despair which is so often levelled against us, seems to me provoked by a mix-up between two parallel planes in our minds which should be kept separate: the plane of detached contemplation in the sign of infinity, and the plane of action in the name of certain ethical imperatives. We have to accept the perpetual contradiction between these two. If we admit that defeatism and despair, even when logically justified, are morally wrong, and that active resistance to evil is a moral necessity even when it seems logically absurd, we may find a new approach to a humanist dialectic. . . .'

XIII. The First Crusade

HAVING taken the plunge I was soon up to my neck in Zionist activities.

Judaism did not attract me. I was brought up in an assimilated environment without roots in Judaic tradition. My mind had been fed on Hungarian, Russian, French, and English literature; the only Jewish literature, as far as I knew, was the Old Testament, and that wasn't literature in the accepted sense. Now, through the Zionist movement, I came for the first time into contact with Polish and Russian Jews who had been brought up in Talmudic schools and in the Yiddish language—a vernacular composed of mediæval German and Hebrew, with Russian, Polish, Lithuanian or Latvian admixtures, according to the region in which it was spoken. This jargon, with its insinuating, lilting sing-song that turned every factual statement into an emotional one, repelled me. It had no fixed grammar and syntax, no fixed vocabulary, no logical precision. It was not spoken but sung, to the accompaniment of gestures. Nothing said in Yiddish seemed to be a flat statement, to be taken at face value; everything was charged with over- and undertones, lubricated with sentiment, shrouded in a kind of logical twilight. I disliked this language, and the mentality which it reflected, from the first time I heard it, and I have never lost my aversion for it.

I read some of the tales of ghetto life translated from the Yiddish and felt even more estranged. They exhaled a stale air, saturated with the smell of narrow streets, of unventilated bedding, mental inbreeding and tortuous ways; they were spiced with over-ripe, self-deprecatory humour. There was in this literature a mixture of servility and spiritual arrogance, of cunning and sentimentality, of mysticism and cupidity, which gave me a feeling of claustrophobia, of wanting to break a window and let the fresh air in.

At that time I did not know that the world is full of ghettos other than Jewish. I did not know that the peculiarities which repelled me were not racial characteristics but products of conditions such as prevail in any hermetically sealed community. Penitentiaries, concentration camps, monasteries, artists' colonies, ethnic minorities, homosexual cliques, tuberculosis sanatoriums, political and religous sects, all develop into little ghettos with a hot-house atmosphere, a peculiar jargon, a private, walled-in universe. Every single so-called Jewish trait can be found in varying combinations in these closed communities. The Jews of Eastern Europe, however, had been exposed to the stuffy atmosphere of the ghetto for some ten or fifteen generations. Their supposedly racial and hereditary characteristics were mostly acquired through social pressure and transmitted through social inheritance. This seems to be true for both mental and physical characteristics. Catholic priests who live in celibacy and fight an often lifelong battle against temptation, frequently develop facial features which give the impression that they belong to a particular race. Convicts who serve long terms in a penitentiary seem to acquire very precise 'racial' characteristics. A furtive and dejected, impudent and servile look creeps into their eyes; their lips become thin, their noses pinched and pointed, their nostrils dilated and waxen; their knees sag, their arms seem to grow to disproportionate length and dangle gorilla-fashion. Similarly the Jews, exiled in Egypt, in Babylon, and later over the whole globe, exposed to strange and hostile surroundings, developed certain peculiar traits :

'. . . Made homeless in space, they had to expand into new dimensions, as the blind develop hearing and touch. The loss of the spatial dimension transformed this branch of the species as it would have transformed any other nation on earth, Jupiter or Mars. It turned their vision inwards. It made them cunning and grew them claws to cling on with, as they were swept by the wind through countries that were not theirs. It increased their spiritual arrogance: deprived of Space, they believed themselves chosen for eternity in Time. It increased the protective adaptability of their surface, and petrified their inner core. Constant friction polished their many facets: reduced to driftsand, they had to glitter if they wanted to avoid being trodden on. Living in bondage cringing became second nature to their pride. Their natural selector was the whip: it whipped the life out of the feeble and whipped the spasm of ambition into the fit. In all walks of life, to get an equal chance they had to start with a plus. Condemned to live in extremes, they were in every respect like other people, only more so. They were a branch of the species touched on the raw, the natural target of all malcontents, because they were so exasperatingly and abnormally human.'

I have quoted this passage from *Thieves in the Night,* a book written twenty years later, for without this anticipatory excursion into a more mature state of mind, what I have said would sound harsh and unjust and might expose me—as happened often before—to the paradoxical charge of anti-Semitism. The fact is, that at the time which I am discussing, I knew little about the fearful power of environmental pressure over mind and body; hence I felt merely bewildered by my first contacts with Eastern European, tradition-bound Jews. Equally bewildering were certain aspects of their religion. Two thousand years after the events on Mount

Golgotha, it was still taboo for practising Jews to mention the name of Jesus of Nazareth—he could only be referred to as 'that man,' or by the Hebrew equivalent, *oto ha'ish*. For centuries on end Jewish children had been educated in the *Yeshiva*, the Talmudic school, where their minds were fed on scholastic exercises based on commentaries of commentaries of commentaries of the Bible. Scholasticism of this type died out in Europe with the Renaissance; in Jewish schools it had remained the almost exclusive discipline of the mind. Simultaneously, the Mosaic ritual had degenerated into an elaborate system of 'interpretations' designed to by-pass the original laws. Generations of Jews were taught in Talmudic schools to interpret a yes as a no and black as white, until this technique became a conditioned reflex of the mind. How far this mental corruption in matters divine was the product of social pressure which forced the Jews to live on the margin of the law, and how far Talmudic mentality reacted in turn on their pattern of social behaviour, is a moot point. The outcome, at any rate, was a vicious circle, a *perpetuum mobile* for generating anti-Semitism, which linked persecution and evasion in a monotonously alternating rhythm.

Yet at the time, I was only dimly aware of the historical background. I was only aware of my revulsion against a form of worship which seemed to consist in cheating the Lord and one's own conscience. I learnt about the practices of orthodox Jews during the Passover Feast, when the Law demands that one should eat unleavened bread and have no crockery that has ever been in contact with leaven in one's house. ' "In your house," ' the scholars declared, 'means "in your possession." Accordingly, you only have to go, on the eve of the Passover, to your Gentile neighbour and make a nominal deal with him—you "sell" him your crockery on the understanding that you will "buy" it back after the Passover for the same sum. The crockery need not actually be moved to the neighbour's; it can stay in your house—for, as it is no

longer "in your possession," the Lord must be satisfied. . . .'
Similarly, to light a fire on the Sabbath is sin; but to pay a
Gentile servant to commit that sin is accepted orthodox practice. A good deal of the Jewish ritual seemed to consist of
such pettifogging practices, and to have degenerated into
manœuvres of evasion. The religion of the desert had
become a religion of the ghetto.

Most bewildering of all was the discovery that the saga of
the 'Chosen Race' seemed to be taken quite literally by
traditionalist Jews. They protested against racial discrimination, and affirmed in the same breath their racial superiority
based on Jacob's covenant with God. Since I had learned at
the age of six that Hungary was the feather in God's cap, I
had become impatient, and indeed allergic, towards all
claims of belonging to a chosen race.

The long and short of it is that the more I found out about
Judaism the more distressed I became—and the more fervently Zionist. The Jewish State was the only cure for a
sickness which I could not name or define, but which seemed
intimately connected with the Jews' lack of a country and a
flag of their own. In the absence of these, they were paying
guests in the houses of strangers, and whether tolerated or
beaten up, were always regarded as different; therein lay
the root of the sickness. When the Jewish State was re-
established, the cure would be automatic and all would be
well.

Perhaps the idea of a 'National Home' had this strong
attraction for me because I had lived in hotels and boarding-
houses since my childhood. A 'rootless cosmopolitan' from
the days of my youth, with a polyglot culture and physically
always on the move, there was perhaps an unconscious
craving in me to grow roots, an urge to create and construct,
to build cities in the desert and gardens out of the swamp.
Besides, to resurrect the State of Israel was something like
building a George Washington bridge across two millennia

of History; a supreme feat of social engineering. Connect, always connect—construct, always construct! Zion was a new version of the song which promised that we would 'lift the globe from its axis.'

However, official Zionism in the 1920s was a depressing affair. It consisted mainly in appeals for money and more money—money for the Jewish National Fund, money for the Jewish Reconstruction Fund, money for the Hadassah Hospital, for the Hebrew University, for the Bezalel Art School; and money for the salaries of those engaged in collecting money. Zionism was meant as an escape from the ghetto, but the ghetto had caught up with it; it hung like a stale fog over Zionist Congresses and the clubs and offices of the movement. The main duty of its rank and file was to rattle a collecting box at a kind of permanent charity bazaar. Hence the old joke: 'Zionism means one man persuading another man to give money to a third man to go to Palestine.'

The great vision of the founders of the movement, Herzl and Nordau, had been whittled down to this dreary bureau-cratised charity. World Jewry had not responded to the historic opportunity offered by the Balfour Declaration; during the ten years which followed it, less than 100,000 Jews had settled in Palestine. The very idea of a Jewish State had been relinquished in favour of the vague term 'National Home' which had no concrete meaning in international law. Immigration was only a small trickle—some ten to twenty thousand people a year. The achievements of the pioneers who drained the marshes and made the stony desert bear fruit again were admirable, and equally admirable were their communal settlements, where the use of money was abolished and all property down to shirts and handkerchiefs was collectively owned. But without a politically and econo-mically solid hinterland, these Utopian enterprises were as certainly doomed to failure as similar experiments in the past.

I was saved from disillusionment by a personality whose decisive part in the establishment of the Jewish State has not been sufficiently recognised. His name was Vladimir Jabotinsky, and he became the first political shaman in my life.

He was, when I first met him, in his middle forties, a man slightly under medium height who carried himself like a soldier and talked like a man of letters. He came from Odessa, like Leon Trotsky, with whom he had some affinities, and whose fate was to some extent paralleled by his own. He had a massive head with Slavonic features and displayed in his manners a strange, eighteenth-century courtesy. Part of his personal magnetism, which captivated his followers and opponents alike, was in his voice : it made every language that he spoke—and he spoke eight to perfection—sound like Italian.

Already in his early twenties, under the pen-name of Altalena, Jabotinsky had achieved celebrity in Russia. A brilliant journalist and lecturer, he had campaigned against the sentimental peasant-cult of the Social Revolutionaries and preached an urbane liberalism modelled on the traditions of the West. He hated the Messianic terrorism of the early Russian revolutionaries and held up against them the example of the great nineteenth-century Liberals and humanists. He was brought up in the enlightened atmosphere of cosmopolitan Odessa, a stranger to Jewish tradition. When he was drawn by Herzl into the Zionist movement, he took towards it the same stand he had taken towards the problems of Russia. He detested the turbid mysticism and confused sentimentality which pervaded the phraseology of the movement; he hated the Talmudic dialectics and roundabout tactics of its leadership. At Zionist congresses he talked a language that was straight, lucid, and European—and utterly un-Jewish in the sense in which the tradition-bound, jargon-bred leaders understood it. Most

Zionists at that time visualised the 'National Home' as a kind of glorified ghetto, without the restrictions but with the traditions and atmosphere of the ghetto—and even the architecture of the ghetto, which the first colonists piously imitated. To Jabotinsky and his followers Zionism meant a complete break with tradition; it meant westernisation, parliamentary government modelled on Britain, education modelled on the French lay-schools, a national army, and, to make the heresy complete, Latinisation of the obsolete Hebrew alphabet. The inevitable result was that he was denounced as a heretic, an anti-Semite, a militarist and later on, of course, a Fascist.

During the First World War, Jabotinsky with patient and persistent effort persuaded the British Government to agree to the creation of a 'Judean Regiment'—the first Jewish fighting force in modern times. It fought under General Allenby in the Palestine campaign; Jabotinsky participated in it with the rank of captain. In 1920, during the first Arab riots, he created an illegal Jewish defence organisation which fought in Jaffa and in the old city of Jerusalem. It was the report of the atrocities committed in the course of these riots which had filled me with such indignation. The Arab instigator of these riots, and Jabotinsky as organiser of the Jewish defence, were both sentenced by British military courts to fifteen years at forced labour. A few months later Jabotinsky benefited by an amnesty; on his release from the fortress prison at Acco he was acclaimed as a national hero. In 1921, he was elected to the Zionist Executive—the shadow government of the nascent Jewish State—but resigned after a short time on matters of policy, foremost among them the whittling down of the 'Jewish State' to the ambiguous term 'National Home.' His prophetic foresight regarding an issue which at the time seemed merely a quibble about words, became evident twenty years later, when the British Government prohibited further entry of Jews into

Palestine on the pretext that the 'National Home' was already established and completed.

In 1924 Jabotinsky founded his own movement, the 'Zionist Activists' whose name was later changed to 'Zionist Revisionists.' Again later, this movement became the cradle of the terrorist groups, Irgun and Stern, who were to play a decisive part in the struggle for an independent Israel. Jabotinsky did not live to see the final victory; nor to be present at the ceremony when one of Tel Aviv's main arteries was named after him. And in 1924, when he visited Vienna on a lecture tour, these developments were still a secret of the future.

The arrival of 'Jabo,' as his friends affectionately called him, was preceded by that of one of his lieutenants, Dr. Wolfgang von Weisl. Weisl had been an officer of the Austrian Army (and, among other things, became later on commander of the Israeli Artillery in the Negeb). He was a lovable and adventurous character, became one of my closest friends, and will frequently figure in these pages. In 1924, when we first met, von Weisl was correspondent of the *Neue Freie Presse* (Vienna's 'Times') in the Middle East, and an old boy of 'Unitas.'

Realising that the Zionist party machinery in Vienna was in the hands of a salaried bureaucracy which had a vested interest to defend, Jabo and his group decided to concentrate their efforts on the *Burschenschaften,* as a reservoir of youthful energy frustrated by the dreary fund-raising tasks imposed on them. Von Weisl took 'Unitas' by storm. At the end of three discussion meetings, we rallied unconditionally to the banner of the Activist opposition. Jabotinsky was elected *Honorary Bursch* of the *Korps*—a distinction which had been previously only bestowed on Herzl and Nordau—and a gold badge was ordered. With this gold badge, encased in a velvet box, I travelled on a May day in 1924 to the frontier station of Lundenburg—in high spirits and third class, accompanied by 'Puttl,' the Falstaffian old boy and terror of the Pan-Germanists (he now runs a bridge club plus a brush factory in Tel Aviv).

On the crowded platform of the frontier station, we recognised Jabotinsky from his photographs, as he emerged from the Austrian customs with a volume of Dante in Italian under his arm.[1] I had the gruesome task of accosting him, welcoming him to Austria and pinning the badge on his lapel under the goggling eyes of customs officials and travellers. Puttl and I, looking like David and Goliath, both wore our shoulder sashes with the violet, white and gold colours. To my relief, Jabo was rather on the David side. He took the whole thing with good grace and acknowledged the honour with a few courteous words. He only drew the line when Puttl tried to place a sash across his chest too. He put the sash in his pocket, remarking that it might frighten the waiter in the dining-car, to which he invited us. He told me later that he had rarely been so embarrassed in all his life. He seemed to take an immediate, amused liking to me, and before the end of his short stay in Vienna, took me as secretary and co-speaker on the continuation of his lecture tour through Czecho-Slovakia. Now I was really launched on the warpath for Zion.

Jabotinsky's speech in the Kursaal, the largest concert-hall in Vienna, was a remarkable event. I have heard many political speakers since, but no one who could cast a similar spell over his audience for three solid hours without ever resorting to cheap oratory. There was not a cliché in his speech, delivered in a German worthy of the traditions of the Imperial Burg Theatre; its power rested in its transparent lucidity and logical beauty. One of Jabotinsky's admirers— either Lord Wedgwood or Anatole de Monzie—has called him the greatest orator of his time and the only man, besides

[1] Jabotinsky has translated, among other classics, parts of the *Divine Comedy* into modern Hebrew.

Lloyd George, who was equally outstanding as a speaker, journalist, and politician.

After Jabo's departure, a few of us started the Austrian branch of the 'League of Activists,' the forerunner of the Zionist Revisionist World Organisation. The founders were, as far as I can remember, Dr. Norbert Hoffman, editor of a Jewish literary periodical; Dr. Paul Diamant, a lawyer and genealogist, now a farmer near Jerusalem; Dr. Benjamin Akzin, now a Professor of international law at the Hebrew University; and myself. From the outset, we were in violent opposition to the Zionist leadership. The main points of our programme were :

That the aim of Zionism was to establish a Jewish State on both sides of the Jordan.

That the prerequisite of a Jewish State was the establishment of a Jewish majority in Palestine.

That a majority could only be established by mass-immigration, facilitated by an international loan instead of by international beggary.

That instead of costly and diminutive, utopian experiments, the Zionist organisation should concentrate its efforts on attracting the capital of Jewish industrialists, and the masses of the Jewish middle classes.

That to facilitate the development of industries in Palestine, temporary protective tariffs should be established.

That a Jewish militia should be legalised under British command for purposes of self-defence, to end the humiliating situation of Jews in their own country having to rely on the protection of British soldiers and taxpayers.

That to break the hostility of the Colonial Office and the Palestine local administration, a mass petition should be organised in which world Jewry laid the facts, and its aspirations, before the people of Britain and its Government.

That after the Jewish State was established, it should be

incorporated as the seventh dominion in the British Commonwealth of Nations.[1]

Most of the points of our—that is, Jabotinsky's—programme were at a later date taken up by official Zionism and eventually became reality. Jabotinsky's tragedy was the classic one of being a few years ahead of his time. There was a fundamental difference in temperament between him and the Zionist leadership, epitomised in the person of Dr. Weizmann. The leadership went out of its way to deny that Zionism aimed at a Jewish State; the term itself was anathema in official Zionist phraseology. Behind the scenes, however, the augurs quoted Weizmann's famous off-the-record remark : 'Always to think of it, never to speak of it.' In other words, the line of official Zionist diplomacy was the traditional backdoor approach—Jabotinsky's the bang at the front door. In retrospect it seems probable that both were necessary to achieve the purpose. Without the caution and Machiavellism of the official leaders on the one hand, and the cavalier approach of the opposition and their offspring, the terrorists, on the other, the movement would either have petered out, or gone down with a quixotic gesture.

But this is wisdom after the event. In 1924, when I became involved in Zionist politics, everything seemed simple and clear; we, the opposition, were in the right and the others in the wrong. This conviction was so deep and intense that even today I have to make a continuous effort to keep bias as far as possible out of these recollections.[2]

One small episode ought to be recorded as a curiosity. One day in 1925 when I was ill in bed, Dr. Hahn and Dr. Diamant came to visit me. We talked about a youth organisation which Jabotinsky planned to create—a Zionist version

[1] This last point was only incorporated in the Revisionist programme of 1927, but was informally discussed and approved before that.
[2] For a more detailed analysis of the whole problem see *Promise and Fulfilment*, published in 1949.

of the Boy Scouts. Hahn, who was good at designing, and Diamant, who knew all about Jewish heraldics, together worked out a sketch for a uniform, sitting on my bed. We sent it to Jabo, and with some modifications this became the uniform of the *'Betar,'* the Revisionist youth organisation which served as a reservoir and training corps for the Palestine terrorists.

At the first elections for the Zionist Congress in Vienna, our party polled exactly seventy-two votes. Seventy of the voters were personally known to us; the identity of the remaining two is still an unsolved mystery.

XIV. The Koestlers are Ruined

THE more absorbed I became in Zionist politics, the less interest I took in my studies. After my third semester I rarely went to lectures; when the time for an examination approached, I shut myself up for a week or two, worked all night long and managed somehow to pass. But as I went on studying steam boilers and compressors, high-tension transmission, electric generators, steel processing and resistance tests, I became increasingly bored. Social engineering had replaced my passion for technical engineering; and applied science had obviously only a very remote connection with the secrets of the universe.

My evenings were given up to political meetings and the related, highly enjoyable activities of the *Burschenschaft*; during most of the day, while I was supposed to be attending courses at the Polytechnic, I led a secret life in a corner of the University library, reading matters which had no connection whatsoever either with my studies or with my politics. I had discovered Freud; after reading through most of the analytical literature I turned to the schismatic schools of Adler, Steckel and Jung, and thence to psychiatry, experimental psychology and the psychology of art. At the same time, I tried to keep abreast with the revolutionary developments in theoretical physics, which were equally unrelated to the curriculum at the Polytechnic. Thus towards the end of my teens the split in personality and aspirations had become quite pronounced: the active half was single-minded, fanatic and intolerant of divergent opinions, while the other dwelt somewhere on the shores of the 'oceanic feeling' and combed its beaches with patient humility.

In that period also started a different type of predicament which has accompanied me through all these years : the conflict of languages in my head.

Until the age of fourteen, I spoke German at home and Hungarian at school. School and ethnic environment were the stronger influence : I thought in Hungarian, and my first juvenile efforts at writing were also in Hungarian.

When I was fourteen we moved to Vienna, and I was sent to an Austrian school; but for a while I still thought and wrote in Hungarian. I saw my name for the first time in print in a periodical to which I had sent some German translations of my favourite Hungarian poet, Endre Ady.

After that, German gradually gained the upper hand. The love poems and the inevitable rhymed epic of adolescence were perpetrated in German, but in between I wrote occasional short stories in Hungarian. Only at twenty-one, when I became a correspondent for German newspapers, was the transition completed. From then onward, until my thirty-fifth year, I wrote and thought in German.

In 1940 I had to change languages a second time, from German to English, this time abruptly and without transition. *Darkness at Noon* was the last book that I wrote in German; all my other books since have been written in English. When awake, I now think in English; when asleep, in Hungarian or German or French. As I am a chronic sleep-talker, my wife is often awakened by my polylingual gibberish.

When I was eighteen or nineteen, my father went bankrupt. He never recovered; a short time after I left home I became my parents' sole financial support.

Like everything he did, the bankruptcy was in the grand style. After we had moved to Vienna he became president of some newly-founded import company. He had an office car, which in the Vienna of 1919 was something of an extravaganza, and we lived in a suite at the Grand Hotel, which was the peak of Viennese *chic*. All this was, of course, too good to last. After a year or two my father left the company to regain his independence, and the suite in the Grand Hotel was exchanged, first, for a furnished flat in the feudal Belvedere quarter, and later for rooms in a boarding-house in the shabbily respectable Alsergrund district.

In 1922 or thereabouts, my father entered into partnership with an old-established Viennese textile importer, Herr W. True to his idea of doing business 'in the American way,' no written contract was signed, and the whole enterprise was founded on mutual trust. But these were the years of the Austrian inflation, when survival had become a racket, when respectable housewives prostituted themselves to keep up the family income and staid business firms went on a spree of currency speculations. Out of that witches' sabbath which forever destroyed body and soul of the Central European middle class, came the fumes of the totalitarian ideologies; it was the beginning of the end of civilised life along the Danube and east of the Rhine. No wonder that Herr W., scion of several generations of respectable merchants, mounted the broom-stick and did my unsuspecting father in.

The procedure employed was astonishingly simple : the financial transactions of the firm were entered in the books a few days or weeks earlier or later than their actual date. In view of the rapid changes in the currency exchange rates which the inflation brought in its wake, these manipulations were sufficient to turn a handsome profit into a catastrophic loss on the books. The books were kept by an old and trusted accountant of Herr W.'s firm, and my father never bothered to check them. He drew money when he needed it, and left the details to his respectable partner. Until the day when

Herr W. came out with the news that there was no more money for my father to draw—it had all been eaten up by losses. And the books were there to prove it.

My father came home in despair, a ruined man. As on the day when the First World War started, I brought him a glass of water with bicarbonate of soda, while he was lying on a couch, tortured by stomach cramps. An hour later that evening, the telephone rang. Old G., the accountant of the firm, wished to talk to my father privately.

He appeared after dinner, a shrivelled little man in a bowler, striped trousers and a cutaway. Old G. had worked some forty years for Herr W.'s firm, under the present W.'s father and even grandfather. He was a sweet old man in his late sixties, a symbol of the old Imperial Austria. He asked to speak to my father alone, and an hour later left, ashen-faced and looking even older. He had been prompted by his conscience to inform my father that for a period of some two years he had, on W.'s direct orders, systematically faked the dates in the account books. Moreover, he had brought with him and left with my father a long statement, written in his own neat, calligraphic hand, containing all the relevant facts.

This, of course, meant prison, disgrace and the end of old G. himself. That he made the confession was not only a tribute to his own honesty and the nineteenth-century world from which he came; it was also a tribute to the endearing personality of my father, to his disarming innocence.

My father went to a lawyer, and Herr W. was arrested on a charge of embezzlement. Old G., for some legal reason, was left at liberty. While in prison Herr W. offered to pay a milliard Austrian shillings if my father withdrew the charge. It was a biggish sum even during inflation days; it represented about half the amount which, according to the accountant's testimony, Herr W. had embezzled. My father's lawyer advised against a settlement and my father refused it. A few days later Herr W. was let out of prison on bail; in another few days the case was transferred from the criminal court to the court for commercial litigation. The lawyer swore that this had been done through bribery; the magistrates, whose monthly salaries during the inflation amounted to the price of a pound of butter or so, were only a little more difficult to buy in those days than their wives and daughters in the bars of the Kärntnerstrasse.

The lawsuit dragged on for a couple of years. Twenty-four hours before it was to come up for a preliminary hearing, old G. was found dead in his dismal furnished room. The autopsy revealed a condition of the brain, which had not manifested itself before and had killed him at a single stroke. Herr W.'s lawyers pleaded that G. had made an untrue deposition out of spite. It was the poor little dead man's word against the powerful firm of W. with its resources and allies. There were, of course, the files of the W. firm, but those had in the meantime been rifled and re-arranged. Their examination dragged on for another year or so. The end of it was that my father could prove nothing, and lost the case. The lawsuit had devoured what had remained of his capital; he was finished.

This story is the material background of the period which I have described. It ruined my father's formerly robust health and his nerves. He never got over his gnawing resentment of the injustice inflicted upon him by this eerie combination of acts of God and human corruption. I felt an aching pity for him and a growing sense of responsibility. My costly education now represented the only investment on which hopes for future returns could be based. In another year I would graduate, and then I would try to find a job as a draughtsman in a factory. In the poor, truncated Austrian Republic sliding from inflation to depression and final decay, jobs for young engineers were hard to find, and grotesquely underpaid. Yet it was the only way. In ten years or so I would probably become Chief Engineer, and in twenty or thirty years Vice President or the like. And meanwhile the arrow, broken or whole, would continue its flight through blue eternity.

XV. The Blessings of Unreason

IN the late autumn of 1925, my father scraped together enough money for a journey to London, to re-establish contact with English manufacturers. Though he maintained a façade of boisterous optimism, and talked of 'colossal' and 'stupendous' projects just about to materialise, his self-confidence was broken, so he took my mother with him for support. I was left by myself in the boarding-house where we had been living for the last three years.

One night in October I came home late after a long discussion on free will and determinism with a Russian student named Orochov. Orochov was a socialist and the nearest incarnation of a Dostoyevskian character that I have met; he seemed to have stepped straight out of *The Possessed*. He was ugly, warm-hearted, tormented and sincere. A year later he committed suicide to escape the squalor of extreme poverty, by jumping at night from a bridge into the frozen Danube.

During that discussion in Orochov's bare room, he had stubbornly defended the determinist position, while I maintained that, within certain limits, man has freedom of decision and ultimate mastery of his fate. We had drunk no alcohol, only pints of weak tea, but I went away feeling drunk and elated. It was raining hard and, having no hat or umbrella, I exulted in getting drenched and letting the rain get inside my collar and slide in an icy trickle down my spine. The streets were deserted; the vast amount of tea we had drunk obliged me to stop at a lamp-post, and this small individual contribution to the downpour seemed to me somehow symbolic and significant. I got home, and in a state of manic exaltation, lit a match and slowly burnt my Matriculation Book. This document, in Austria called *Index,* was the student's sacred passport; in it were entered the examinations he had passed, the courses he had attended and other relevant details concerning his studies. It was extremely difficult if not impossible, to replace, as the overcrowded Polytechnic only had records of examinations, but not of attendance at courses, which in some cases were compulsory. The burning of my *Index* was a literal burning of my bridges, and the end of my prospective career as a respectable citizen and member of the engineering profession.

The act was unpremeditated. No doubt it must have been maturing for a long time in my unconscious mind. But in my conscious mind I had never before dared even to contemplate it. To abandon my studies in the seventh—that is, the last but one—semester, and thereby to renounce a hard but solid professional career at a time when my parents' only hope rested on it, was indeed the peak of unreason and irresponsibility.

The motives which prompted that sudden decision are difficult to explain. This story would be much simpler to tell if I could fall back on the comfortable cliché that I was driven by an 'irresistible urge to become an artist.' But at that time I did not think of becoming a writer. My adolescent effusions, embodied in a few poems and stories, were embarrassingly bad, and I knew it. Zionist politics I took seriously, but it did not enter my head to go to Palestine at once. Zionism was primarily a political task of organising the Jews in Europe and America. So this was not an explanation either.

The reason for that act of apparent lunacy was a sudden enamouredness with unreason itself. The discussion with Orochov had brought on a condition which I can only describe as a severe shock of 'oceanic feeling'; and in that condition all values are reversed. The experience as such has no verbal content; it is merely an inchoate, luminous euphoria; but it sometimes has the power to crystallise the amorphous underground processes of the mind. It appeared to me as a self-evident truth that reason was absurd. Already Kant had proved that reason had to abdicate before the problems that really mattered, like eternity and infinity. Einstein had given the *coup de grâce* to commonsense. Freud, in a different sphere, had completed the process. The inflation, with prices of a thousand Kronen for a loaf of bread, had reduced economic standards to complete absurdity. Old G.'s end had demonstrated what a life guided by homely reason and respectability led up to. Life was a chaos, and to embark on a reasonable career in the midst of chaos was madness. All this may sound like a tenuous intellectual construction; but at the time I felt it very intensely—so much so that people who ordered their lives according to the dictates of reason appeared to me as only deserving contempt and pity.

I had no plans except 'to lead my own life.' In order to do that I had to 'get off the track.' This metaphorical track I visualised very precisely as an endless stretch of steel rails on rotting sleepers. You were born on to a certain track, as a train is put on its run according to the timetable; and once on the track, you no longer had free will. Your life was determined, as Orochov maintained, by outside forces: the rail of steel, stations, shunting points. If you accepted that condition, running on rails became a habit which you could no longer break. The point was to jump off the track before the habit was formed, before you became encased in a rattling prison. To change the metaphor: reason and routine kept people in a strait-jacket which made their living flesh rot beneath it.

These theories I expounded with great eloquence to my

friends—an eloquence which became the more voluble as, after the momentary illumination had passed, I became very frightened of what I had done. Their answer was unanimous : 'You are simply fed up with the idea of becoming an engineer. Maybe that is indeed not your vocation; but for God's sake stick out the remaining six months until you have your degree, and then do whatever you like. Thus you will always have a diploma to fall back upon. Whatever your future projects are, to throw away a safe profession in the last minute is to act like a complete fool.' 'But I want to act like a fool,' I kept repeating stubbornly.

The night after I had burnt my Matriculation Book I had a vivid dream. I was walking as a small child hand in hand with my governess along a street in Budapest. We passed an ironmonger's shop and I tore myself free, entered the shop and bought a spade. . . .

The dream was a transparent recollection of one of my favourite childhood reveries. Before I went to school, in the period of great loneliness around my fifth year, I had often daydreamed of running away from home, buying a spade, and earning my living like the men whom I always saw digging up trees and tram-tracks in the streets. That I had no money to pay for the spade bothered me no more than the remaining difficulty of getting enrolled in a municipal work-gang at the age of five.

The spade-reverie, and the dream which recalled it, seem to reveal a basic escape pattern, an urge to run away and burn my bridges, which flared into the open on the night of my discussion with Orochov—and on some later, equally decisive occasions. This 'bridge-burning pattern,' with its morbid undertones and unexpected rewards, will gradually unfold, in successive episodes of throwing up jobs, breaking off personal relations and tearing up roots in a number of countries where I tried to settle.

The four or five months between that night and my departure for Palestine were a turbid nightmare. The decision to abandon my studies was made in the rarefied atmosphere of the 'tragic plane' where questions like Free Will and Determinism are all that matter, and practical considerations do not count. But the major part of a twenty-four-hour day is usually spent on the 'trivial plane' of routine, where the big words have no currency or meaning, and are shrugged off as an expression of overstrung nerves.

During those months of transition, I lived in a purgatory of guilt and remorse. My parents were stuck in England. I suspected that they did not have the fare to get back. My board-bill in the Pension Glaser was often overdue for several weeks, but somehow my father managed to send the proprietor an occasional pound or two, and as we had some furniture and luggage stored as security, I had my board and lodging assured. This only added to the load of my guilt, for I could imagine how hard it was for my stricken father to rake up those few pounds—and here I was, wasting my time in the University library and writing lying letters to maintain my parents in the belief that in a few months I would graduate, earn a salary and support the household.

The pressure of guilt became so intense that I could not get myself out of bed in the morning, and read or dozed or daydreamed until two or three in the afternoon; and there were days when I did not get up at all. During my whole life, with the exception of this nightmarish *inter-regnum,* I have stuck to the habit of getting up at 7.30 a.m. and rushing under a cold shower or dipping into a cold bath. If I occasionally oversleep, I feel as guilty as a schoolboy. Thus, rotting in a crumpled bed until afternoon meant for me sinking into an abyss of depravity—and yet I could not get up. The force which paralysed me in this daily dismal struggle was obviously fear. As long as I stayed in the womb of my bed I was protected against the pressures which tried to force me back to steam boilers and electric generators, back to reason and a draughtsman's office in some small-town factory. At the same time the warm bed was a safeguard against more irrational fears—the expectation of some vague but terrifying form of punishment, designed by the old enemy Ahor. When at last I managed to get up in the early afternoon, I got straight into my clothes, dodging the cold shower which, with its blast of hostile reality, would have broken the dreamy haze that still enwrapped me. I ambled off to the library without being able to force myself to wash or change my shirt.

During that time I wrote the only poem which I believe was any good. It was the prayer of a young automobile coming off the assembly belt and out of the factory on an icy morning. Its engine had been cranked for the first time; its body was trembling in fear of the road ahead. It prayed : Lord, give me a little respite before thou lettest the clutch in.

Yet in spite of all, I stuck to my decision and never again set foot in the Polytechnic building on Karlsplatz. There are two kinds of courage : the brave man's and the coward's. Mine has always been the coward's courage, which is often the more stubborn variety. I was mortally afraid of the course I had chosen but stuck to it, having written this motto on a piece of cardboard and propped it against the foot of my bed : COURAGE IS NEVER TO LET YOUR ACTIONS BE INFLU-ENCED BY YOUR FEARS.

I needed that constant self-admonition, because I have never before or after lived through a period so haunted by guilt and fear, not even during the outwardly more dramatic episodes of later years. While I am no longer plagued by dreams of being back in prison, I do, to this day, occasionally dream that I have been sent back to the Polytechnic, and am desperately trying to pick up my studies where I left them, and to make up for the wasted years.

The only person who seemed to approve of my decision

was a chance acquaintance whom I only met once for a few minutes. Among the guests of the Pension Glaser were two curious people—the first highbrow intellectuals I had come across. One was Dr. Theodore Wiesengrund-Adorno, the music critic, pupil of Schoenberg. He was a shy, distraught and esoteric young man with a subtle charm which I was too callow to discern. Thomas Mann is said to have drawn a pernicious caricature of him in one of the characters in *Dr. Faustus*. He shared a small table in the dining-room with a blonde and equally withdrawn woman : the actress Anny Mewes, who had been a friend of Rainer Maria Rilke; some of Rilke's letters are addressed to her. Adorno and Anny Mewes occasionally spoke a few friendly words to me from their remote intellectual heights. They could not, of course, take seriously a half-baked *Burschenschafter,* parading with a three-coloured sash across his chest; but they seemed to watch my antics with a trace of detached amusement.

One day Adorno and Miss Mewes had a guest at their exclusive table : a sturdy woman of middle age with brisk movements and an ugly, attractive face. She was, as I later learned, Regina Ullman, a Swiss poet who had won high critical acclaim though her work remained practically unknown to the public at large. After dinner Miss Mewes asked me over to their table and presented me as a kind of curiosity, I suppose, to Regina Ullman. Miss Ullman stared at me and asked me whether it was true that I had given up my studies in my parents' absence and without their consent. But her question was asked in such a matter-of-fact voice, free from pedagogical overtones and moral judgment, that my shyness vanished and I launched into an exposition of my theories about the necessity of jumping off the rails and the blessings of unreason. She listened attentively, then said : 'You seem so convinced of your ideas that you can no longer understand people who do not share them—is that so?' I concurred eagerly, and she said : 'Well, young man, maybe you are right.'

That was all. I never saw or heard of Miss Ullman again and I haven't read any of her books. But that brief dialogue gave me an immense feeling of reassurance.

The decision to go to Palestine and till the earth seems like a logical consequence of the burning of my bridges, yet it came to me only a few weeks later. The mind is not a logical machine; ideas and decisions grow with the jerky, spiral movements of a plant rather than in the manner of a blueprint; and what seems the only obvious solution of a problem is only obvious in retrospect.

To get to Palestine as a 'Khaluts' or pioneer—that is, as an agricultural worker without capital—was not quite as difficult as getting on the American Immigration Quota, but difficult enough. The British Mandatory Government each year provided the Zionist Organisation with a limited number of immigration certificates, and these certificates were distributed by the Organisation among the several Zionist parties. As the number of certificates given to the various parties determined their relative strength in Palestine, they fought and haggled for certificates even more stubbornly than for their share of the Organisation's funds. The certificates for 'Khalutsim'[1] without capital practically all went to the Left-Wing Zionist Groups. These ran farm-schools in Europe where candidates received their basic training in agricultural work, and a thorough political indoctrination. The preparatory training lasted for a year or two and sometimes longer, according to the number of certificates available.

The newly founded Revisionist Party had as yet received no certificates. But my case was a rather exceptional one, as it rarely happened that budding Zionist politicos and

[1] im is the Hebrew plural suffix for nouns.

Burschenschaft-leaders chose to become hewers of wood and drawers of water. So, after some wire-pulling, eloquent entreaties, and the passing of an examination in modern Hebrew, the Palestine office of the Zionist Organisation in Vienna, presided over by a benevolent lawyer by the name of Dr. Blauer, put me on their waiting list for a certificate of immigration as an agricultural labourer. I still remember mild Dr. Blauer's doubtful look as he talked to me. He probably also had a son at the University and would have very firmly objected to his embarking on such a wild adventure. To be a Zionist was one thing; to let 'a boy of good family' go out into the wilderness among the mosquitoes and Arabs was quite another.

The Hebrew examination was the easiest part of the preliminaries; I had learnt to speak the revived language of the Bible with tolerable fluency, by a kind of pressure-cooker method, in a few weeks. The most difficult part was waiting; and the uncertainty whether I would finally get that certificate on which everything now depended. If it was refused, I saw no way of getting out of the nightmare in which I lived.

I received my certificate towards the middle of March, 1926. My parents were still in England. I wrote them a long letter, probably the most eloquent and dishonest piece of writing that I ever produced. I explained to them that I was going to Palestine for a year as an assistant engineer in a factory, and that by acquiring in this way practical experience, it would afterwards be much easier for me to find a job in Austria and to make a quick career. It is the highest tribute I can pay to my parents that instead of threats and curses they sent me their blessings—together with my mother's admonition to keep out of bad company 'in the Orient,' and to wear a scarf round my neck on the ship, as boat decks tend to be draughty.

I left Vienna and the parental home on a symbolic date : 1st April, 1926. The fact that it was April Fools' Day did not

F

mar the solemnity of the occasion. The entire *Burschenschaft* turned out in 'full colours' and sang the Zionist Anthem on the platform while I stuck my beaming face out of the third-class compartment window. Then came the loveliest music to the ears of a young man heading for adventure: the whistle, puff and jolt of the train pulling out of the station. It also contained a hidden message whose meaning I could not decipher at the time. It meant that my childhood fantasy had at last come true: I had escaped, and I had bought myself a spade.

Part Three

A VAGABOND AT LARGE

1926–1927

'But, although M. de Pontverre was a
good man, he was certainly not a virtuous
man; on the contrary, he was an enthusiast.'

ROUSSEAU:
Confessions

XVI. Weighed and Found Wanting

'THE Zionist settlers started from the conviction that the Jews could only be reborn as a nation if they acquired a social structure like other nations, with a solid base of farmers and manual labourers. In order to become normal again, they had to reverse the social pyramid of the ghetto where for centuries they had been condemned to the parasitic existence of money-lenders, traders and middlemen. The promised land could only become truly theirs if they tilled its soil with their own hands. "If I spend not my strength I shall not gather the crop," wrote the Hebrew poet Byalik.

'This new insight shaped the character of the Zionist movement. The cry "back to the land" did not spring from a romantic whim; it expressed a historical necessity.

'Once this necessity was recognised, it was developed with characteristic Jewish exuberance into an almost mystic worship of manual work, of labour which ennobles." The cult of labour became ideologically fused with Marxist class-concepts, with Tolstoian ethics and Jewish messianism. This curious blend of national renaissance and socialist Utopia, became incarnated in its purest form in the collective settlements or communes, which gave Israel its unique character as a social experiment.'[1]

My destination was one of these collective settlements—*Kvutsa Heftsebā*—in the Valley of Yesreel, *Kvutsa* means

[1] *Promise and Fulfilment.*

'group' or 'community' and is used to designate the smaller type of collective settlements—the larger ones are called *Kibuts*. Heftsebā is the Arab name for the hillside where the settlement was established.

The Valley of Yesreel sweeps in a broad arc from the Mediterranean to the Jordan. In Biblical times it was, and it is again today, the most fertile plain in Palestine. In 1926 it was still mostly a stony desert, infested with malaria, typhus, and marauding Bedouin tribesmen. The hills bordering the valley were dotted with Arab mud villages, dissolving by an act of natural mimicry in the violet haze of earth and rock. Down in the plain sprawled the first Jewish pioneer settlements, a conspicuous eyesore with their white, cubic concrete buildings. They were a challenge to the landscape and its native inhabitants.

Heftsebā was at that time the settlement farthest to the East, that is, deepest in purely Arab territory. It also had the worst climate, for it lay some three hundred feet below sea level. (The Valley of Yesreel slopes down towards the East until it reaches the Jordan valley, the deepest depression in the surface of the earth.) In summer the heat was stifling, aggravated by the Khamsin, a hot desert wind with a peculiarly unnerving effect—ancient Turkish law considered it a mitigating circumstance if a murder was committed during a Khamsin. Mosquitoes, flies, cockroaches and bugs of all varieties abounded—the only abundance which nature provided in that region, for the earth was arid and stony, and had not seen a plough for a millenium and a half before the settlers of Heftsebā arrived. The settlers were nearly all lawyers, architects, doctors of philosophy from Vienna and Prague. They had had no previous experience in agriculture and in hard manual labour. The settlement was built at the foot of Mount Gilboa, the hill where Joshua defeated the Amorites and bade the sun stand still.

I arrived at Heftsebā one evening in April, 1926. The first

sight of the settlement was a shock. I had disembarked at Haifa a few days before, and was still dazed by the picturesque and colourful Oriental scenery of its port and Arab bazaars. Now I found myself in a rather dismal and slumlike oasis in the wilderness, consisting of wooden huts, surrounded by dreary vegetable plots. The huts were not the log cabins made familiar by illustrations of the American pioneering age, but ramshackle dwellings in which only the poorest in Europe would live, as an alternative to the discarded railway carriage. The only buildings made of concrete were the cowshed and a square, white house where the children of the settlement lived together, separated from their parents. I don't know what I had imagined the settlement would look like; but certainly not like this.

It was dinner-time when I arrived; the men and women were assembled in the wooden barrack that served as a communal dining hall. They sat on benches at tables made of rough deal planks on trestles. Most of them were between twenty and thirty but gave the impression of being much older, for they all looked weary and physically exhausted; they slumped over their plates, elbows on table, and spooned their soup in silence, too tired to talk. Their faces were sunburnt but not healthy. Many showed the yellowish tint of malaria; the women's features were coarsened by the climate and hard work. Nobody asked what my business was or took any interest in me as I came in. At least so I thought; only later did I become aware of the silent, intense scrutiny to which the newcomer's smallest actions were subjected by the community.

I asked for Guetig, one of the leaders of the commune and once a member of 'Unitas,' who had been advised of my impending arrival. I was told that he was ill with malaria. Without further comment, the man to whom I had spoken moved closer to his neighbour on the bench to make room for me. I sat down, and from the head of the table a plate of soup and a chunk of bread were passed along, but still neither of my neighbours inquired who I was or what I wanted. It was, and still is, one of the basic rules of the Palestine communes that the wayfarer be given food and a bed without payment or questions asked.

Dinner consisted of onion soup, bread, goat's cheese and olives. The midday meal on the next day was the same; breakfast consisted of tea and a salad of onions and raw vegetables. Meat was served once a week, on the Sabbath.

Eventually I got into conversation with my right-hand neighbour. He was dark and haggard, with thick-lensed glasses on a deeply-furrowed face which expressed strength, intelligence and mildness. His name was Loebl—Dr. Loebl, in fact; it appears in the dedication of my novel on Palestine, *Thieves in the Night*.

I explained to Loebl that I had come with the intention of joining the commune. 'For good?' he asked, without looking up from his plate. I said I didn't know; that I would like to work here for a year or two, and later perhaps find a job in Tel Aviv, or go into politics. Loebl said nothing. He was spooning his soup and chewing his bread, concentrating on his food in the manner of men who are engaged in a constant struggle to keep up their physical strength. The gravely ill eat in that way, and people in concentration camps who know that every lost calory is a lost chance of survival. After a while he explained that because of the economic depression there were more candidates for the collective settlements than these could absorb. On seeing my dismayed expression, he added that he would talk to the Secretary—the Secretary is the mayor and leader of the commune—and see whether it could be arranged that I should stay for a few weeks on probation.

Before being accepted as a member of a commune, each candidate has to pass through a probationary stage—a kind of novitiate—during which his physical qualities and social adaptability are weighed and measured by the community. As I found out much later, during that short talk with Loebl I had in fact already been weighed and found wanting. One did not enter a commune, any more than a convent or a monastic order, 'for a year or two.' In more recent times it has become a custom for young people to spend six months or a year on a collective farm before embarking on a career in the towns. But in the early days, to enter a *Kvutsa* meant dedication for a lifetime.

I was given a bed in a bare, stiflingly hot little room which I shared with two other men. The room was part of a hut, the other half of which was occupied by a married couple. Through the thin wooden partition we could hear every word and every sound as if they lived in the same room with us. This lack of privacy, which extended to the communal shower-room and the communal latrine, was an even greater nervous strain on the settlers than the fight against disease and physical exhaustion. It was a principle of all communes that the care of children and cattle came first, and care of the adult human element later. Thus the first concrete building to be erected had been the cowshed and next had come the children's house; while the men and women of the settlement continued to live in tents and shacks, often for many years. This self-imposed hardship was partly dictated by poverty, partly by the settlers' collectivist ideology. The *Kvutsa* was regarded by its members as a mystic community in which not only property but also one's thoughts, feelings, and the most intimate aspects of life ought to be shared— with the only exclusion of sexual life. Promiscuous tendencies were considered signs of individual selfishness and social maladjustment. Sexual conflicts and tragedies did, of course, occur but they were exceptional—mainly, one may suppose, because the sexual appetites were blunted by fatigue and by the neutralising effect of familiarity. This, incidentally, led to the curious phenomenon of a kind of incest-barrier develop-

ing between men and women within the same commune—
with a resulting trend toward exogamy, a preference to
marry outsiders.

The morning after my arrival I was assigned to work on a
steep, sloping field, which was intended to become a future
vegetable plot. As yet it was only a staked-out stretch of arid
waste which seemed to contain more stones than earth. The
stones had to be picked up one by one and carried away in
baskets. When a small area was cleared of the bigger stones,
it was hacked up in ridges with a hoe. After an hour or two
of this work, my hands were blistered, my head, covered with
a wet handkerchief, swam, and my bones felt as if stretched
on the rack. Loebl, who was in charge of the gang working
in that field, watched me out of the corner of his eye and
repeatedly told me to fall out and take a rest. The second and
third days were no better; only towards the end of the first
week did I gradually begin to pick up the rhythm of the
work and the technique of economising energy with every
movement.

Even after the physical strain had begun to ease, work
in the field remained torture. I have always liked manual
work such as carpentering, scrubbing floors, or making electrical installations; even today I regard it as a treat to take a
day off and do odd jobs around the house. But digging and
hoeing I have always hated—though I had to do a lot of it
later as a soldier in the Pioneer Corps. I hate the monotony
of it, and the fact that it is work which is never finished, and
never gives one the satisfaction of having completed a tidy
job. But work in the fields was, of course, the only occupation
in the collective settlements at which young members could
be employed; carpentering and technical jobs were the privilege of elderly, specialised workers.

My probationary period lasted some four or five weeks. I
did my best to hide my aversion for the spade—that rusty,
clotted spade, so different from the gleaming symbol of my

dreams of freedom. But in a small community, where every-body is constantly under the scrutiny of everybody else, it is impossible to hide any trait of character; even a passing mood, a momentary shadow of discontent, the first hint of friendship and animosity are immediately known to all. This is not a result of gossip or spying on each other, but rather of a kind of sixth sense which the closely knit community develops, and which registers individual disturbances with the precision of a seismograph. It gives the member of the *Kvutsa* a curious feeling of being transparent, as if he were living under an X-ray camera and had nowhere to hide. This leads in most cases sooner or later to a psychological crisis. About one person out of every two is unable to stand up to the strain and leaves the *Kvutsa* in the second or third year. The remaining half become more or less permanently adjusted; and in another few years they become unfit for any other form of life.

After a few months I would perhaps have developed a taste for digging, but my initial dislike could not be con-cealed. Other factors which weighed against me were that I only intended to stay for a limited period—which was con-sidered as a flippant and 'worldly' attitude; the fact that there were three or four times more candidates than the existing communes could absorb; and finally my political affiliation. The collective settlements stood ideologically on the extreme left, regarded Jabotinsky as a militarist, and his party as a Fascist movement.

At the end of my probationary period, Loebl told me with great gentleness that the Members' Assembly had decided to give preference to two other candidates who were physically and mentally better equipped for *Kvutsa* life than I. I received the news with mixed feelings of dejection and half-conscious relief. The handicaps which I have mentioned were real; but had I felt the true vocation, I would probably have overcome them. At the same time, the collapse of my plans was a bitter disappointment, and though it is obvious that I was completely unfit for that kind of life, it is even today painful to remember that I failed.

No doubt my dismay was partly caused by hurt pride; but to an equal extent by the fact that during those short weeks I had grown very fond of Loebl, Guetig and others, and had come under the strange lure of *Kvutsa* life. The nature of this attraction is difficult to convey. The *Kvutsa* in its early days was a socialist monastery and at the same time a wildly romantic pioneering adventure. To stand guard in the moonlight with an old rifle at the foot of Mount Gilboa was an experience not easy to forget. Nor the bliss of the peaceful Sabbath mornings when physical rest, the clean shirt from the communal laundry, and the meat at dinner were savoured as rare luxuries. Nor the undefinable feeling of growing roots in an untamed spot, and of growing human ties of a quality unknown elsewhere—organic ties as binding as the climbing plants which make separate trees grow into an indivisible living tangle. I believe that never since the primitive Christian communities have such strange brother-hoods existed as in the early days of the communal settlements in Palestine.

Life in a *Kvutsa* meant—and still means in some parts of Palestine, such as the Negeb Desert—a life of heroic poverty and of grim struggles on the borderline of human endurance. The institutions and amenities of normal society were absent. No uniformed policemen or gendarmes protected the settlers in a hostile land; they had to wield with one hand the plough and with the other the sword, as in the days of Ezra after the return from the Babylonian exile. All forms of hired labour were barred from the communal settlements. So was private property and the use of money. The member of the commune was supposed to work to the limit of his capacity and receive the bare necessities of existence in return. He was housed and fed and provided with soap and toothbrush, working clothes and reading matter, postage stamps and contraceptives, from the communal store, free of charge. His children were brought up under the care of nurses and teachers in the communal children's house. Money was only used by the Treasurer of the commune in his transactions with the outer world; but even these transactions were largely on paper. The necessities of the commune were bought on credit from the co-operative stores of the Hebrew trade unions, and the produce of the commune was sold to another branch of the same co-operative organisation. Children born and brought up in a collective settlement never saw a banknote or a coin; they had literally no notion of the value of money and the ways of handling it.

All this led to a curious estrangement from reality. Life in the *Kvutsa* was hard, but at the same time free from economic cares, from the worries of a normal social existence. The commune took charge of all of man's needs from the cradle to the grave.

After five or six years spent in this intense and artificial environment, a great many of the members of the communes became unfit for any other form of life. They could no longer face the struggles in a competitive society. They could not re-adapt themselves to the social values and relations, the problems and uncertainties of the outside world. In this respect, paradoxically, they resembled habitués of tuberculosis sanatoria, who, like birds with clipped wings, never stray far from the protective shelter.

At the time of my first stay in *Kvutsa* Heftsebā, there existed some twenty or thirty collective settlements in Palestine. When the independence of Israel was proclaimed, their number had grown to some one hundred and twenty; as this is written there are more than two hundred. Unlike other Utopian experiments, from Spartacus' Sun City to the 'New Harmony' of the Owenites, which all have collapsed after a short time, the Palestine communes have succeeded in establishing themselves as stable forms of rural society; in some of the oldest settlements the children now belong to the third native generation. Indeed, the most remarkable thing about the *Kvutsa* is that it has survived.

It would be a mistake, however, to overestimate the social significance of these unique communities, or to use them as models for experiments on a mass scale. The members of the collective settlements are an élite of volunteers; the rigours of their existence are self-imposed. It would be impossible to build any similar society by compulsion, just as it would be impossible to compel a large section of the population to take monastic vows. Even the voluntary settlers, with their spirit of fervent self-sacrifice, had to make concessions and mitigate the harshness of the original collectivist doctrine. During the forty years which have elapsed since the first collective settlement was founded in Dagania on the shores of Lake Tiberias, the structure of the *Kvutsa* has undergone a gradual reform. The settlers are now permitted certain private possessions, from clothing to radio sets and other small comforts of life. In most collective settlements small children are allowed to live with their parents instead of being segregated in the communal children's house. Some settlements have ceased to be purely agricultural and run industrial plants and craft shops of their own. Others allow their members pocket money which they can spend as they please. Mixed forms, half-way between collective and co-operative farming, are springing up here and there. But this organic evolution does not diminish the value and achievement of the early pioneers, and the moral inspiration which the budding nation of Israel derived from them.

I have frequently re-visited Heftsebā—and many other collective settlements—since my abortive attempt to settle in the shadow of Mount Gilboa. The idea of writing a novel around life in a *Kvutsa* attracted me from the beginning; it was the first subject for a novel which occurred to me. It did not materialise until twenty years later, in *Thieves in the Night*, written in 1945. '*On revient toujours à son premier amour*,' sometimes also applies to writers and their subjects.

XVII. Mostly about Hunger

I NOW entered upon a period of poverty and semi-starvation, which lasted for about a year.

I had arrived in Palestine with a little less than a pound in my possession. My luggage consisted of one suitcase, which contained a spare suit and a pair of shoes, six shirts and Schopenhauer's *The World as Will and Idea* in two paperbound volumes—one of which had been stolen on my arrival at Haifa. The other volume, together with the suit, shirts, etc., I had intended to surrender to the communal store at Heftsebā. I had not worried about money, for as a member of a collective settlement, I would need none.

By the time I left Heftsebā I had only some twenty piasters, or approximately four shillings, left. I had to walk back to Haifa on foot. The distance was less than forty miles; but owing to the tropical heat, the necessity of carrying my suitcase and the fact that I had contracted a mild form of dysentery, the trip took me three days. After every mile or so I had to hide behind a bush, and bushes were rather scarce in those days in the Valley of Yesreel. In spite of this predicament I rather enjoyed the adventure. For meals and shelter I stopped at other collective settlements along the road—Tel Joseph, Ain Herod—or at one of the new villages, such as Nahalal, where the farmers were equally hospitable. The language spoken in the Valley—the rural nucleus of the future state—was exclusively Hebrew. In Haifa and Tel Aviv one still heard Russian, Polish, Yiddish or German in the streets, but the settlers in the Valley were purists in the matter of language as in everything else. They were hard, taciturn men; what distinguished them from farmers elsewhere was their Biblical hospitality, and the sophistication which emerged when one succeeded in establishing contact with them. In spite of their kindness, I unconsciously regarded them as inferior to the crowd at Heftsebā. Though my stay had been short and had ended in my rejection, I had acquired some of the parish pride of the true settler.

I reached Haifa with my twenty piasters still intact, and the dysentery cured. I had no idea what to do next, but I hoped that the Revisionist Party would help me to find a job.

On my arrival from Europe, and before setting out for Heftsebā, I had called on the leader of the Party's Haifa branch. Dr. Abram Weinshall was, and still is, one of the leading lawyers of Palestine. He was then in his early thirties, tall and boyish looking; his shy, modest manner, dry humour and a tendency to understatements, gave the impression that he had been brought up in an English public school. Only when pleading in court, or when launched on a political argument, did his restrained passion and intellectual brilliance break through. He came from Baku, had studied in Germany and Switzerland, and was married to a beautiful Russian actress. When we met, he had just taken on what was probably the most famous law suit in the history of the Middle East : a claim brought by the heirs of the last Turkish Sultan, Abdul Hamid, against the British Government for possession of the lands formerly belonging to the Turkish Caliphate. The suit was to drag on for years before various local and international courts, and for all I know is still going on.

Our first meeting had started early after lunch in Abram's office, the day after my arrival in Palestine. It had continued through the whole afternoon, during dinner at his house, and until three in the morning—altogether for some twelve hours. We were both devoted admirers of Jabotinsky; we compared developments in our party in Europe and Palestine, and talked of plans for future political campaigns. Apart from the identity of our political views, we had taken a spontaneous liking to each other—the beginning of a friendship which has lasted to this day.

On my return from Heftsebā, I rang up Abram at his office. He said he was glad that I had not become a farmer, and at once invited me to stay with him and his wife as long as I liked. I accepted with alacrity and betook myself to their flat, spending half a piaster for bus fare, and another five on flowers for beautiful Zina.

Their flat was in a new residential suburb half-way up the Carmel. Although Abram had said that Zina was at home, nobody answered the bell. Finding the door unlocked, I entered the large sitting-room which was shrouded in semi-obscurity, and saw some twenty young men and women lying motionless on the floor, along the walls, under tables and on sofas, shielding their eyes with their arms and emitting plaintive sighs and groans. In the middle of the room sat Zina with a gong in her hand, whispering from time to time: 'Lehitrakez—lehitrakez,' the Hebrew for 'concentrate!' On seeing me enter with my suitcase, she motioned me to the next room, explaining in a whisper: 'Shsh, we are concentrating.' She was holding her theatrical class for amateurs; 'concentrating' in relaxed positions was an exercise prescribed by some avant-garde Russian school of acting. Much as I like Zina, these classes, accompanied by gong-beatings, spoken choruses, growlings and yellings, were rather a nightmare.

My stay with the Weinshalls was a highly enjoyable interlude which gave me a few weeks' grace before the hunger period started. Abram and I burst into a frenzy of joint political activities which crystallised around three enterprises. The first was a Hebrew weekly newspaper called

Zafon—'The North' (Haifa is the centre of Northern Palestine). The second was a Political Press Service for Europe, *Sokhnut Medinit Leumit*—which, literally translated, means 'National State Agency.' The third was *Sehuténu*—'Our Right'—a kind of League for Civil Liberties, designed to provide legal aid for Jews against abusive practices of the mandatory administration. These three enterprises—known, as a family joke, as 'the three S's'—kept us every evening busy until two or three, while in the next room Zina's pupils howled and declaimed. The Hebrew weekly was set up and printed by hand in a little printer's shop down in the Arab bazaar. As my Hebrew was far from adequate for editorial tasks, my main job was to collect advertisements for the paper. This meant trudging along the hot, dusty streets of Haifa for some eight hours a day, and using my eloquence on shopkeepers, businessmen and café owners. But it also meant learning to know rapidly and intimately the mentality of this industrial pioneer town with its heterogeneous population.

The Civil Rights League was Abram's baby; the Press Agency mine. It was a one-man show; I wrote most of the material, typed it on stencils, mimeographed it, put it in envelopes and, as a matter of pride, dropped these myself into the letter-box. The bulletin came out once a week, on Thursdays, in approximately ten closely-typed pages; it contained articles and news items, and was sent to some fifty Zionist periodicals in Europe and in the United States. After a month, it had two regular subscribers : one in Riga, Latvia, and one in Brno, Czecho-Slovakia, at five Palestinian pounds per annum each. But much of our material also appeared in Zionist papers of various languages, though without acknowledgement or compensation. This was a minor political victory, for the claims of the Revisionist opposition were systematically ignored by the Zionist leadership, and our aim was to break through their wall of silence. The bulletin had the moral advantage of coming out of Palestine itself—the land on which all Zionist eyes were focused, but to which few Zionists betook themselves. Hence, every voice from Palestine had a ring of authority, like a voice from Russia among Communists. A few weeks after the Agency was founded, the leading organ of official Zionism in Europe, the *Jüdische Rundschau,* found it expedient to print a full-page article of mine outlining in detail the Revisionist programme. This created quite a stir; we felt that at last the Walls of Jericho had fallen, and Abram, Zina and I celebrated with an orgy of ice-cream in Haifa's best Greek café. Ice-cream 'at the Greek's' was our favourite treat; once I had set foot among the abstemious pioneers in the Holy Land I had forgotten even the taste of alcohol.

There were only two other kinds of recreation in the Haifa of 1926. On the rare nights when we were not working on one of the three S's, we would go to an Arab open-air café which had a cinema screen. Its name was, if I remember rightly, 'The Garden of Eden,' and it was indeed a paradisiac place. The films were silent Western serials with Arab subtitles, and were accompanied on an upright piano by a one-eyed Arab whose repertoire consisted of the Toreador's March from *Carmen* and the Letter Aria from *La Tosca*. The former served to accompany hold-ups of the mail-coach, pursuits and shootings; the latter to create atmosphere for the love scenes. As the essence of Arab music is monotony and repetition, everybody was satisfied. You sipped your sweet, hot coffee from tiny cups, smoked a water pipe, looked at the starry sky or at the events on the pale, rainy screen which on moonlit nights were hardly recognisable, and felt a profound contentment. It was not exactly as Europeans imagine the mysterious East, yet, even without the Arab headgear of the guests and the occasional quiet party of Bedouins from Transjordan among them, 'The Garden of Eden' had the lotusland mood of the real Orient.

Our remaining choice for a binge was to hire a taxi-cab
on a night of full moon and drive along the sandy beach to
the ancient fortress of Acco. At that time Haifa Bay, now one
of the world's oil refining centres, was still a desert; there was
nothing to see except the moon and the sea, a few palms on
the dunes, and an occasional Arab sleeping in the moon-
shade of his camel. Half-way down the Bay we would stop
and take a swim in the moonlight, our bodies shining in the
water like silvery fish. Then, if the Greek was still open, we
would have another ice-cream for a nightcap.

After a month or so the Weinshalls moved to a new flat,
and I felt that it was time to stand on my own feet. Our
three S's had been financed mainly out of Abram's own
pocket, so naturally I had worked without a salary. Now we
agreed that until the Press Agency became self-supporting, I
should draw one pound a month which would pay for a bed,
and that I should also draw a ten per cent commission on
the ads I sold for our weekly. Unfortunately, the day after I
left the haven of the Weinshalls we discovered that an
employee by the name of Rabinowitch had collected the
advertisement fees from most of our clients and had then
vanished in the general direction of Bagdad. This was a
severe blow to the paper, and to myself. I declared jauntily
that nevertheless I would manage somehow, and though
Abram and Zina knew that I was not exactly rich, they had
no idea exactly how poor I was.

With my first monthly salary of one pound, and nothing
else, in my pocket, I went in search of a bed. I found one in
a room in the German colony, a garden suburb of Haifa. I
shared the room with a Jewish policeman named Danzig,
and his eighteen-year-old sister. They came from Russia, had
the innocent minds of Russian students, and thought such an
arrangement quite natural. By a different interpretation of
naturalness I found it rather tantalising, the more so as Miss
Danzig was rather pretty, and her brother, of all things, a

cop. However, they only wanted eighty piasters a month for my bed, which left me with twenty to start on my independent career. By living on two piasters a day I managed to make this sum last for ten days. The two piasters bought one cup of black coffee, one *pitta*—the flat, round, unleavened Arab bread—and half a pound of olives. I drank the coffee in the morning, and munched olives and *pitta* during the remainder of the day whenever the pangs of hunger became acute.

During the next several months I felt constantly hungry. I became soon accustomed to that condition, though in the beginning I had some difficulty in falling asleep on an empty stomach. On the whole, I found the experience not particularly painful or depressing, except for a certain diminution of physical vitality. But that, too, had its advantages in view of the tempting closeness of Miss Danzig's bushy head on the pillow, and the sound of her Aeolic breathing next to her snoring brother. Besides, my reduced vitality put me in a detached philosophical mood, and occasionally wrapped me in a pleasant haze. I walked through the Arab bazaars, dreaming—mostly of food—amidst the gay, colourful and yet unhurried jostle of camels laden with durra flour, short-legged donkeys mounted by long-legged Biblical elders, and Arab urchins in garments resembling striped nightshirts. I loitered around the open-air stalls with their exciting smells : the hundred spices of the spice dealers, the fresh smell of leather from the saddlers and cobblers, the charcoal-and-burnt-flesh smell from the makers of *kebab*, the honey and mutton-fat smell from the pastry shops; and all these suspended in the general aroma of dust and sun, camels' urine and roasting coffee beans. This symphony of scents made one feel less hungry—provided that one steered clear of the *kebab* stalls.

More painful than hunger was the craving for cigarettes. An acquaintance from Vienna, an architect called Sobelson,

had an office half-way between the German colony and the
centre of the town; I used to stop by daily, purportedly for
an hour's chat, in fact to smoke a few of his cigarettes. This
mean calculation brought an unexpected reward, for just on
the day after my last piaster had run out and my hoard of
olives was reduced to less than a handful, Sobelson found me
a job with an architect, Mr. Boutagi. The Boutagis were one
of the leading Christian Arab families of Haifa; they owned
department stores and garages, ran a law office and sat on
the municipal council. One of the members of the Boutagi
clan, an old, mellow and rapacious gentleman, had made a
fortune as a builder of small, slummy houses for Arabs. He
had no architect's licence, and under Turkish rule had not
needed one. In those days building-permits were obtained by
bakshish; the contractor sent a couple of his men to the site,
where by means of mud and sun-baked bricks they slapped
together something like a house, with no plan to guide them
except tradition and experience. Now, under British rule,
blueprints had to be submitted, sanitation provided and fire
ordinances observed; so old Boutagi felt compelled to engage
a European architect who could cope with all these chican-
eries. I wasn't exactly an architect, but just for this reason I
could be hired for four pounds a month; and in the course
of my studies at the Polytechnic I had in fact passed a per-
functory examination in the elements of building—though
'building' here referred to pump houses, small transformer
stations, and the like simple concrete structures which an
electro-engineer may have to deal with on installation work.
However, we were not bothered by such fine distinctions and
I embarked with enthusiasm on the blueprint for a two-
family, two-storey, stone dwelling-house with balconies, a
bathroom, pillars, Moorish arches, and lots of gingerbread.
It would have been a headache even for a full-fledged architect; though old B. and I did our best, the result was a blueprint which for some time remained a source of merriment

in the District Commissioner's Building Department. Apart from other minor blemishes, the pillars supporting the roof had nothing to stand on—the result of some mix up between inches and centimetres. That, after about three weeks, was the end of my architectural career.

I had been too bashful to ask my employer for an advance; by the time I was fired I owed most of the three pounds that he paid me to the Danzigs, from whom I had borrowed small sums for my bread-and-olive diet plus two or three hot meals a week. It is curious how physical hunger often generates an abnormal pride. During my hungriest period Abram and Zina constantly asked me to meals which I refused on the pretext of being busy. When, about once a week, I accepted their invitation, dinner became an ordeal, for I felt bound to refuse second helpings and to conceal my greed, suspecting that my friends read my thoughts and watched me put every blessed fork-load of steaming pilaff into my mouth. Apart from Knut Hamsun's novel *Hunger,* there is curiously little mention in literature of this elementary physical experience. Apparently there is a modesty in civilised man with extends to all basic bodily functions; he feels an instinctive need to cover up his hunger as a naked person covers his sex. George Orwell was one of the few contemporary writers who has lived in a state of semi-starvation for a lengthy period; but in his autobiographical *Down and Out in Paris and London* there are again only the scantiest references to physiological hunger itself. And, though I often intended to discuss the subject with Orwell, it was probably the same odd modesty which made me forget it each time we met—until it was too late.

Having failed as an architect, I made a half-hearted attempt to become a lemonade vendor in the bazaar.

Lemonade was a flourishing item of trade in Palestine. On almost every street corner one could see so-called 'gazoos' stalls. 'Gazoos' is a corruption of the French *eau gazeuse,* used as a collective name for all kinds of coloured, fizzy drinks served out of huge balloon bottles. These stalls with their rainbow spectrum of orange, lemon, lime, tamarind, date, and melon-flavoured liquids, added much to the colour of the street scenery—they have practically vanished now, together with nearly every other trace of the Orient, from the diligent, drab and industrious State of Israel. Apart from these *gazoos* stalls, there were ambulant vendors who walked the streets carrying a kind of copper gourd, filled with iced lemonade, on a belt around their rumps, yelling '*Ya lemoun —ya lemoun*' and clicking a pair of copper castanets between their fingers. So one day, when I was again running out of olives, I borrowed this equipment from an Arab *gazoos* stall, started walking up and down the bazaar yelling '*Ya lemoun,*' and trying to make the castanets click in a workmanlike manner. It couldn't have been very workmanlike, however, because the whole *sūkh* seemed to grin at me. I only managed to sell, during a couple of hours, two glasses of *lemoun* at half a piaster each—which did not cover the stall-owner's outlay for ice.

Selling lemonade has, like any other trade, its tricks and secrets. You have to return every half-hour to the stall to get a fresh supply of ice. After two re-icings you have to put more flavour into your mixture, lest it become too watery. Apart from the lemon gourd or jug, you have to carry a bottle of water to rinse the glass before each customer's eyes. Your cry and castanet-play must be sufficiently shrill to attract attention, but at the same time you must sing out the word *lemoun* in a languid, heart-rending quaver which conjures up before your prospective customer's mind the image of caravans dying of thirst in the desert. In short, lemonade-selling, too, has its Napoleons and Babe Ruths; and if you are not a 'natural,' you had better give up. It is practised in temperatures around ninety degrees, and involves carrying over twenty pounds of equipment on a leather harness. After three more attempts I gave up.

Shortly after the lemonade venture I left the room at the Danzigs', and for a few days slept on the floor of a paint shop which belonged to a friend's uncle. The reason for my leaving was a cake of soap moulded in the likeness of a rabbit. Our room was bare except for the three beds, a couple of chairs and a shelf. On the shelf Miss Danzig, who had a craving for beauty, displayed what she called her 'museum.' The museum consisted of the frontispiece of a Zionist calendar portraying Dr. Theodore Herzl against a rising sun; a reproduction of Boecklin's 'Island of the Blessed,' and the rabbit made of soap. The rabbit, whose ears were beginning to melt, was my last sight of this world when I fell asleep, and the first when I opened my eyes again; soon it began to intrude into my dreams. Even the concrete floor of the paint shop was better than that. The more so as, without that rabbit, I would in the end probably have married Miss Danzig and her museum for the sole purpose of getting our beds five inches closer.

In the paint shop I had for a few days quite a cosy time. The friend to whose uncle the shop belonged was a *Burschenschafter* from Vienna and a former officer of the Austro-Hungarian Imperial Cavalry, by name of Buxbaum. He had huge cauliflower ears, a shaven skull, and a round, humorous face which was a landscape of duelling scars stitched in a geometrical pattern. Buxbaum too was an engineer—that is, a real one, who had actually graduated from the Vienna Polytechnic; and, like myself, down and out without a job. He had, however, to my envy, a girl friend with a room of her own, in whose arms he slumbered while I had to make do with the hard floor in the paint shop. The night I moved into the shop, we discovered a forgotten sack of rice in one of its dark recesses. Mice had built a nest in it, but there was enough rice left to last us a year—if we could only cook it.

Being both of us engineers, we managed to solve the problem. Our only source of heat was an oil-lamp; this we put on the floor and built a kind of chimney around it with bricks; on top of this we put an empty paint tin, having cleaned it with turpentine, and filled it with water and rice. Even for engineers it was a surprise how little heat and how much soot an oil-lamp gives out: to cook our can of rice took the best part of four hours. But it provided us with the wonderful sensation of going to sleep with a full stomach, and Buxbaum with manly vigour for his amorous pursuits.

I could only stay in the paint shop from closing time until it opened in the morning, from 8 p.m. to 8 a.m. For a few days all went well; we cooked our rice, and Buxbaum even got hold of a bag of salt. The taste of turpentine in the can either wore off or we grew accustomed to it. But one fateful day Buxbaum brought back a bottle of vodka, a gift from his girl friend. We finished it in the small hours of the morning, assuring each other that the more we drank the more sober we felt. In our undernourished state, the effect was disastrous. Buxbaum's uncle, a hard little orthodox Jew with a black skull cap, found us in the morning laid out between the barrels of paint. I remained unconscious for nearly twenty-four hours, hidden away in a small room at the back of the shop.

The next day I found myself a new abode. This was a leather sofa in a dentist's surgery. Again I only had possession of it at night—but it only cost fifty piasters a month. The surgery was unbearably hot, even by Palestinian standards; its window opened upon a narrow passage in the old city; and across that passage, less than five yards away, were the headquarters of a left-wing Hebrew youth group. There were meetings and discussions every night, carried on with Marxian acrimony; and what was worse, most of the speakers hollered not in Hebrew, but in Yiddish. Marxist dialectics is a method which enables an idiot to sound extremely clever—a discovery which, alas, I soon forgot. The shrill, self-righteous voices invaded my sleep, as the rabbit had done; minor irritations of this kind have always tormented me more than dramatic predicaments in a major key. So, at the end of the month I fled the surgery, and went to camp at the Revisionist Club.

Our Club, of which I was Honorary Secretary, consisted of one room and a balcony. The room was bare, except for four wooden benches and two tables covered with newspapers and magazines, which made a hard but relatively cool bed. My remaining shirts and socks, which I washed and mended every other night, were in the process of disintegration. I could not face the idea of calling on the Weinshalls, or any other acquaintance, in this dilapidated state. Buxbaum had gone to Tel Aviv and thereby drifted out of my life for ever— as so often happens in such fraternal but short chance-friendships.

One day in July, my capital fell to absolute zero. I had spent my last piaster. At midnight, when the last visitors had left our club, I ate my last olive and stretched out on a table. There were plenty of cigarette stubs left around, and I still had some cigarette paper with which to put them to use. Lying flat on my back in the dark room, and chain-smoking on an empty stomach, a great exhilaration came over me. I knew I only had to think matters over calmly and Babo would come to my aid, showing me how to pull myself out of the bog.

Sure enough, after the third or fourth cigarette, I had an inspiration. The idea had struck me that in our civilisation it simply does not happen that a young man starves to death —I mean, that his body is actually found starved to death. At least, I had never heard or read of such an event. *Ergo,* I reasoned, it was impossible that this fate should befall me. And if it was impossible, there was no need to worry. I did not know how people with absolutely no money managed not to die of starvation. But since I had proved that it was impossible something to prevent it must of necessity turn up. Hence the solution was, particularly in view of my weakened physical state, to do nothing and to wait for the event which was bound to prevent the impossibility, according to the rules of logic. With that I went contentedly to sleep.

The next day I spent at the Club, reading newspapers, arguing with visitors about protective tariffs for Palestine, or sitting on the balcony and looking down into Allenby Street with its mixed traffic of camels, motor cars, donkeys, Arab women in black veils, Jewish girls with thighs bulging out of khaki shorts, *lemoun* vendors and the rest. At night I slept or dozed on the table, perfecting the technique of using newspapers for a mattress and pillow.

This restful existence continued for four days, without a bite. I felt only a little hungrier than usual, and otherwise perfectly at peace. I was playing a private game with myself and with fate, of the kind which my friends of 'Unitas' with their shaggy-dog humour would have hugely enjoyed. The impossibility that I would just starve to death in this manner was more evident to me than ever; and my curiosity as to the nature of the event which would prevent it provided me with a pleasant thrill of expectation.

On the fifth day of my career as a fasting fakir, I was sitting as usual on the balcony, when an *arabadshi,* a horse-drawn Arab carriage, aroused my curiosity. Its occupant was a tall Arab in Bedouin head-gear with an unlikely amount of luggage around him. As if attracted by my gaze, the voyager looked up at me on the balcony and yelled out a greeting in Viennese. Upon closer inspection he turned out to be Dr. von Weisl of 'Unitas,' then Middle East correspondent of the Ullstein newspapers.

He stopped the *arabadshi* and came racing up the stairs, two steps at a time, with his Arab headgear and cloak flapping behind him. He was on his way back from the Djebel

Druze—wherefore the Arab costume—to his permanent headquarters in Jerusalem. After exchanging our news he invited me to the Greek's for an ice-cream, and off we went in the *arabadshi*.

To eat ice-cream after having eaten nothing for four and a half days is an interesting experience. The first mouthful cuts into your stomach like a razor blade; after the second or third, you get the queer sensation that a deep-freeze plant has been installed in the centre of your body. The temperature at the Greek's was over eighty degrees, but my teeth began to chatter and I broke into a cold sweat; then I had to go out and be sick. After holding my head under the water tap, I suddenly felt surprisingly well and sat down again in a state of euphoria. Weisl asked what was the matter with me, and I told him that I had recently had a bout of *papatatchi* fever—which was quite true. *Papatatchi* fever is a disease caused by the bite of a fly of the same name, which drives your temperature up to somewhere round one hundred and three or four, lasts four days, and then wears off without any further ill effects. Weissl, being a doctor, suggested a cup of hot tea instead of ice-cream. With the tea came a plate of *petits fours* which I devoured with relish. We continued to talk animatedly until Weisl had to leave in a hurry to catch his train. He asked me to pay the bill, pressing a pound note into my hand, and dashed towards his waiting *arabadshi*. I objected that the bill would hardly be more than five piasters. Weisl yelled, 'Don't be an idiot,' climbed into the carriage, hitching his cloak up over his striped trousers, and was gone.

That meeting seemed to have effected a magic change. The next day, adorned in a new shirt and new socks, and with a solid breakfast of coffee and two eggs inside me, I went for a swim on the beach of the German colony. While I was basking on the sand, a red-faced young man came up to me and greeted me with great warmth. As I did not recognise him, he explained that his name was Reich, that his father had been Chief Rabbi in Baden, where I had gone to school, and that he had recognised me.

'I never thought that you would become such a famous man,' he added.

'Famous for what?' I asked.

'What do you mean "for what?"' Reich asked back rabbinically. 'A man who is printed on the front page of the *Neue Freie Presse* is a famous man.'

The *Neue Freie Presse* was, as I have already said, something like *The Times* of Central Europe, and held in awe and respect by every citizen of the former Austro-Hungarian monarchy. Months before, in a moment of reckless daring, I had sent them a travelogue piece called 'Arrival in Palestine,' knowing that it had about as much chance of being accepted as I had of winning the Irish Sweepstake. In fact, I had so little hope that I had forgotten all about it. Young Reich's announcement meant more than a momentary triumph; it was indeed the starting point of my career as a journalist and writer; and at that moment on the sun-baked beach, I had a strangely intense awareness of this.

I have mentioned that I had articles published in the Zionist press before, but that was a different matter. The Zionist papers were a family affair, written and read by members of a small, hardly known sect. The difference in professional terms was about the same as between taking part in amateur theatricals at the parish house, and singing at the Metropolitan Opera.

In great spirits, we walked to Reich's room to look up the paper. As he treated me already with the deference due a famous man, I felt I had to live up to standard by asking him to stop for an ice-cream at the Greek's. When at last we were in his room and I had the paper in my hands I felt a terrible disappointment. The article was there all right on the front page; but in the second phrase of the third paragraph, where I had said that 'the water in Haifa harbour was still like green glass,' the printer had put 'grass' instead of 'glass.' I was heartbroken and suspected the editor of having deliberately murdered my article out of jealousy. Reich's lack of comprehension for the horror of having one's good name put to a text which compares still water to grass made me even more furious. It was a thoroughly professional reaction.

A second, more bitter disappointment awaited me a week later. My parents had returned from London to Vienna, and my mother wrote me a congratulatory letter which contained a discreet mention of the fact that through a friend of hers, who was a friend of the paper's editor, she had pulled some strings to get my article accepted. I have never quite got over this anticlimax.

In due time I received a cheque from the *Neue Freie Presse* for one pound, ten shillings. This, together with the remainder of Weisl's loan, put my capital up to nearly two pounds. I felt that it was time for a change of scenery and a new start. I talked the matter over with Abram and we decided that I should go to Tel Aviv, where the chances of finding a job were slightly better, and that I should continue the Press Agency from there.

To save money and see the world, I again travelled by foot; but my suitcase, minus the spare suit and shoes which had fallen into rags, was lighter this time.

XVIII. The Bohemia of Tel Aviv

Among the three main cities of Palestine, Haifa with its waterfront and factories was a vigorous industrial pioneer town. Jerusalem, with its Holy Places, its University, monasteries and convents, was the spiritual centre and seat of Government. Both had mixed Christian, Jewish, and Moslem populations. Tel Aviv alone was purely Jewish—the first Hebrew town founded since the destruction of Jerusalem by Titus. It was an old dream unexpectedly come true; and like all dreams it was disorderly, irrational, difficult to define, with an occasional tendency to turn into a nightmare. Even its name was a paradox: 'tel' means 'hill,' 'aviv' means 'spring'; but the city is flat, and the winter rains are followed by summer heat without much transition. I have tried to describe the puzzling atmosphere of the town in a novel which is part autobiography, *Thieves in the Night*:

'Each time Joseph came to Tel Aviv he was torn between his conflicting emotions of tenderness and revulsion. Tenderness for the one and only purely Hebrew town in the world, and the jostling vitality of its citizens; revulsion from the dreadful mess they had made of it. It was a frantic, maddening city which gripped the traveller by his buttonhole as soon as he entered it, tugged and dragged him around like a whirlpool, and left him after a few days faint and limp, not knowing whether he should laugh or cry, love or hate it.

'The adventure had started less than a generation ago, when the handful of native Jewish families in Arab Jaffa decided to build a residential suburb of their own, on what they imagined to be modern European lines. So they left the Arab port with its labyrinthine bazaars, exotic smells and furtive daggers, and started building on the yellow sand of the Mediterranean dunes the city of their dreams : an exact replica of the ghettoes of Warsaw, Cracow and Lodz. There was a main street named after Dr. Herzl with two rows of exquisitely ugly houses, each of which gave the impression of an orphanage or police barracks. There was also a multitude of dingy shops, most of which sold lemonade, buttons and flypaper.

'In the early nineteen-twenties, with the beginnings of Zionist colonisation, the town spread with increasing speed along the beach. It grew in hectic jumps according to each new wave of immigration—an inland tide of asphalt and concrete advancing over the dunes. There was no time for planning and no willingness for it; growth was feverish and anarchic like that of tropical weeds. Each newcomer who had brought his savings started to build the house of his dreams; and for a decade or so, the source of inspiration of all these petrified day-dreams remained the stone-warren of the Polish small town : the Hill of Spring became a maze of peeling stucco, which after the first rains looked as if it had contracted the measles.

'However, life in Tel Aviv during those early days owed its peculiar character not to the people who had built houses, but to the workers who built them. The first Hebrew city was dominated by young workers of both sexes in their 'teens and twenties. The streets belonged to them; khaki shirts, shorts and dark sun-glasses were the fashionable wear, and ties, nicknamed 'herrings', a rarity. In the evening, when the cool breeze from the sea relieved the white glare of the day, they walked arm in arm over the hot asphalt of half-finished boulevards which ended abruptly in the dunes. At night, they built bonfires and danced the *horra* on the beach; and at least once a week they dragged pompous Mayor Dizengoff or old Chief Rabbi Hertz out of their beds and took them down to the sea to dance with them. They were hard-working, sentimental and gay. They were carried by a wave of enthusiasm which had a crest and no trough. There were few cafés in those days but many workers' clubs; the cheap restaurants sold meals on credit and got their supplies on credit; landlords let rooms on credit in their houses which were built on credit; and yet the town, instead of collapsing into the sand on which it was erected waxed and grew....'

I arrived in Tel Aviv at the peak of an economic depression. During the previous months immigration had slowed down to a trickle, partly owing to the restrictive measures of the British administration which put immigrants without capital on a quota, partly to the unwillingness of Jewish capitalists to go to Palestine. No immigrants meant no building; and as building was the main industry in Palestine, large-scale unemployment resulted.

It was nearly as impossible to find a steady job in Tel Aviv as it had been in Haifa. The second article which I had sent to the *Neue Freie Presse* never appeared; manuscripts sent to other European papers were returned with printed rejection slips. Bread, olives and pressed dates, which were as cheap as olives, became once more my regular diet.

For a while I had a job with a tourist agency; I was supposed to handle their English and French correspondence. But it was one thing to talk English and French with tolerable fluency, and another to write business letters whose language had to be not only correct but idiomatic and salesmanlike. I was fired after a fortnight.

My next job was more satisfactory: I became a land surveyor's assistant. The surveyor was Abram's brother, Ilyusha Weinshall, an engineer and the notorious Don Juan of Tel Aviv. He was tall, dark and dashing, with slanting eyes and that faun-like smile which women in all climates are alleged to find irresistible. He was the only one of the Weinshall brothers with whom I did not become friends; the reason was that I envied him. My job consisted in trudging through the dunes carrying a twelve-foot pole with black and white horizontal stripes, and setting it up at certain points as a landmark for Ilyusha while he took his bearings by peeping through his sextant. As we were often separated by a mile or more, he had to signal me by waving his arms or by blowing a whistle, which made me feel like a sheep-dog. During an eight-hour day I would march some fifteen miles across the sand in scorching heat, sometimes on an empty stomach. Yet it was a leisurely and easy job; trudging along the yellow dunes under the blue haze of the sky, I could spin lazy dreams around the question mark which was my future, and the thirty-five piasters, Union rate, which the day's work would earn me. Unfortunately Ilyusha could only employ me once a week, which meant living on a shilling a day.

The strip of desert we were surveying has now become the orthodox Jewish colony, B'nai Barak. I visited it some twenty years later with a certain feeling of proprietory pride. In the meanwhile, poor Ilyusha had fallen into the clutches of a hysterical woman from Berlin, and died from an overdose of sleeping pills.

As I am writing this chapter about life in Tel Aviv I feel that my memories are shapeless and sprawling. Unlike the periods which preceded and followed it, these three or four months are difficult to bring into focus. This may be a reflection of the shapelessness and diffuse character of Tel Aviv itself. As with those printed horoscopes which say that you have artistic inclinations but also a down-to-earth mind and that you are a cheerful companion though subject to fits of depression, every statement about Tel Aviv is true, and its opposite equally true. In daylight it looks like Whitechapel and at night like Monte Carlo; it is a cheerful town and a depressing town—a town without a profile. The streets have no perspective and no skyline, for the houses neither adjoin nor are they separated by gardens; there are just gaps between them, untidy and pointless little areas like gaps between teeth set too far apart. The people are equally difficult to define. They are admirable in some ways, contemptible in others; they have ceased to be Europeans, refuse to be Asiatics, and resent being called Levantines.

I shared a furnished room with an engineer, later with a bank clerk; I remember nothing about them, not even their names. One day, feeling lonely, I picked up a pariah dog on the street, took him home and shared my bread with him. For two days he didn't leave me for a minute; on the third he vanished and was never seen again. That, I thought, was typical of Tel Aviv. I also had a love affair with a girl from a respectable Tel Aviv family. One day she told me that there were urgent reasons for us to get married at once. Half delighted, half in despair, I borrowed the wedding rings of my friend Jasha and his wife, borrowed a dark suit from another friend, and went to call on my fiancée's papa. She met me in the street and told me that the urgent reasons for our marriage no longer existed. We met again once or twice, got bored with each other and never met again—that, too, was Tel Aviv. But most typical of Tel Aviv at that time was my last job there.

For a month or two I sold advertising space for *Commerce and Industry*—a periodical published in Hebrew and English by the Palestine Manufacturers' Association. The magazine paid me a fixed salary of five pounds per month. But only one pound of the salary was paid out in cash. The remaining four I received in the form of a voucher which entitled me to two meals a day at a certain Mr. Altshuler's restaurant in Allenby Street. Mr. Altshuler passed the voucher on to the cigarette factory of Dr. Walter Moses and obtained for it four pounds' worth of cigarettes. Dr. Moses passed the voucher on to *Commerce and Industry* in payment for advertising space. So the circle was closed.

It was a perfect example of a self-contained economy based on mutual credit. The only trouble with it, as with all perpetual-motion machines, was the frictional losses, and these were made up by donations from abroad.

The summer went by and I got nowhere. My weekly letters to my parents, full of elaborate lies about my dazzling prospects, were a constant headache. My twenty-first birthday was approaching. What was it all leading up to? I was constantly hungry. I could sit in the evening for a whole hour on my favourite bench on the shore and watch people walk by. Not far from this bench there was a fruit stall which sold bananas and little round coconut tarts. The bananas were hung up in bunches and could easily be counted. Their number was always between ninety and a hundred and ten. They gradually became an obsession : I kept stupidly arguing with myself whether, if I had the money to buy the whole stall, I could eat a hundred bananas at a stretch or whether I would be sick. Two years later, as a prosperous news correspondent, I returned to that stall and started on a banana-eating marathon, explaining to the proprietor that it was for a bet. I got to twenty-six; but that was three hours after a solid luncheon, so the experiment was not conclusive.

Once my boss on *Commerce and Industry* caught me in the street wolfing a huge, half-melted chocolate cake, which on an irresistible impulse I had bought at a stall. He gave me a surprised stare and looked away. The humiliation of that moment illustrates what I have said before about the feeling of shame which makes people place a kind of fig leaf before their naked hunger.

In Haifa my spirits had been kept up by frantic political activity. The Revisionist Party had mainly consisted of Abram and myself; in that industrious town people were too busy to bother much about politics. But Tel Aviv was the centre of political life; it was also the seat of the Revisionist Central Committee with its inevitable factions and internal feuds. The single-minded devotion with which Abram and I had run our 'three S's' looked here provincial and out of place. Nobody seemed to take much interest in my press agency, and as I didn't have the money to pay for the stationery and postage, I closed it down. All my enterprises seemed to come to nought; I had taken and lost about a dozen jobs in half as many months : obviously I was a complete failure.

That was also the opinion of my friend Dr. Har-Even, the first psycho-analyst to set foot in Palestine, and a member of the Revisionist Central Committee. He kept telling me that I ought to go back to Vienna and the Polytechnic. 'If you don't finish your studies,' he kept saying, 'you will remain a vagabond. No matter how successful you are, you will always be a runaway and a fugitive on the earth, and all respectable people will smell out the tramp in you.'

Mosche Har-Even was a former assistant of Professor Stekel's (who, like Jung and Adler, had left Freud and founded a school of his own).[1] A Russian by origin, he had worked with Stekel in Vienna, and had arrived in Palestine a year or two before me. He was in his thirties, a tall, bony, bald-headed man with a good-humoured Tartar's face, who looked more like a Cossack *hetman* than a Jewish psycho-analyst. During the three years which I spent in the Middle East, he was my nearest friend; and he never tried to analyse me. 'You are a hopeless case,' he used to say, 'the type who after the first half-hour starts analysing his analyst and drives him nuts.'

At that time Har-Even was as chronically hungry as I. One would imagine that a psycho-analyst, and the only one to boot, would have thrived in all-Jewish Tel Aviv like yeast

[1] Stekel's school called itself the Psychanalytical School, without the orthodox 'o' in the middle.

in a barrel of malt. The opposite was true. Har-Even, in spite of his high qualifications and attractive personality, had only two or three patients, at ten piasters an hour. Tel Aviv's cold reception of its first psycho-analyst may have been due partly to the fact that the majority of its population came from Poland and Russia, countries which at that time had not yet been bitten by the bug. But there was, I believe, a deeper reason for it. The Palestinian Jews, and particularly those of the second or third generation, have a mental attitude and culture-pattern completely different from Jews anywhere else. Jewishness is essentially a minority status. What in Europe and America is known as Jewish humour is the salty product of a victimised minority. In Palestine, it is drying up. The typically 'Jewish' jokes are imported.

With regard to neurosis the situation is much the same. I am not sure whether Jews in Palestine are less neurotic than elsewhere, but they are certainly less aware of and preoccupied with their neuroses. The pressure of a hostile environment—whether it is exerted through overt persecution or the subtler forms of discrimination—increases the tendency towards introversion. The Palestinian Jew, as a member of an expanding pioneering community where pressure works from the centre outward, becomes transformed into an extrovert. This may sound like a sweeping generalisation, but it seems to be borne out by the strikingly 'un-Jewish' appearance and mentality of the new, native generation.

If I was a runaway student without a profession, Har-Even was an accomplished scholar without patients and, though for different reasons, as hard-up as I. But analysts are supposed to have a superior grip on reality; this Har-Even proved by teaching me an ingenious method of how to go less hungry, which we called the Credit Rotation System.

During the great depression, most Tel Aviv restaurants gave their regular customers a limited amount of credit when the latter ran out of funds. The Credit Rotation System consisted in having breakfast regularly in one restaurant, A; lunch in another, B; and dinner in a third, C. When you got hold of a little cash, you paid A where you were most heavily in debt; the next time B; and so on in rotation. If A, or even both A and C, stopped your credit, you thus always had B to fall back on for at least one meal a day. Never since have I seen an analyst achieve such effective therapeutical results.

Later on, when I became a foreign correspondent stationed in Jerusalem, I spent all my week-ends with Har-Even in Tel Aviv. My friendships have always tended to fall into two distinct categories : intellectual relations and *camaraderies*. The two rarely overlapped; for the men from whom I derived intellectual stimulation were usually much older than I, or else their tastes and habits were different from mine. The *camaraderies,* on the other hand, were either chance encounters of the Buxbaum kind under conditions of stress—in prisons, concentration camps, in the Army—or they were based on some shared taste in dining or wining or playing poker, with no other interest in common. Har-Even is one of the few men in whom I have found both; and that is the nearest definition of friendship that I know. The last I heard of him is that he has become a successful psychoanalyst in Geneva, Switzerland.

As I have said before, Tel Aviv lacked, among other things, two essential atmospheric ingredients : a touch of Freud and a touch of humour. While Mosche Har-Even was trying to provide the first, I embarked with another friend on a plan to provide the second in the form of a Hebrew cabaret.

Avigdor Hameiri came, like myself, from Budapest. A Hebrew poet and novelist, he had achieved a certain reputation by his daring, hyper-modern experiments with the petrified language of the Bible. Our friendship started when I translated two of his poems into German. The translations appeared, accompanied by a somewhat turgid eulogy—my first literary essay—in a Berlin Zionist weekly. Hameiri—now a civil servant of the Israeli Government—was a shortish, stocky man of terrific dynamism, a volcanic talker, enthusiastic, quarrelsome and given to violent tantrums. Once, during a quarrel on the merits of Rilke, he smashed his glasses on the floor and performed on them a frenzied tap-dance until they were ground to powder. His bureau drawers were full of unpublished manuscripts; he was nearly as penniless as I, and had a wife and a daughter to support. I often slept on the floor of their little slum-flat in the Yarkon district, which at that time was on the distant outskirts of Tel Aviv, where the city merged into the dunes. For breakfast we had hot water and a few tea leaves, and each of us an onion, large as an apple, with a chunk of bread. Eating raw onion was a welcome change after the date-and-olive diet, and useful for keeping up my vitamin balance.

Talking of vitamins, I should mention as a curiosity that during that hunger year, which was my twenty-first, I kept growing until I outgrew my last and only suit. Yet, as far as I know, I have never had any glandular disfunction.

Having agreed that Tel Aviv was a provincial and humourless place with no feeling for true genius, Avigdor and I decided to found a politico-literary cabaret. We had both grown up in the town which, next to Paris, had produced the best *chansonniers,* witty *compères* and satirical one-act plays on a miniature stage. Our associates were two other Hungarians : an industrial designer, and a young actor named Donath. We had night-long discussions in the *Café Hungarith,* at that time the main haunt of Tel Aviv's bohemia—the painters Rubin and Mane Katz, the poet Uri Zwi Greenberg, and others who have since become celebrities in Israeli arts and letters. The cabaret, called 'Matateh' (The Broom), did actually materialise—but only a few months later, after I had left Tel Aviv. Under a less aggressive name—'The Samovar'—it still exists and, as far as I know, is still the only literary cabaret in Israel.

Simultaneously with the cabaret project, I branched out into a new line of activity : I started to write Hebrew fairy tales. These were inspired by a snub-nosed little boy named Arik, the son of the third of the Weinshall brothers. Jasha Weinshall, the surgeon, was an extremely good-looking, quiet and dreamy man, who in his spare time wrote biographical studies of cranks and eccentrics in Jewish history. He was married to a lovely young woman who that year had been elected beauty queen of Tel Aviv. Arik was as handsome as his parents. When I had tea with the Weinshalls he used to sit on my knee and pester me for stories which I improvised for his benefit. Of one of them I still remember the beginning :

'There was once a king in Israel who had three hundred wives. The first had red hair, the second green hair, the third had a hunchback and the fourth a pimple on her nose. . . .'

'Why ?' asked Arik.

'I don't know,' I said, 'they just were like that.'

'*I* know,' said Arik, 'they were like that so that the king could tell one from the other.'

This one remark seemed to me to contain the essence of fairy-tale logic. For a while I was engrossed in thinking out stories for Arik, and writing them down with a view to collecting a volume. Jasha encouraged me :

'Tel Aviv needs fairly tales,' he said dreamily. 'We have no folklore. What is a nation without fairy tales ?'

Everybody had a pet theory of what Tel Aviv needed most : fairy tales, a cabaret, municipal autonomy, a repertory theatre, a town-planning council, the prohibition of Sabbath traffic, a zoological garden, a museum, authorised bordellos. It was a town without a past, sprung to life like a phantom out of the gap of two thousand years in Jewish history. It was a town whose population could not quite believe in its own reality, while they watched it grow with awe and wonder. One day the Mayor, Dizongof, dropped a stone into the sea to inaugurate the beginning of work on the future harbour. When the water had plopped over the symbolic stone, he turned round and said solemnly : 'Citizens, I can still remember the days when Tel Aviv had no harbour. . . .'

I actually finished only three out of the prospective volume of fairy tales. They were published in a Zionist year book in Czecho-Slovakia. When I started on the fourth, I received a call from von Weisl in Jerusalem with a surprising offer. Would I go with him to Cairo and edit there a German-language weekly newspaper? Of course I would. At last, so it seemed, I was getting somewhere.

XIX. Dead End

THE newspaper was called *Nil und Palestina Zeitung*—the *Nile and Palestine Gazette*. Half of it was printed in German, half in Arabic; it was financed by the German Legation in Cairo who wanted to boost German export trade, and directed by von Weisl who wanted to make Zionist propaganda among the Arabs. It lived for exactly three issues and then folded quietly up like my previous hopeful ventures, from architecture to the selling of lemonade.

But the three winter months which I spent in Cairo added a new dimension to my experience. I was not conscious of it at the time; I was merely soaking in new experiences, as a sponge feeds on its nourishing environment. Von Weisl, an Austrian painter and I shared a small flat with a large terrace on the *Sharia Falaki*. The painter, Robert Hoffmann, took me round on his sketching expeditions in the native quarters and along the banks of the Nile. Through him I learnt to see, without thinking, in purely visual terms, and to perceive human beings—some sailors on the Nile or a beggar on the steps of a mosque—as incidental figures in a timeless landscape.

Most of my time I spent in the Egyptian Museum, loitering round the mummies, and the statues of the Eighteenth Dynasty. The strands of limp, flaxen hair on the skull of Rameses II looked as if a damp brush had just been passed over it. I had a dizzy feeling as if I were bending over a dark, murky well into which somebody had dropped a stone a long time ago. To my science-trained mind it seemed atrocious that however deep it travelled into the past, the stone would never reach bottom. It was the image of the arrow in reverse; the arrow travelled in pure, rarefied space, the well of history opened into a more intimate, humane dimension. Thus my first groping steps away from the scientific and towards a humanistic view of man were induced by a detour *via* the Pharaohs of the Eighteenth Dynasty. This is less paradoxical than it sounds; towards the end of his life, Freud seems to have passed through a similar experience. His only work which can be called humanistic in spirit—*Moses the Egyptian*—was inspired by Akhnaton, the mad Pharaoh who initiated the cult of a single and invisible god.

After the teeming bustle of Jewish Palestine, which made one feel as if one were a damp rag being passed through a mangle, Egypt induced a feeling of sudden stillness and peace —as if a radio had been switched off next door. The respite was of short duration. The *Nile and Palestine Gazette* had been a still-born idea—the outcome of Weisl's fertile imagination which had momentarily bowled over some enterprising diplomat of the Weimar Republic. When the first difficulties of policy and financing arose, the impracticability of the scheme became obvious, and the paper closed down.

It was equally obvious that I had again reached a dead end. For a few weeks I worked as Weisl's secretary. Then an unexpected opportunity turned up.

The international Revisionist movement was growing; its headquarters had been transferred to Berlin. The organisation needed an Executive secretary, and Jabotinsky had proposed me as a candidate for that post. If I went to Berlin to talk the matter over with the International Executive Committee, there was a good chance that I would be accepted. I went at once.

I chose the then cheapest route, by small Roumanian steamer from Alexandria to Constanza, and then by train to

Budapest, where I could break the journey to see my parents. It was not exactly a glorious return. But the journey through the Dardanelles and the Bosphorus, followed by a spectacular storm in the Black Sea, was too exhilarating for worries about the future. Besides, I travelled in the company of a very lovely dancer born of a German father and a Javanese mother. She was returning from an engagement tour in Egyptian cabarets, and nearly as broke as myself. Towards the end of the long train journey I ran out of my last penny, and she paid for our breakfast in the restaurant-car. Thus, in addition to the other experiences gained in that short year, I also had a taste of life as a gigolo, to the extent of one cup of hot coffee and two rolls with butter and jam.

I found my parents living in a furnished room, in the town which my mother so much disliked, and to which my father's bankruptcy had forced them to return. But my dancer friend had continued the journey to Berlin, and I was too entranced with love and longing to feel depressed. I did not have the fare to Berlin, and could not ask my father for it; so I went to see the editor of the *Pester Lloyd*, Hungary's old-established German-language paper. Old little Mr. Vészi-Weiss, the editor, looked me up and down and asked me what I wanted. I said that I came from the Middle East, where I had written articles for the *Neue Freie Presse*; the plural was an exaggeration which I found justified by the circumstances.

Old Weiss shook his head. 'Tell that to your Aunt Hatty,' he said. 'You look like a schoolboy and talk to me of the *Neue Freie Presse*!'

I produced my passport, and the one article which my mother had planted in that paper. Old Weiss asked me whether I had brought some manuscripts. I handed him five travelogues on Palestine and Egypt. He picked out three and, without reading more than the titles, made out a voucher to the cashier for immediate payment. 'If you are good enough for the *Presse,* you are good enough for me,' he said, 'and now scram, I am busy.'

Old Weiss—short, bald, with the head of an ostrich—had befriended many young writers in this gruff paternal manner. Newspaper editors of his kind still existed in pre-war Europe; now you only see them on movie screens.

I split the proceeds with my father, and set out for Berlin.

There a major and a minor disappointment awaited me. My dancer friend had gone on to Paris without so much as leaving her address or writing me a picture postcard. And the Revisionist Party was lacking in funds. I got the job, together with the high-sounding title of World Executive Secretary; but it was only a half-time job, at the miserable pay of a hundred marks—five pounds—a month.

My work consisted in dictating letters to the various branches of the movement, explaining to them the decisions of the Central Committee, answering their queries and spurring them to greater activity. It was not an inspiring job; but it taught me much about political psychology. The Zionists were a minority within the various Jewish minorities. The Revisionist movement was a minority to the third power, as it were. But in every single branch there was an opposition within the opposition, and factions which fought each other tooth and nail. It was the same story, the same futile little drama re-enacted from Kovno to Paris, from Berlin to Salonika. The issues were either personal or ideological, but mostly a turbid mixture of both. I learnt to dismiss most of these local quarrels about doctrine or tactics as mere projections of personal rivalries. But I also learnt that the smaller the group, the more it was apt to produce experts in ideological hair-splitting and sectarian monomaniacs.

At the time I thought that these were traits peculiar to Jewry, or to the Revisionist movement, and felt pretty disgusted. A few years later I found a very similar pattern in the Communist International (which, contrary to popular belief, counted many Jews in its lower strata but few among its leaders). It was partly due to this feeling of *déjà vue*, of having gone through all this before, that I never had any ambitions to play a political part in the Communist movement, though I stayed in it for seven years. When, at last, I broke with the CP, I was again saved by that early experience from joining, as most of my renegade comrades did, the Trotskyites or some other Left-Wing splinter group.

So, in retrospect, my political apprenticeship had its uses. But the three or four months that I spent in Berlin were among the dreariest I remember. To be a penniless tramp in the Orient is adventure; to be an office worker in Berlin at a hundred marks a month is not. I found a furnished room, in the proximity of proletarian Alexander Platz, for sixty marks including breakfast. That left me with a little over one mark a day, the equivalent of one hot meal, with nothing to spare for theatres, movies, or taking out a girl friend. Berlin in the 'twenties was the most cosmopolitan capital in Europe, throbbing with life and excitement. I felt left out, starved in body and spirit, greedy, lonely and envious.

I knew nobody in Berlin except an uncle, who lived in a suburb—and my boss, Richard Lichtheim, a banker and member of the Revisionist Central Committee. Lichtheim represented the best type of the Jewish European, to whom German culture owes so much, and against whom it committed one of the most hideous crimes in history. He had a penetrating intelligence, great organisational capacity, humour, civilised tastes and personal integrity. Later on he broke with Jabotinsky on political grounds, and after that played no prominent part in the Zionist movement.

Some twenty years after our Berlin days, during the Arab-Jewish war, I again met Lichtheim in Tel Aviv. He had emigrated with his family to Palestine, and was without a job. He would have made an admirable ambassador for

Israel to any Western European country. But as he did not belong to the ruling Party, or any other political coterie, he could obtain no Government appointment. We sat in a noisy café on the Tel Aviv sea-front and talked of bygone days, of our dreams of the future Jewish State, and of the present reality which, as always, was an illegitimate child of the vision. Lichtheim said quietly and without bitterness, 'I am a forgotten man.' His fate is typical of what happened to the Old Guard of the Zionist movement. But at least they were spared the fate of the Old Guard of the Russian Revolution.

The only other family which befriended me in Berlin was that of my mother's brother, Otto Devrient. His story is also typical, though in a different way, and deserves to be briefly told. Uncle Otto was a boy of nineteen or twenty when the respectable Hitzigs were ruined by the machinations of the dashing villain, and my grandfather was packed off to America. He must have felt the hurt and the humiliation very deeply, for he ran away from home to Berlin, embraced the Lutheran faith, and even changed his name from Hitzig to Devrient. About his early years in Berlin I know little. When I was a child, he was mentioned at home as a prosperous man who unfortunately . . . and at this point voices were always lowered to a hushed whisper. When I grew older, I gathered what Uncle Otto's dark secret was: he had married a 'sandwich-damsel.' When I grew even older, I understood that a 'sandwich-damsel' was a young lady who walked about in Berlin nightclubs and other disreputable places selling flowers, chocolates and ham sandwiches to the customers. To make the disgrace complete, the damsel's first name was Henne—which means, simply, the hen.

On my arrival in Berlin in the spring of 1927, I stayed for a couple of weeks in Uncle Otto's and Aunt Henne's house. It was a nice house with a garden near the pleasant lake of Coepenick. The peculiarity of the house was that the floors in all the rooms were covered with Oriental rugs—including the bathrooms, kitchen and lavatories. Otto was the head of a firm which imported carpets and he had such a passion for them that he kept bringing home rare collector's pieces until there was no place left to put them. This led to my only friction with Uncle and Aunt, for I like to take splashy showers —which, on account of one Tabriz and two Bokharas on the bathroom floor, was much resented. Otherwise we got on excellently. Uncle Otto was a quiet little man with a gentle face, large brown eyes, and a peculiar, baroque sense of humour. Aunt Henne was a beautiful matron with snow-white hair and regal manners. The two were childless, deeply devoted to each other and to their preposterous mongrel dog —twelve years old, gouty, mangy and smelly—whom my uncle addressed as 'Baron Tassilo.' Otto had just retired from business; he spent most of his time pottering in the garden, adorned in a green Tyrolean hat, and alarming the children of the neighbourhood by suddenly breaking an hour's complete silence with a wild and blood-curdling yodel. He had a strange power over children, who ran after him as if he were the Pied Piper of Hamelin.

I visited the Devrients for the last time in 1932, a few months before the Nazis took power. They were both over sixty then, but still gave the impression of a couple of young lovers. Baron Tassilo was buried in a corner of the garden, and his place taken by an equally preposterous puppy called Tassilo II. Though Otto was slightly ailing, they seemed destined to a long and graceful old age among their flowers and carpets, worshipped by a probable Tassilo III. Instead of which came the Nuremberg laws, the curse upon mixed marriages, the shadow of the concentration camp, and finally the gas chamber.

Aunt Henne could have saved herself by deserting Otto. She refused. In 1939, a few months before the outbreak of the war, a friend of mine, Francine F., was sent from Paris to

Berlin as a courier of one of the German underground parties. Her mission was, among other things, to smuggle out people from Germany. I asked her to look up Otto and Henne, and to see what could be done for them.

I had not written to them since the beginning of the Nazi régime, that is, for seven years, for I was proscribed in Germany as a Communist, and a letter from me would have put them in additional danger. I gave Francine a password: she was to say that she came from 'Dundy'—my nickname as a little boy—and to follow this up by a private joke referring to the games of chess which I used to play with Otto, and which no outsider could possibly know about.

On her return to Paris, Francine described her visit to me. She rang the bell at the garden gate; for several minutes there was no answer except the fierce barking of a dog. She kept ringing, and at last a white-haired matron appeared who spoke to Francine across the fence without opening the gate. Francine asked to see my uncle; Henne replied that he was ill and did not see anybody. Francine said that she came from 'Dundy', and added the chess-joke. My aunt looked at her for a second; then said, 'We know no Dundy,' turned her back and slowly walked into the house.

The end of the story I learnt in 1946 when my mother, who had been caught by the war in Budapest, came to join me in London. During the first war years she had kept up a cautious correspondence with the Devrients by means of greetings on picture postcards—which were least likely to attract the censor's attention. In the summer of 1942, when the Jews of Europe had reached the last stage of their calvary and the gas chambers were put into operation, she received two successive postcards on which Otto's end was recorded by Henne. One evening he took an unusually large amount of sleeping pills, and walked out into the garden. Henne heard the rattling of the chains of their little boat on the lake, and followed him. When she reached the mooring he was already away out on the water, rowing away from the shore. She called and entreated him to come back; he answered with a single phrase: 'Don't make it so difficult . . .' The next morning the boat was found, drifting upside down on the lake.

Otto was my mother's only brother. A few months after his suicide, her only sister, Rose, was gassed at Auschwitz— together with her daughter, my cousin Margit—the one who had taken me to her lecture at the metal works—and Margit's two children, Kate and Georgy. Kate was seventeen and dark, Georgy twelve and blond. Kate wanted to become a pianist, Georgy a doctor.

XX. The Turning Point

THE opportunity to start on a stable professional career came at long last in September, 1927, just before my twenty-second birthday. Von Weisl, Middle East correspondent of the *Neue Freie Presse* and of the Ullstein chain of papers, received a new assignment: he was sent on a grand tour of India, Malaya and the Far East. His post, with headquarters in Jerusalem, was temporarily vacant. He proposed me for it and I got it.

The House of Ullstein was at that time at the peak of its glory. It was a kind of supertrust; the biggest enterprise of its type in Europe and probably in the world. It published four daily newspapers in Berlin alone. These were the venerable *Vossische Zeitung*, founded in 1704; the *Berliner Morgenpost* with the largest circulation of any newspaper in the German language; the *B.Z. am Mittag*, a midday paper which broke all news-speed records, and *Tempo*, a tabloid-style evening paper. There were more than a dozen weekly and monthly periodicals which catered to all tastes and strata of the population: from the highbrow *Querschnitt* to the popular *Grüne Post*, from the science magazine *Koralle* to the ladies' fashion journal *Die Dame*; not to forget the *Berliner Illustrierte,* the largest illustrated weekly in Europe. The Ullsteins were, furthermore, among the leading book publishers in Germany; they ran their own travel agency, photo agency, and finally the Ullstein News Service, with subscribers from Scandinavia to the Balkans. In short, to be a correspondent of Ullsteins was every newspaperman's dream and placed you in the ranks of the European journalists' aristocracy—or at least made you feel terribly important. Particularly at the age of twenty-two, as the youngest person on record to ascend to such dignity.

The atmosphere of the 'House' in Berlin's Kochstrasse was more that of a ministry than of an editorial office. The firm was owned by the Ullstein brothers, the sons of old Leopold, founder of the dynasty. They were five, like the erstwhile Rothschilds, and also Jews. The motto of the House was political liberalism and cultural modernism. It was anti-militarist, anti-chauvinist and Pan-European; the great vogue of Franco-German friendship during the Briand-Stresemann era was largely due to the influence of the Ullstein press. It was a political power and at the same time the embodiment of everything progressive and cosmopolitan in the Weimar Republic.

I got the job by shameless bluffing on von Weisl's and my own part. The length of his absence from the Jerusalem post was undetermined—perhaps one, perhaps two years. During that time the Ullsteins did not want to send out a highly paid correspondent, and preferred to make do with a local string-man. So we both pretended that I lived permanently in Jerusalem, and was only on a short visit to Berlin. I had a few articles in various papers to my credit and was warmly recommended by Weisl; but even so my future chiefs were sceptical. The decision rested with Dr. Magnus, head of the Personnel Department and Dr. H., head of the News Service. Against me spoke my cursed schoolboy appearance and my timidity, which during the decisive interview practically paralysed me and, after a sarcastic remark by Dr. H., changed into sudden and very ill-timed aggressiveness. H. took an instant dislike to me, under which I was to swelter for years. But Magnus, a dry, taciturn little man from Hamburg, took a more paternal attitude—perhaps because he too suffered from incurable shyness, disguised by a nutcracker-cum-martinet pose. At the end he said: 'All right, we'll give you a try out. Two hundred marks a month plus what you earn by your articles. But remember, you are on probation.' H. shrugged without comment; his opinion of my future chances was written on his face.

I walked out and along the sound-proof corridors of the awe-inspiring building with my heart still in my pants and my head in the clouds. Two hundred marks was a small sum, I was employed only on a temporary basis, and the hostility of my immediate superior was a grave handicap; but, although my self-confidence was often wanting where human relations were concerned, it was unlimited on the professional plane. There was no doubt in my mind that, if only given a chance, I would within a short time become a star of the journalistic profession. Now my chance had come.

One difficulty remained: to get back from Berlin to Jerusalem. As previous passages may have indicated, I had a nearly insurmountable psychological block when it came to borrowing money, even from friends. The same inhibition cropped up each time I had to discuss my salary or expenses with my employers. This complex—for once an entirely honourable one—is in an obvious manner related to my father. The feeling of guilt for having abandoned my studies and thereby cheated him out of his last investment, never entirely left me; and employers are always father substitutes of sorts. In short, I couldn't bring myself to borrow the fare either from my uncle or from Lichtheim or Weisl, both of whom would have gladly obliged. Instead, I started on a grotesque Odyssey towards the south.

The first step was Vienna; that was as far as my cash went in terms of railway mileage. In Vienna I called on the famous *Neue Freie Presse* and, with the credentials of the Ullsteins in my pocket, obtained without difficulty a contract for two articles per month. This already doubled my future income. But to ask for an advance would have been bad for my prestige; besides, when it came to matters of cash, the block made its inevitable appearance. In the end, my old comrades of 'Unitas' came to the rescue. We had always shared what cash we had, and redeemed each other's dinner-jackets from the pawn shop; they were a fraternal and not a paternal symbol. After two nights of revel, and a *Kneipe* to end all *Kneipes,* they emptied their pockets, whose contents were just sufficient for the next stage southward, to Budapest— and even then only by the cheapest means of transportation; by Danube steamer.

Back in Budapest, I went to see old Weiss, and made the psychological mistake of showing him my credentials. 'You are a big shot now, so what do you need me for?' he said in a peeved tone. 'Scram.' So I was stuck again. For two days I made the round of the second-hand bookshops, selling what remained of my school-books and other battered treasures of my childhood. My father managed to rake up a few pengoes, and my mother pawned the one diamond ring which had survived the shipwreck. It was the greatest psychological hurdle which I had to overcome, and the last sacrifice which they had to make on my behalf. Three months later I was able to start sending money home, and a year later to take entire charge of their support; and my neurotic behaviour decreased in proportion to the increase of my cheques.

I left Budapest with exactly the amount that would enable me to reach Palestine by Danube steamer down to Giurgiu, from there by slow train to Constanza and then by a Roumanian boat to Jaffa. On the way from Giurgiu to Constanza I had to change trains in Bucharest, where I paid a visit to the local leaders of the Revisionist Party. These kind and hospitable people, whom I had never met before, saved me from a major predicament. When on the next morning I arrived in Constanza I learnt that my boat would be two days late. I not only had to live for two days, but also to pay an embarkation fee which I had not foreseen; and all I had left was some small change, as I had counted on the food being provided on board ship.

In my despair I went to the British Consul with a cock-and-bull story of having had my wallet pinched on the journey. Constanza is a Roumanian harbour full of the dregs and driftwood of humanity which accumulates in ports. The Consul or Vice-Consul, who received me on the strength of an impressive visiting-card that I had had made en route, listened to me politely and with a complete absence of sympathy.

'You are the third visitor this week whose wallet has been stolen,' he remarked dryly. 'If you are a correspondent of Ullsteins, why don't you go to the German Consul?' I explained—quite truthfully—that if I went to the German Consul my employers would be bound to learn about the incident through the German Foreign Office, and that this would very much embarrass me. But such psychological subtleties cut no ice at a British Consulate—particularly if you travel with a Hungarian passport as a correspondent of German newspapers. I did not have the money to send an SOS either to Vienna or Berlin; I had just enough to send a local telegram to my new friends in Bucharest. They promptly wired the sum for which I had asked—and yet I must confess to my shame that I have completely forgotten not only their names, but even what they looked like and what kind of people they were. A fortnight later I returned the money from Jerusalem with a warm covering letter; but they did not answer, and I never heard of them again.

I arrived in Jerusalem at the end of September, 1927, almost exactly two years after the night when I had burnt my Matriculation Book—and my bridges. At this point ends the narrative of my apprenticeship; of confused wanderings, starvation and false starts. The next four years are the more or less banal success story of a European newspaperman in the Middle East, Paris, and Berlin; of dogged work, straining ambition and vain satisfactions—until the next turning point in 1931, when I burnt my bridges a second time and joined the Communist Party.

During those two tramp-years I had mostly felt like the bewildered hero in Petronius' *Satyricon* : 'You leap about and fuss and worry like a busy mouse caught in a chamber pot.' But in retrospect the hectic jumps, the wild goose chases and escapades of that time fall into a different and meaningful pattern. On the other hand, the four following years when I 'made good,' and behaved according to the rules of reason and respectability, seem now the dreariest and most sterile though outwardly they were full of colour and change, ranging from visits to Arab kings to a Zeppelin expedition in the Arctic. In the rectifying mirror of time, the meagre years which seemed to carry me nowhere appear rich with the fullness of experience; whereas the years of purposeful striving and success were spiritually but a period of marking time.

Part Four

THE ROAD TO RESPECTABILITY

1927–1930

Es pocht eine Sehnsucht an die Welt
An der wir sterben müssen.
ELSE LASKER-SCHULER

XXI. King Feisal of Iraq

In the spring of 1940, shortly before the German invasion of France, detectives from the Préfecture de Police made a search of my Paris flat. They took away, among other things, the collection of newspaper articles that I had published during the preceding fifteen years. The articles were pasted in several bulky scrap-books; I have never seen them since. With the exception of two unpublished manuscripts which they overlooked (one of them was *Darkness at Noon*), everything that I had written from adolescence to the age of thirty-five was gone.

I was surprised to discover how little I regretted the loss. Though in subsequent years I often worked in public libraries, it never occurred to me to look up my lost articles in their newspaper files. Not until the spring of 1951, when I started writing this book and it became necessary to fill in blank spots in my memory, did I force myself to do so. I went to the New York Public Library and was referred to its down-town Newspaper Division where the back files of the *Vossische Zeitung* and the *Neue Freie Presse* are kept.

The Newspaper Division occupies two stories in a dreary office building on Twenty-fifth Street; it completely lacks the glamour of the main building on Fifth Avenue. It has a large, grimy and depressing reading-room where bored research workers dig for items of information in the past. I handed in my order form and sat down on a bench at an ink-stained table. It was very hot, the room smelt of sweat, and I was filled with a guilty apprehension—quite unlike the feeling of excitement and curiosity which I had experienced when I went to look up the 'secular horoscope' of my day of birth.

After a few minutes a boy laid before me several dusty, brown paper parcels held together with string. I opened the first; out came a cloud of more black dust and what looked like a shower of confetti. At first I thought that mice had nested in the parcel, but the attendant explained that the quarter-century-old newspapers had just disintegrated. Respectable English and American journals are bound into volumes to preserve them. But the venerable *Vossische* had been bundled helter-skelter—the dates were all mixed up—in common brown paper. Days, weeks and entire months were missing; and a good part of what was left had crumbled into yellow confetti.

To leaf through the remaining pages, which had a tendency to disintegrate under one's touch, was a melancholy business. When I had worked through two entire months—August and September, 1927—without having come across my name, my apprehension began to verge on panic. Perhaps I had only imagined the past? Or some unknown power had erased every trace of it? I had told the library attendant that I wanted photostats made of my articles. From time to time he looked my way expectantly—there was nothing. Drops of sweat fell from my face into the confetti and dust; not only did the attendant take me for an impostor, but I felt like one myself.

At last!—on a torn page of the *Vossische* of 6th October, 1927, there was an article 'by our Correspondent in Jerusalem' entitled '*Die Erbschaft Zaglul Paschas*.' Reading my name under it, in Gothic type, I felt as proud and elated as when it had first appeared in print, some thirty years ago.

This episode seems typical of my ambivalent attitude towards my own youth. The panic which had seized me when I could find no documentary evidence of my past—

accompanied by a fleeting but genuine doubt whether it had really existed—illustrates that incomplete identification with my former self which I have mentioned before. The silly feeling of pride which came after indicates on the other hand how gladly the past is recognised—provided that it offers cause for pleasure and satisfaction.

However, satisfaction soon turned into embarrassment as I read the recovered opus, and those which followed. Now I understood why I had been so reluctant to look them up before. Their style was insupportable; their manner and approach dated from a dead era—removed from the present not by twenty-five years but almost by centuries. It was a ghastly experience; the more decaying parcels I untied, coughing in the clouds of dust which they exhaled, the more I felt like an archæologist breaking into a Pharaoh's tomb.

There was a subjective and an objective side to my dismay. E. M. Forster once wrote to me that he could think of his early work only 'with rage and shame'. This is probably a common reaction among writers who have a stronger relationship to their work than to their ego. But the commonness of an experience makes it no less painful. In my particular case, the effect was increased by a contrast in languages. Those lost articles were written in German. By the time I recovered them, I had for more than ten years written and thought in English.

Now there is a basic difference between Anglo-Saxon and German journalism—a difference that is relevant to this story. British and American newspaper correspondents aim, at least theoretically, at an impersonal and objective reporting of facts. Political bias and personal idiosyncrasies are supposed to be kept down to a minimum and make themselves only indirectly felt, through the inevitable selection of material and distribution of emphasis. To express opinions and judgments is the prerogative of leader-writers and columnists. German journalism, particularly during the

H

Weimar Republic, took a diametrically opposite course. Its starting point was the Correspondent's *Weltanschauung,* and the political philosophy of the paper for which he worked. His job was not to report news and facts (that task was contemptuously left to the news agencies), but to use facts as pretexts for venting his opinions and passing oracular judgments. 'Facts,' a famous German editor said, 'are not fit for the reader when served raw; they had to be cooked, chewed and presented in the correspondent's saliva.' Fed on this kind of diet, the German reading public never developed an empirical approach to world affairs; it never learnt to face the facts and weigh the evidence. Its approach to reality was distorted by *Weltanschauung*; and the more you become addicted to *Weltanschauung,* the easier you are swept off your feet.

This tendency towards subjectivity determined not only the content, but also the style of German journalism. A foreign correspondent was expected to be more of a *littérateur* than a reporter, and to have an 'individual style' like a creative writer. One of the most celebrated Ullstein correspondents, Richard Katz, caused a minor sensation when he wrote a front-page editorial in metric verse. (The editorials of most German papers appeared on the front page, thus illustrating the priority given to comment over news.)

As if to underline the subjective nature of his reports, the correspondent's full name appeared over each of them, and even a two-line cabled item—say, a railway accident or a heat-wave—was signed with his initials. And a considerable part of a correspondent's time was devoted, not to reporting, but to the writing of *feuilletons.*

The *feuilleton* was the curse of Continental, and especially of German journalism. It was a perverse blend of travelogue, essay and short story, bringing out the worst side of each. It was always written in the first person singular, and mostly in a knowing, whimsical style. While I was looking for my own articles I reread several *feuilletons* by the celebrated masters of that time—let their names be mercifully forgotten —whom I had so much admired, and on whom I had modelled my style. It was like a visit to the waxworks; though I suppose that a quarter-century from now, a collection of *The New Yorker* magazine will appear just as ghastly and dated. Works of art survive; fashions and 'schools' don't.

The badness of the writing of my more famous colleagues of the period comforted me, but it did not diminish my distaste for my own. I looked at the titles over my articles : 'The Vices of Beirut,' 'The Shadow-Cæsar on the Caliph's Throne,' 'The Café of the Arabian Nights,' and writhed in embarrassment. The worst of it was the silly waste of the rich factual material that I had accumulated in three years of travelling through the various countries of the Middle East.

Only a few among my articles of that period bear rereading today, and these are pieces that I wrote in a hurry, without whimsy and *Weltanschauung*. The more pains I took in rewriting and polishing a piece, the more embarrassing the product appears now. If only some experienced craftsman had given me a good dressing down, had beaten the smartness and the purple patches out of me, it would have saved me years of wandering in the desert. But the editors in the various newspaper offices in Berlin, Vienna and Prague preferred gingerbread to factual fare; they suppressed figures but let the adjectives stand, and sometimes added a few of their own. Their papers were the most staid and respectable journals in Central Europe; so the fault was not entirely my own but shared by a culture which was rapidly losing touch with reality. The demand for gingerbread and purple patches was determined by the same mentality which, a few years later, wallowed in the turbid flow of Nazi *mystique*.

One of the idyllic aspects of the Arab countries at that time was that, if you were a visiting European journalist, you went for information straight to the reigning King, Emir or Pasha, and were usually asked to stay for lunch. Thus at the age of twenty-three I could—and did—boast of the acquaintance of King Feisal of Iraq, the Emir Abdulla of Transjordan, the Egyptian Prime Minister, Nahas Pasha, the President of the Lebanese Republic, and so on. Only two of them made a lasting impression : the jovial, shrewd, irascible Abdulla and his brother King Feisal.

Feisal, friend of Lawrence and hero of the revolt in the desert, was probably the last great Arab of our time; a lean, majestic, melancholy figure. I have never known a human being with an aura of such utter loneliness.

'. . . I felt at first glance that this was the man I had come to Arabia to seek—the leader who would bring the Arab revolt to full glory,' said Lawrence about his first meeting with Feisal.

'His Majesty plays an excellent hand at bridge. He is a very nice man,' said the wife of a European Consul at Bagdad when she heard that the King was to receive me in audience.

'I hope His Majesty will be cautious in his statements,' the British High Commissioner in Iraq remarked with a worried smile.

The room in his palace where Feisal received me appears in my memory octagonal in shape, dazzling white, with a high ceiling supported by eight marble pillars. Feisal was seated on a settee, alone. He wore European clothing, except for an *iraquiya,* the black, two-cornered Mesopotamian headgear. He was at that time forty, only ten years older than in the portrait by Augustus John which appears in *The Seven Pillars of Wisdom*; yet he could have been the father of John's romantic figure. The pointed beard and the lean features in the narrow face had remained the same, but the light had gone out of them; and this impression was so strong that although he sat facing the sun, his face in my memory is steeped in shadow. He was still 'tall, graceful, with a royal dignity of head and shoulders', as Lawrence describes him, but 'the pathetic frailty' had deepened and the vigour was no longer there. Disenchantment had transformed the desert hero into a shadow-cæsar.

Lawrence, too, had been destroyed by disenchantment, but not before he had set up the *Seven Pillars* as a memorial to Feisal and to himself. I doubt whether Feisal derived much consolation from it. I doubt whether he had even read the *Seven Pillars,* and whether he appreciated that gift of immortality made by a prince of letters to his royal brother in arms. Feisal was not a *littérateur;* his nature 'grudged thinking, for it crippled his speed of action'. His failure surrounded him like a bitter desert; he did not possess Lawrence's unclean magic of the word which made water flow from the rock of defeat.

The excerpts which follow are from an article in which I reported my visit to Feisal (*Vossische Zeitung,* March, 1929):

'As my name was announced by Tahsin Bey, the King's tall and slender figure rose, silent, unsmiling, with a movement so quiet that it gave the impression of immobility.

'I knew that the King spoke French and was disappointed when he called in his Private Secretary to act as interpreter. We sat in armchairs with an ivory smoking table between us and I asked for His Majesty's opinion on the perspectives of a Pan-Arab renaissance.

'The King spoke slowly, as if tasting each word on his tongue. The Unity of Arabia, the rebirth of the once so mighty Empire was every Arab's wish. But progress was slow and hampered by the present "peculiar circumstances". He seemed to swallow down what he was about to say, then said it nevertheless : "The foreign influence is not favourable to this development."

'How much bitterness, pain and impotence, how many shattered dreams this single phrase contained. The flight from Damascus, from the cannons of the French, at night, disguised, in a truck—the headlights bore blindly into the desert, the last lights of the town which he had conquered at the head of his victorious army, where the Constituent Assembly had jubilantly elected him Monarch of the great Arab Empire, fade in the dust. Then the exile's entry into Bagdad, his coronation by Britain's favour as ruler of this wretched country of beggars, bandits and nomads. . . .

'The King continued :

' "However—history will take its course, and in the end our idea will triumph. It is a slow process but sooner or later the rebirth of Arabia will become a fact."

'I remarked that I had been travelling in Syria, Palestine and Transjordan, and had seen the beginnings of a Pan-Arab movement; but that it seemed to be lacking a co-ordinating centre.

'This was an unmistakable allusion to the part which Feisal himself had played in the past. The King answered with evasive courtesy : "You have travelled and studied a great amount and it was good of you to undergo the great trouble of a long journey to Bagdad. . . ." But again diplomatic caution succumbed to sudden impulse, for Feisal added, as an afterthought : "A co-ordinating centre, as you say, may exist even if not easily visible from outside. . . ." '

I turned the conversation to the border incidents between Iraq and the Wahabi Kingdom in Central Arabia—which at that time looked as if they might lead to war. I was careful though to avoid mentioning Ibn Saud by name—the Wahabi leader who had chased Feisal's father, and the whole Hashimite dynasty, out of the Peninsula. Feisal's father, Hussein, the old and foxy former sherif of Mecca, who had a few years before proclaimed himself Caliph of all Arabs, was now dying in exile on Cyprus. According to Arab tradition it would have been incumbent on his sons—the rulers of Transjordan and Iraq—to avenge the shame inflicted on them. But both countries were controlled by Great Britain; the days when an Arab prince could observe the sacred code of honour were past. Here lay the core of Feisal's tragedy. He, too, avoided mentioning his father's conqueror by name; his voice remained courteous, but it had lost its resonance and become a shade more shrill—as if to compensate for the awareness of his impotence, for the humiliation which was destroying him.

'No,' he said in answer to my question, 'developments in Central Arabia do not affect the Arab renaissance one way or another. Never, not even at the peak of the Caliphate, did the Peninsula share in the high civilisation of the Arab Empires—and it would be too much to hope that this will be different in the future. Central Arabia is today more than ever a country of ignorant fanatics. . . .'

At this point Feisal caught himself and, continuing in more diplomatic language, denied that there was any danger of war; border clashes between tribes were a normal, seasonal recurrence whose importance had been exaggerated by the press. If only the newspapers could be restrained from adding to the tension all would be well. . . .

He ended the audience on this note of pathetic anticlimax. As I was bowing myself out, anxious not to fall over my feet, I saw Feisal smile for the first time. His face was not made for smiling—rather for sudden quick bursts of laughter, which, I imagined, would appear and vanish without warning and transition—so his smile had a rare and disarming quality. He said: 'You are still very young; let us hope that by the time you return to this remote country you will find us a great deal nearer to Arab unity.'

It was obvious he did not believe a word of it. I was glad when the Adjutant closed the door, extinguishing from my view the oppressive dark figure standing alone in the dazzling white room. King Feisal died three years later. He was the last, lovable incarnation of an anachronistic ideal which a queer genius from Oxford had tried to revive by a remarkable *tour de force*; and which History has passed by with a shrug.

XXII. Farewell to Jerusalem

THE Middle East is proverbially a land of contrasts. When I returned from my visit to King Feisal to my head-quarters in Jerusalem, a cable was waiting for me with urgent instructions to find out whether the opera *Turandot* had been written by Puccini or by two sisters named Ruben-sohn in Tel Aviv who were accusing Puccini of having cribbed the opera from their unpublished score.

I went to Tel Aviv and found in a desolate furnished room two sweet elderly spinsters from Prague who flapped around me like excited hens. One of them made her living by playing the piano in a cinema (those were still the days of silent films), the other by giving music lessons. They showed me the score of a Chinese opera that they had written some twenty years earlier; a testimonial from the Grand Rabbi of Tel Aviv according to which parts of the score showed a great resemblance with *Turandot*; and told me a long and involved story to the effect that they once had shown the score of their opera to a friend of Puccini's. It was of course all nonsense, but to please the two old dears I wrote a *feuilleton* about them in their beloved *Neue Freie Presse*, which, I imagine, they are still showing round to this day, together with the Rabbi's testimonial.

The Holy Land exerts a strong attraction on eccentrics, prophets, monomaniacs and reformers; there are probably more cranks to the square mile in Jerusalem than in any other town. One of them made a strong impression on me at the time.

He lived in one of the seventy burial shafts known as the 'Tombs of the Judges' on the outskirts of Jerusalem, where the city ends and the desert begins. I had read a notice in small print about him in one of the local papers; it said that he was worshipped by the oriental Jews in the Bokharian Quarter who on every Sabbath flocked to his cave and believed that he was Messiah. So one afternoon in December, 1927, I walked out to the Judges' Tombs. On my way I was caught in one of Jerusalem's famed tropical cloudbursts. The white chalk-dust on the streets, product of the decaying rock on which the city is built, was instantly transformed into mud. Blinded by rain, I waded through an ankle-deep morass to the tombs; a little Bokhari boy, who was my guide, pointed out the cave in which the Messiah lived, then ran away. I climbed down the shaft into a small, damp burial chamber steeped in a foul smell and muddy twilight; and there was the prophet. He was short, and thus able to stand almost upright in the low cave; he had black, tangled hair which fell in locks on to his shoulders and around his rotting shirt; a bloodless face, and large, gentle eyes. He was young, under thirty, and talked in a pleasant, normal voice. He seemed to take my visit for granted, and explained quietly that some people thought him mad, but that more believed in him; that he had been a physician, and had several times tried to commit suicide when the spiritual torment had become too great for him; that later on he had lived as a hermit in the desert of Sinai, and after that on Mount Nebo, where Moses had died. 'I had a peaceful time on Nebo,' he said thoughtfully, 'only the Bedouin were a nuisance; once I had to kill three of them.'

He went on to tell me in the same quiet, convincing manner that at the age of four he had predicted every event that had happened since; that 1928 would be the year of the Last Judgment, when God would again walk through the streets of Jerusalem; and that God would be a woman from top to waist, a man from waist to toe. Out of every nine people seven would die. 'But you,' he explained, bringing his shining eyes uncomfortably close to mine, 'will be among the remaining two.' He added : 'Have you got a cigarette? I am not an ascetic.'

We lit cigarettes—he standing in the smelly burial chamber which only had space for one, I crouching on the slippery steps dating from Roman days that led down to it. He accused me in a mild voice of being a sceptic; of not really believing in him; of suspecting that he had an *idée fixe*— whereas in fact he was working on a book that would decipher all the secrets of the universe contained in veiled hints in the Bible. As I had always wanted to decipher the secrets of the universe myself, I felt a growing sympathy for him. The prophet, however, lost interest in my presence, squatted down on the damp sand of the cave, and sang one of those heart-rending Eastern Jewish songs that are irresistible because of their unrestrained self-pity. The effect was enhanced by the hollow acoustics of the cave and the drumming of the torrential rain outside.

When the song was over, he said : 'I know you want proofs. That is simple. Think of the earthquake' (there had been that year one of the worst earthquakes in Palestine's history). 'Four hundred dead! I did it. It was simple. Like this . . .' He picked up two stones which were the only furnishings of the cave, and hit them against each other in a sudden fury. 'That is how I made the earthquake. Are you convinced now?'

I said I was, promised I would come back, handed him the sopping loaf of bread that I had brought, clambered out of the shaft into the rain and plodded back towards the veiled lights of the city—steeped in that peculiar kind of depression which I had named for myself 'Jerusalem Sadness.' In the depths of the cave, Messiah was again singing.

A week or so later, I heard what I then thought was the

end of the prophet's story. One of his numerous disciples in the Bokharian colony, a young girl who had often taken bread and water to his cave, was with child. I remembered the prophet telling me that he was not an ascetic. The Bokharians, who have maintained themselves as a small enclave in Central Asia from the destruction of the Temple until their return to Palestine 1,800 years later, are the most puritanical and fanatical Jews on this earth. They decided to stone the false Messiah to death. Fortunately a pious Rabbi from Holland, on a tourist trip, happened to be visiting the Tombs of the Judges when the angry Bokharian crowd appeared. The Rabbi, on hearing their story, made a beautiful speech in Hebrew, with many little known Talmud quotations. The Bokharis, who are connoisseurs in matters of the Talmud, listened appreciatively and went home, appeased. The Dutch Rabbi took the frightened prophet to his hotel; from there he was transferred to a mental home.

In January, 1951, nearly twenty-five years after these events, I received a letter addressed care of my publishers. It was on expensive notepaper, with an embossed address, and had been dictated by Messiah to his private secretary. He said he had read my last book; had remembered my name from an article which I had published on 29th January, 1928, in the *Neue Freie Presse* after my visit to his cave; that it had been a fine article and a fine book; that he too had meanwhile completed the book about the mysteries of the universe that he had mentioned to me on that visit; that I could procure it at the preferential subscription rate of five dollars and fifty cents by signing the enclosed printed form; and that, generally speaking, it was time I joined the several thousand distinguished followers of the new cult he had founded, and who met weekly in their elegant little temple in the St. Lenardo Valley, California, the land of Faith and Sunshine. Which brought on another attack of Jerusalem Sadness.

Jerusalem Sadness is a local disease like Bagdad Boils, due to the combined effect of the tragic beauty and inhuman atmosphere of the city. It is the haughty and desolate beauty of a walled-in mountain fortress in the desert; of tragedy without catharsis. The angry face of Yahveh is brooding over the hot rocks, which have seen more holy murder, rape and plunder than any other place on this earth. Its inhabitants are poisoned by holiness. Josephus Flavius, who was a priest in the city and suffered from Jerusalem Sadness, has this strange phrase: 'The union of what is divine and what is mortal is disagreeable.' The population of the city is a mosaic; but every portion of it is disagreeable. Perhaps the most disagreeable are the clergy, Moslem, Christian and Jewish alike. The Moslem clergy in my time used to call on the average twice a year for a holy blood-bath. A peaceful Arab landlord would joke with the family of his Jewish tenants some Friday morning during the Ramadan, go to the Mosque, listen to the Imam, run home and slaughter tenant, wife and children with a kitchen knife. The Greek, Latin, Syriac, Coptic, Armenian and other Christian clergy would come to blows over such questions as to whether the Greeks had a right to place a ladder on the floor of the Armenian chapel for the purpose of cleaning the upper part of the chapel above the cornice in the Basilica of the Nativity in Bethlehem; and whether the Greeks must attach their curtain tight or in natural folds to the lower Nail No. 2 at the foot of the pillar which lies south-east of the left-hand set of steps leading to the manger (both examples are authentic, and I may add to them the regulation 'that the Latins should have their curtain fall naturally down the same pillar, leaving a space of sixteen centimetres between it and that of the Greek Orthodox').

The Jewish clergy was engaged in feuds with the Moslems about rights of way to the Wailing Wall, and among themselves about the correct method of ritual slaughter; they also encouraged their orthodox disciples to protect the sanctity of the Sabbath by beating up the godless who smoked cigarettes in the streets and by throwing bricks at passing motor cars.

The political atmosphere was equally poisoned. The Husseini clan murdered members of the Nashashibi clan; during the riot season they both murdered Jews; the Jewish Parties hated each other, the British, and the Arabs, in that order; the British sahibs, here called *hawadjas,* behaved as British sahibs do.

There were no cafés or night clubs, no cocktail parties, and no night-life of any kind in Jerusalem. People kept to themselves, their church, clan or party. It was an austere, pharisaic town, full of hatred, distrust and phoney relics. I lived at No. 29, Street of the Prophets, at five minutes distance from the Via Dolorosa, another five from the Mosque of Omar where for a shilling you are shown the Archangel Gabriel's fingerprints on the rock. I have never lived at such close quarters with divinity, and never farther removed from it. The whole unholy history of the city, from David to Herod, from Pilate to the Crusaders, from Titus to Glubb and Bernadotte, is an illustration of the destructive power of faith, the failure of man's attempts to come to terms with God, and the resulting unpleasantness of the union of the mortal and the divine. It is this awareness of defeat, driven home by the haughty silence of the desert, of dry watercourse and arid rock, which causes the Jerusalem Sadness.

My social position was difficult. The papers that I represented gave it a certain weight. My income rose rapidly, thanks to the prodigious number of articles I wrote for the numerous Ullstein publications, and after the first year my employers raised my guaranteed monthly minimum from two hundred to seven hundred marks. In fact my income amounted to approximately a thousand a month, which in the Middle East of the late 'twenties was a lot of money, and although I now had to provide for my parents, enabled me to lead a very comfortable existence. Yet, as a member of the Revisionist opposition, I was boycotted by the Zionist bureaucracy and ostracised by official Jewish society. As a Zionist, I was barred from social contact with the Arabs; as a foreigner, ineligible for the British club and British colonial society. Nevertheless, I was not lonely. I had a few friends in Jerusalem. There were rides on horseback in the Judean desert, and night rides on donkeys. I spent my week-ends with Har-Even in gay Tel Aviv. I had my dog Jessy—the first of a long series of Alsatians, Welsh sheep-dogs, Boxers and St. Bernards; and I made frequent trips to Galilee and the neighbouring countries.

My beat included Palestine, Egypt, Transjordan (now Jordan), Iraq, Syria and the Lebanon. I also had to cover Ibn Saud's Wahabi kingdom from a distance. From my return to the Middle East in the autumn of 1927, until my transfer to Paris two years later, I wrote on an average three full-length articles a week for the host of newspapers and magazines owned or serviced by Ullsteins. About half of these dealt with political developments, the other half were travelogues and *feuilletons* about cabbages and kings: about the Hebrew theatre and the brothels of Beirut, about Byzantine mosaics and Bedouin costumes, about the Queen of Sheba and the potash works on the Dead Sea. One of them, which unfortunately had fallen to dust in the New York Public Library's file, dealt with the remarkable adventures of Jessy, by full name Jessica Kovács de Kovácsházi, culminating in the arrest of a criminal gang known as 'The Black Hand of Jerusalem.'

Jessy was the first Alsatian to take up residence in the Holy City, and hence a celebrity. (The only other Alsatian in Palestine at that time, a vulgar and common animal called Pasha, lived in Tel Aviv.) I had imported Jessica from Budapest, on my return from my first leave in Europe. As a matter of fact, I had wanted to bring back a wife, to help combat Jerusalem Sadness; but the girl I had in view decided at the last moment that she was afraid of mosquitoes and Arabs, and married a dentist in Subotica, Yugo-Slavia (where mosquitoes are fiercer than in Palestine). So I brought back Jessy instead. I had met her under dramatic circumstances. One dark night I was tiptoeing in my socks, with my shoes in my hands, along a dark garden path, for purposes that have nothing to do with this story, when a fierce puppy darted out of a house, wrenched one of my patent-leather boots out of my hand, and made off with it. The next morning I succeeded in locating her proprietor, recovered what remained of my shoe, and bought Jessy on the spot. The story of my journey with Jessy from Budapest via Subotica (to prove that I didn't mind), via Athens (where she got lost and was found on the Acropolis by a tourist party), via Crete (where she got lost in the labyrinth of Minos), via Alexandria (where she got lost, chewed up a hotel carpet and bit a veiled Moslem lady's calf), to Jerusalem (where she started her public career by desecrating a mosque)—I intend to tell in a chapter, 'About Dogs,' in a later volume. The climax of the journey occurred in the sleeping-car from Belgrade to Athens, in which I shared a compartment with a detestable merchant from Salonika. While we were having a night-cap in the dining-car, Jessy had chewed up the merchant's gift for his fiancée : a dress from a Paris couturière which he had kept in its original cardboard box in the luggage rack; and, no doubt finding it distasteful, had been sick on the bridegroom's bed.

For Moslems, of course, a dog is an unclean animal, and the Street of the Prophets where Jessy and I lived was in the Arab Musrara quarter. In consequence I became known to the grocer, lemonade-vendor and the urchins in the street as Abu Kalb—'The Father of the Dog.' After a few weeks I gave up my efforts to prevent Jessy from getting lost, and let her lead an independent existence. After breakfast she would depart and pay courtesy visits to several of my friends: Steinmatsky, the librarian; Pikovsky, the engraver; and a Hungarian doctor who was also called Kovács (*kovács* in Hungarian means smith, and Jessica's full pedigree name meant: J. Smith of Smith's Manor). About 1 p.m. she would be back home, have her lunch, and then retire for her afternoon nap.

One day, however, Jessy did not turn up for lunch. Knowing her punctual habits, I got worried and rang Major Harrison of the Palestine Police. He promised to do his best to recover her.

Now during the previous weeks several rich Jews had received threatening letters, signed 'The Black Hand,' in which they were asked for huge sums of money—or else . . . One of the victims was a gentleman called Picotto who lived in the suburb of Talpioth. He was told to carry five hundred pounds in cash in his wallet until the Black Hand contacted him. Two days after he had received the letter, a man in police uniform called at the Picottos' house. Led into the host's study, he declared in Yiddish that he was the Black Hand, and had come for the five hundred pounds. Mrs. Picotto, however, overheard the conversation from the next room, and, being a resolute woman, locked both the policeman and her husband into the study, then yelled for help. At this, the phoney policeman jumped through the window and escaped.

Jessy's trail led to a camp on the outskirts of the city. It was a camp of young Jewish labourers engaged on road construction, members of an extreme Left group who shared their earnings and led the collective life. Several Arab boys had seen 'a dog like a wolf with a blue collar round its neck' being dragged on a rope towards the camp. So two policemen betook themselves to the camp. The people in the camp, who did not know the reason for this visit, behaved so suspiciously that the police made a search. They found Jessy tied to a tent pole, having the time of her life as a new member of the Collective; and in one of the tents a crude imitation of a policeman's uniform, together with a false moustache. That was the end of the Black Hand in Jerusalem. Incidentally, the gang had of course acted for purely idealistic motives, inspired by the example of the early days of the Russian Bolsheviks, when Stalin himself had participated in a number of 'expropriations' for the benefit of the Party fund. Their methods had been so amateurish and unsuccessful that they got away with a few weeks of prison. But that did not diminish Jessy's glory.

Some time in 1928, Jabotinsky visited Jerusalem and took over the oldest Hebrew daily, *Doar Hayom* ('The Daily Post'). I became a member of the editorial board and wrote a weekly column on world events. But my main interest regarding that paper lay in a different field. The Hebrew press was unbearably solemn, provincial, and stuffy. I wanted to give our daily a more human, European, mundane touch; to reduce the volume of acrid polemics in favour of more factual news; to combat Jerusalem Sadness. Among other steps in this direction I proposed a week-end page devoted exclusively to entertainment: quizzes, jokes, competitions, acrostics, a chess column. Jabo agreed, and made me editor of the week-end page—frivolous innovation the like of which the Holy City had never seen. It became a success, in spite of a grave initial mishap. In the first issue of my page, I had printed 'Twenty Questions' which I had culled from the Ullstein magazine *Uhu*. The answers were to appear the following week-end. But before that following week-end, I had managed to lose the copy of *Uhu* that contained the answers, and despite desperate efforts was unable to get hold of another copy. Most of the questions were of the type 'How long is the Great Wall of China?' and 'Who invented fly-paper?' and I was able to find the answers in the encyclopedia; but two or three of the answers I had to suck out of my thumb. One nightmarish question I still remember : 'Which of the rodents has the longest life-span?' I asked the Hebrew University, the Agricultural Department of the Zionist Executive, and one young Englishwoman who was a bird-watcher; nobody knew. So I decreed that the rodent with the longest life-span was the squirrel. Nobody has ever challenged this statement.

Encouraged by the success of the week-end page, my ambitions grew : I decided to introduce the crossword puzzle into Hebrew culture. This was a tricky business, because the Hebrew alphabet consists of consonants only. A system of vowels was devised in the sixth and seventh centuries A.D., but these are almost never used, either in long-hand or in print; and when they are used, as for instance in first readers, the vowels are written underneath the consonants and not in a row with them. So Hebrew crossword puzzles could only contain consonants, which made both devising and solving them extremely difficult. I found a young Hebrew philologist who took a sporting interest in the problem, and between us we manufactured the first six specimens. Then the problem arose under what name we should introduce them. Jerusalem being Jerusalem, the name *cross*word puzzle would have provoked a hue and cry among our orthodox readers. Even Jabo shrank from the risk of such a scandal. So we settled on the name '*Hidud Hamo'akh*'— 'Brain Acrobatics.' I shall never cease to be proud of the fact that I am the father of the Hebrew crossword puzzle.

In spite of these and other diversions, I grew increasingly tired of Palestine. Zionism in 1929 had come to a standstill. Immigration had been reduced to a mere trickle. Nazism, which was to turn it into a flood, was still a monster being hatched in the womb of the future.

I had gone to Palestine as a young enthusiast, driven by a romantic impulse. Instead of Utopia, I had found reality; an extremely complex reality which attracted and repelled me, but where the repellent effect, for a simple reason, gradually gained the upper hand. This reason was the Hebrew language. It was a petrified language which had ceased to develop and been abandoned by the Jews long before the Christian era—in the days of Christ, they spoke Aramaic—and had now been revived by a *tour de force*. Its archaic structure and vocabulary made it totally unfit to serve as a vehicle for modern thought, to render the shades of feeling and meaning of twentieth-century man. By making Hebrew their official language, the small Jewish community of Palestine cast itself off not only from Western civilisation, but also from its own cultural past.[1]

I felt that to undergo the same process would be spiritual suicide for me. Out of loyalty to Zionism, I had acquired Palestinian nationality and a Palestinian passport, a step which few Zionists were willing to take—even Dr. Weizmann only gave up his British passport after he was elected President of Israel. I could renounce European citizen-status, but not European culture. I was a romantic fool, in love with unreason; but on this point my instinct allowed no compromise. I knew that while in a Hebrew-language environment I would always remain a stranger; I would at the same time gradually lose touch with European culture. I had left Europe at the age of twenty. Now I was twenty-three and had had my fill of the East—both of Arab romantics and Jewish *mystique*. My mind and spirit were longing for Europe, thirsting for Europe, pining for Europe.

My next leave was due in June, 1929. I made up my mind

[1] About the consequences of this choice for Israel's future, see *Promise and Fulfilment*.

not to return afterward. I did not write my employers for a transfer to another post for fear that they might refuse; since I was by now regarded as a specialist for the Middle East, it would obviously be more convenient for them if I were to stay there. I decided to confront them with a *fait accompli* and take a gambler's chance : either they would give me a new post, or I would start again from scratch. The bridge-burning pattern was once more asserting itself.

This time I took a French boat from Haifa to Trieste. On the boat I made friends with a pretty girl who was travelling steerage. She was eighteen or nineteen, dark, petite, and wore a kind of blue girl guide's uniform with a red scarf round her neck and a leather bag like a postman's hanging by a strap from her shoulder. On the second or third evening she told me her story. She was a member of the Komsomol, the youth organisation of the Communist Party, and on her way to Soviet Russia. She had come to Palestine with her orthodox Jewish parents who were now dead; had graduated from the Herzlia School in Tel Aviv, and then worked in a collective settlement in Galilee. She had not liked the narrow, nationalistic outlook of the Zionist movement, and had decided that Russia was the real thing : 'If a Messiah is really necessary, we have already got him. The Messiah of humanity is Lenin.' She said it in dead earnest, and it did not sound ridiculous at all. An uncle in Russia had obtained a visa for her (her parents had been of Russian origin, and those were the golden days of 1929). So now she was on her way from the Promised Land to the Land of Promise.

On arriving in Trieste, instead of taking our respective trains for Moscow and Berlin, we took a train for Venice. I then discovered that her entire luggage consisted of the leather bag on the strap which she carried on her slim shoulder. We spent two days in Venice which I knew from previous visits with my parents, but which she had never seen and would never see again. She had had no experience of palazzos, paintings or men, yet had the sureness of instinct of a bird or a saint; her whole person, body and soul, had been purified and freed from dross by her communist faith. Here, if ever, the arrow in the blue had become flesh.

We parted on a platform between our two trains at a railway station—Bolzano or Merano, I believe. She had purchased her railway ticket all the way to Moscow at a travel agency, but had only a few coins left in her leather bag. I forced some money on her, and her last words that I remember were: 'You know that one cannot send money from Russia, so I can only repay you after the world revolution— and that may take three or four years.'

I received one letter from her, one month later, from Moscow. It was noncommittal and sounded unhappy. I answered immediately, but never heard from her again. The members of the Children's Crusade, who were sold into slavery to the Moors, wrote no letters home either.

I have recorded this episode because, though I have forgotten even her name, the memory of the girl with the red scarf and the leather bag has remained, together with Chopin's Funeral March and the giant red globes of Budapest, one of the landmarks of the unconscious which determine one's future path.

In Berlin, I left my luggage at the railway station and went to see my immediate superior, the head of the Ullstein News Service, Dr. Magnus. On the outcome of my talk with him depended whether I would go to a good or a cheap hotel.

When I had told Magnus that I would rather part from Ullsteins than go back to Jerusalem, he gave no sign of surprise. He nodded, as if he had expected something of the sort, looked at me for a few seconds, then said with his dry smile:

'If you are fed up with holiness—how would you like to go to Paris?'

In subsequent years my interest in Zionism faded, and became absorbed in the larger context of social problems.

It was to be reawakened, with a vengeance, thirteen years later, when Hitler's gas chambers and crematoria began to function.

XXIII. From the Mount of Olives to Montparnasse

U NTIL June, 1929, my address had been : 29 Street of the Prophets, Jerusalem. In July it became : 23 Rue Pasquier, Paris.

I have said before that my education seems always to have proceeded by shock and jolt. To each of these I responded by a mental jump, some sudden mutation of consciousness. The process of quiet maturing I can find nowhere in my past.

The most wonderful of these jolts was the change of scenery from the Judean Desert to the Luxembourg Gardens, from the Holy City to Sodom on the Seine, from the Levantine fringe of civilisation to its luminous centre. After three years of cultural exile and starvation of the senses, the first contact with Paris, at the age of twenty-four, was bound to have the intensity of a chemical reaction. This was indeed the case; but the reaction was entirely different from what I had expected.

It was my good luck—though I did not appreciate it at the time—that, owing to illness on the staff, I had to start work almost at once. From the day following my arrival, I was on duty from 9 a.m. to 1 p.m., from 3 p.m. to 7 p.m., and from 9 p.m. to 11 p.m. For two months I did not even have a chance to look at the Louvre from inside. Thus I never saw Paris through the eyes of the tourist; I grew into her life functionally as it were, sharing from the outset the routine of a French office worker of average modest income. I went native from the first day, with an ease which revealed a profound affinity—not with French art, architecture, or literature—but with that most conservative and oppressive form of existence, the life of the French *petit bourgeois*.

Yet the paradox is only an apparent one. I was a rootless vagabond, and as one is always attracted by a form of life which is the direct opposite of one's own, I delighted in becoming assimilated, temporarily but wholeheartedly, to that form. I mostly took my lunch in the same little restaurant in the Rue des Mathurius near the office, where my table napkin was kept in a ring with my name on it. At 7 p.m. I went by Métro from Chausée d'Antin to Place de la Bourse, where I took my *apéritif* at the Café Vaudeville. There I played a game of billiards with two of my French colleagues on night duty, one a legman with the Agence Fournier, the other with Havas; after which we had our dinner, with half a litre of red wine each, at a *prix fixe* in the Rue des Petits Champs.

By 9 p.m. we sat at our ink-stained, cigarette-burned desks in the airless, smoke-filled basement of the Stock Exchange Building, called *Salle des Journalistes*. This was a kind of newspaperman's purgatory; it served as a common press-room for the smaller fry among the foreign journalists, and the legmen of the big news agencies, known to the profession as *nègres* or *pompiers*. At 11 p.m., when my last call to Berlin had gone through, I either went straight to bed or sat with my girl-friend for half an hour on the terrace of the Dôme. By midnight I was asleep; by seven-thirty in the morning my routine started again. In due time I acquired a tiny second-hand car, which allowed my friend and me to spend every other Sunday, when I was off duty, rowing a hired boat on the Marne or picnicking in the forest of Fontainebleau. I never got drunk, never slipped up on the job, and was, generally speaking, a paragon of *petit bourgeois* virtue. Thus passed my first three or four months in Paris—the Paris of Hemingway and Cocteau, of the hectic 'twenties.

Out of the ten years that I lived in that town, these few months were the dullest in appearance, and yet the most deeply satisfactory. I had settled down to married life with Paris in shirt sleeves and slippers on the first day of our acquaintance; the courtship and the falling in love came long afterward. Thus from the start I became immune against future disenchantments. My first impression of Paris was the sleep-swollen, unwashed faces of the crowd enveloped in the cosy stink of a second-class carriage of the Métro at eight-thirty in the morning; the dreary *prix fixe* restaurants around the Bourse; the hopeless drudgery of the *nègres* in the basement. I saw their meanness towards each other and their unattractive mistresses; and, above all, I learnt the motto of the French little man : *il faut se défendre.*

I heard this phrase on the third or fourth day in the basement when one of the old hands of Fournier's said to a colleague, referring to me : *'Il ne se défend pas mal, le petit.'* I heard it from the instructor of the driving school in the thick of the threatening Paris traffic : *'Vous vous défendez assez bien.'* I heard it, by way of explanation, when I discovered that Monsieur Robert, the old Havas legman, was willing to sell me his news flashes at half the official subscription price : *'On se défend.'* Monsieur Robert, by the way, was sixty-two and had seen forty years of service in that basement. His salary was about one-fourth of mine. At fifty-five he had intended to retire with his wife to a little house in the suburbs. One year before his retirement he lost all his savings in one of the periodic French financial scandals. He now had another ten or fifteen years of drudgery ahead of him before the dream of the little house could materialise. Actually, he did not live to see it; he died in 1935 of a heart attack in the self-same basement. He had 'defended' himself stubbornly and yet had been defeated.

I soon began to suspect that this motto, 'one must defend oneself', was symbolic of the France of our day. The French, next to the Americans, are probably the most individualistic people in the world. But whereas American individualism is youthfully aggressive, aimed at outsmarting the other fellow, French individualism is resigned and defensive. French foreign policy between the wars was obsessed by the idea of *sécurité*, of hiding behind the Maginot Wall; the private life of the French little man was modelled on a similar pattern. He defended himself in his underpaid job; he defended himself against the State by cheating on income tax, against his fellowmen by an attitude of suspicion and defiance, a manner of sour surliness. He lived entrenched in his oppressive little flat, in his unaired clothes, like a cockroach in his carapace. And yet his manner of living attracted and fascinated me. Partly, as I have said, because it was the opposite of mine: tenaciously rooted in his country, town, *quartier,* family and habits; and also because he never went abroad, had no curiosity about other countries and other lives; because he regarded any idea of change with contempt; because he was smug and self-satisfied, and for all his narrow-mindedness and meanness, lived in a profound harmony with himself and enjoyed his food, wine, fishing and sex in his grumbling, sour, deprecatory manner more than people in any other human community that I had seen. I liked the French *petits bourgeois* without respecting them—and this in itself was a new experience for the green romantic which I essentially still was.

The contrast between my past and my present job was as marked as the change in scenery. In Jerusalem I had been my own master; in Paris I had a boss and was forced to keep regular office hours. On the other hand, the Middle East was a political backwater, and Paris the centre of Europe.

The 'Ambassador' of Ullstein's in Paris, Dr. Leo Stahl, was my senior by some twenty years. The word 'Ambassador' is not entirely out of place, for, as correspondent of the greatest

German newspaper chain which was also the main public support of the Franco-German *rapprochement,* he wielded considerable political influence. He was a square, heavy Bavarian of Jewish faith, a veteran of the First World War which had gained him the Iron Cross and a game leg. He had been the first German correspondent accredited to France after the Armistice, and had witnessed the historic meeting in the Chamber of Deputies, when a flushed Briand, thumping the desk with his fist after each phrase, made the revolutionary pronouncement: 'The French are a great nation' (thump). 'The Germans, too, are a great nation' (thump, dead silence). 'Let them get together, *nom de Dieu*' (roaring ovation).

It was the first and, as far as I can remember, last anecdote which I heard from the lips of my new chief. He was a scrupulously honest man and conscientious about his job to the degree of pedantry, but unfortunately more of a bureaucrat than a journalist, and the atmosphere at our headquarters was that of a boys' school or a military barracks rather than of a newspaper office. Our bureau was in the elegant Madeleine district (the Press Room in the Stock Exchange basement was only used when on night duty). The regular staff comprised the chief, his two *nègres*—Brix and myself—and a secretary, whom I shall call Irmgard. Brix was a rotund, jovial, good-natured native of the Saar, completely devoid of any ambition, conviction or personal problems; he provided the soothing, neutral element in our tense quartet. Later on he was to serve his new Nazi bosses with the same honest, detached *bonhomie* as he had served the liberal Ullsteins, yet he is one of the few people whom I am unable to blame for it. As for Irmgard, or Bébé, as her friends called her, I have to write with restraint, for my happiest memories of Paris are the few months when we lived, loved and laughed together, and as she vanished during the German occupation, I don't know whether she is still alive. Bébé was the brilliant late-born daughter of a stuffy Austrian army officer; she had run away from home at nineteen, and after various adventures in Berlin and Paris, had landed her first promising job at our Paris office. She was now twenty-one, lithe, with an innocent baby face that was more piquant than pretty, a bizarre, surrealistic sense of humour, and a knack of producing the most hair-raising or absurd statements with a thoughtful childlike air. On one of our Sunday excursions on a tramcar in the suburbs she almost got us arrested by turning the brake-wheel on the rear platform and bringing the crowded car to a stop; another time, on the Marne, she deliberately capsized our boat to find out how I would function as a life-saver in my new flannels and suèdes. These and other misdemeanours she committed with that expression of wide-eyed, angelic, half-witted innocence which, many years later, made the fortune of Harpo Marx. Unlike Harpo, however, Bébé had her articulate moments. Their sum total constitutes her first novel, published in the late 'thirties by Gallimard—shortly before she disappeared without leaving a trace.

On my first day at the office, I discovered an entry in her diary—which involved no indiscretion because she used for a diary the flowery French wallpaper behind her desk :

'Today arrives the prodigy from the Wailing Wall, now all will be well.'

That acquainted me with her style. One of her favourite pastimes was to fabricate apocryphal news items which, when news was short, I telephoned to Berlin—from where they made the rounds of the various '*Faits divers*', 'Miscellaneous' and '*Kleine Nachrichten*' columns. One of the most successful of her plants ran something as follows :

'A traffic accident which could easily have turned into an appalling catastrophe occurred today at the level crossing on Kilometer 32 of the railroad from Paris to Orleans.

A truck, loaded with fresh eggs, collided because of the drunkenness of its driver with a freight train carrying butter and other dairy produce to Paris. As a result of the crash the truck caught fire. Nobody was killed, but the eggs and the butter were fried into an enormous omelette weighing more than a ton.'

What with Bébé, and easy-going Brix, and the comfortable flat on the Rue Pasquier which served as our office, we all could have had a wonderful time, if only the Chief had allowed us to take things a little easier. Stahl was neither a bully nor a tyrant, and each time he went to Berlin he came back with a raise in our salaries; but he reduced journalism entirely to office work. He kept us locked up all day in the office, regardless of what events took place outside. He did not believe in first-hand reporting; our job was to read the French newspapers, agency bulletins and broadsheets, and to collate and paraphrase them. Thus during my entire year at the Ullstein office in Paris I was allowed only once to attend in person a meeting of the Chamber of Deputies, whose proceedings I reported and commented upon day by day—and that unique experience came after three months. Only twice was I allowed to leave the fortress in the Rue Pasquier during office hours to interview people in person instead of by telephone : one was the Duc de Broglie when he won the Nobel Prize for physics, the other Carlo Roselli when he escaped from Italy. The first of these occasions was, as will be seen, fraught with personal consequences. My only other outdoor mission during that year was a trip to the inundated territory in the Tarn-et-Garonne Department.

The Chief himself also left the office only on rare occasions —so rare indeed that each time we practically went off our heads with the unexpected sensation of freedom. His contacts with the other world were transacted partly through our French parliamentary and diplomatic informers, and partly at official luncheons and dinners. Incidentally, our parliamentary informer was a Socialist deputy; had it been known that he was 'in German pay' it would have led to a major scandal. As for the diplomatic informer, he worked, of course, for the *Deuxième Bureau,* and the Chief instructed us that we should carefully stick to the fiction that we didn't know that he knew that we knew it. These, and other characters who came to the Rue Pasquier to earn a casual five hundred francs by selling some doubtful item of inside dope, were ushered with a great show of discretion by Fräulein Irmgard, alias Bébé, into the presence of the Chief. Brix and I never had any dealings with them; nor did the Chief encourage other contacts between us and the outside world; nor were we ever invited to the Chief's house. And yet, as I have said, Stahl was a well-meaning and kindly man; he just happened to have his own ideas about journalism, and he stuck to them with German thoroughness.

The consequence of all this was that during my first year in Paris I hardly met any Frenchmen. I had no name, and no social position and no introductions to French families. There was only one French house to which I was from time to time invited, Professor Julien Luchaire's, and even there the hostess was German. Otherwise I never saw the interior of a French household.

This experience is, of course, by no means unique for a foreigner in Paris. The French middle class is probably the most centripetal, closed society in Europe. If you meet a citizen of London, or Rome, or Stockholm, or Vienna and get on reasonably well with him, you are at once invited for a week-end or a meal at his house. In Paris you may know the same type of person for years and lunch with him in restaurants from time to time, and yet never set foot across his doorstep. The last war has loosened things up a bit, but by and large it is still true that the average French middle-class family makes a clear distinction between friends and acquaintances whom one meets occasionally on neutral ground, and those whom one asks to the house. The latter are either relatives or 'friends of the family' whom one has inherited with the piano and the household silver, and with whom one maintains an institutionalised relationship, accepting and returning invitations to the end of one's life. In other words, the life of the Paris *bourgeoise* is essentially provincial. At sixty the circle of your 'friends of the family' will be substantially the same as it was at twenty. In all probability you will have married inside that circle and your children, after a few reckless sallies, will return to live and die in it.

Thus, like most foreigners, I was cut off from French family life. But in Paris this does not mean loneliness. In London or New York you will quickly make a few friends— and yet you may feel as lonely as a dog. In Paris the houses are closed to you, but the sidewalks are yours, the cafés are yours, the town is yours—and you are part of the town whether its stuffy citizens admit it or not. In fact, you have a more intimate and sensuous relationship with it than they have. They live in their hermetically closed circles, you live in the open air; they live in their *quartier,* you live in Paris. For this is an adulterous town: frigid to her legitimate masters, passionate to the passing stranger.

XXIV. An Elegy on Bawdy Houses

M OST of the day we spent, as I said, in the office; then Brix and I took the night-duty shifts in the basement of the Stock Exchange building.

During the first three months I had the easier shift : from 9 p.m. to 11 p.m. Then Brix went on leave and, in addition to my own, I had to take over his shift from 4 a.m. to 8 a.m. —with time off for sleep from 9 a.m. till lunch-time. This brought my sedate existence to an end, and started a new chapter in my relationship with Paris.

Brix had worked the morning shift for years, and got accustomed to it. For me the problem arose whether it was preferable to go to bed at midnight and be woken up at 3.15 a.m. by the shriek of the alarm clock, or not to go to bed at all and make do with four hours' sleep in the morning. But to stay up, night after night, until 4 a.m. and then go to work is not easy—not even in Paris, not even at the age of twenty-four. My companions, including Bébé, dropped off one by one, and I was left alone to roam Montparnasse, until the waiters started putting the chairs upside down on the tables and throwing sawdust on the floor—the most melancholy of all sights for the night-bird reluctant to go home.

But I was not a real night-bird; I was marking time to avoid the torture of sleeping three hours and being jerked out of sleep by the alarm clock. So I went and sat in some all-night *brasserie* on the Boulevard Edgar Quinet, frequented almost exclusively by tired street-walkers; or to the *Chope du Nègre* in the rue du Faubourg Montmarte,

I

frequented by the same patrons plus their protectors—the
maquéraux and *souteneurs* of all ages, whose main occupation was to play belotte while keeping an eye on their dames
and their clients. Or I sauntered round the *Halles,* and
watched the unloading of the mountains of vegetables and
fruit, fish and beef, eggs and hens, into the giant belly of
Paris—envying Zola who wrote his famous novel on the
Halles without ever having been there at night (he preferred
to rely on the eyewitness reports of the Goncourt brothers).

Sometimes I ate out of sheer despair and boredom two or
three dozen oysters at the *Chien qui Fume,* swilling them
down with Alsatian wine and following this up with onion
soup—the traditional fare of revellers who wind up the night
at the *Halles.* I looked at them with the same bitterness as
the milkman and the dustman and the street-cleaner, whose
day starts at dawn, watch those sodden parties in dishevelled
evening dress drive past. Like all professional night-workers
I developed a profound contempt for the drunk, and a
natural *camaraderie* for the pariahs of the entertainment
industry—waiters, café artistes, doormen and tarts. As I still
looked like a schoolboy, and as I was nearly always sober,
dragging myself from one of these places to another, carrying
a book and looking unhappy and bored, I became soon quite
well known among the tarts and their friends under the
name of *le petit journaliste.* They knew that I was always
good for a *café-crème* and a brioche, or for a *crème de
menthe au cassis,* which for some inscrutable reason is the
street-walker's favourite drink.

By and large the women fell into two categories: those
who were *sérieuse* and those who were not *sérieuse.* The
latter were tramps by temperament, morally irresponsible,
with a low I.Q., and a tendency to alcoholism, or drug addiction, or more frequently a pathological addiction to some
particularly unattractive, seedy, weedy, greasy, swaggering
pimp. The pimps were almost without exception wholly lack-

ing in masculine sex appeal. They acted tough without looking it; the predominant type was pigeon-chested, sallow-faced, with sloping, padded shoulders, short, bandy-legged. They had no physical prowess and relied, if it came to a fight, on their switch-blade knives, razors and, rarely, on revolvers. They had no sexual prowess either. Many of them were impotent or nearly so; many suffered from chronic gonorrhoea. And yet one woman after another told me: 'You will never understand that. But if he touches me with the palm of his hand I feel more than if other men make love to me with ten horse-powers.' (This is not quite idiomatic, but let's leave it at that.)

The secret of this pathological relationship seems to lie chiefly in the pimp's brutality to his women. It is a calculated and nauseating kind of brutality which has its own ritual and cant. There are, of course, other factors which vary from case to case, but brutality is the common denominator, and its obvious function is to satisfy the tramp's craving for punishment—a craving the more consistent as it is mostly unconscious. 'I will punish you' is a favourite expression in the *souteneur's* vocabulary, and the threat alone seems to have the required effect. 'Punishment' consists mostly in slaps, kicks or mere verbal abuse; overtly sadistic practices hardly ever occur. They would defeat the purpose of the whole relationship, which is based on the axiom that the punishment is an act of justice which the victim deserves for being 'bad'. In short, the prostitute creates her own ritual of penance; the kick on the shin and the slap in the face represent the act of absolution; the unsavouriness and repellent physique of the protector and avenger are a logical part of the pattern.

The experience of that period taught me a lesson of which I only became conscious years later. It was a meeting with the sense of guilt in its crudest, most primitive and tangible form. It was startling to see how powerfully this complex of guilt acted upon creatures apparently devoid of any sense of moral responsibility. It was even more startling to discover that the sense of guilt and craving for atonement did not procure them grace, but drove them even deeper into perdition. This is a point which, I believe, Dostoyevsky has always missed—by a hairbreadth. His guilt-ridden drunkards who wallow in self-abasement, ask to be spat in the face, and get their devious satisfaction out of the procedure, are entirely convincing. But his redeemed prostitutes are mostly unconvincing because in Dostoyevsky's panorama of the underworld the most important character, the pimp, is missing. Yet the pimp is the real hero of the show. He is the false Messiah of the fallen woman, who makes her suffer without offering redemption. But that suffering without redemption may exist, and that an awareness of guilt may serve the purposes of the devil, was an idea too frightening even for Dostoyevsky to face.

The tramps who were *sérieuses* were of a quite different mettle—as different, in fact, as conscripts are from professional soldiers. They had no *souteneurs,* or, if they got into trouble, took a protector out of sheer necessity on a strictly business basis. They preferred to work not in the streets but in 'Closed Houses', as the brothels were politely called.

Among the Houses again there were 'serious' and less serious ones. The serious Houses watched carefully over their reputation; no drunkenness, bawdy behaviour or fleecing of the clients was tolerated; and the girls had to observe a strict code of etiquette. There existed a number of luxury establishments like the 'Chabannais', the 'Sphinx' or the place in the Rue des Victoires which specialised in *tableaux vivants*—featuring monks, nuns, princes and shepherdesses in Rabelaisian poses. But such establishments, like everything else connected with the tourist industry, were regarded by the trade with some contempt. The serious Houses catered to the people who lived in the *quartier,* had their more or less stable clientèle, reasonable tariffs and a cosy atmosphere where a man could sit for an hour over a glass of beer or brandy, pay and go home without having been molested—which is exactly what about half of the guests did. Not infrequently they brought their wives or mistresses who wanted to satisfy their curiosity and see a 'House' from the inside; only in the cheaper establishments were female visitors excluded for fear of competition.

The average, serious, well-spoken House had a large parlour on the ground floor, equipped like a café, with leather benches around the wall, tables and chairs. The only visible difference between a House and a café was that the women had little or nothing on (except of course those who had come as guests); but one got as quickly accustomed to this circumstance as in a nudist colony. There was little lewdness, hardly any drunkenness, no jealousy and no quarrels. If a client wished to retire with a lady upstairs, they left the drawing-room separately, and did or did not reappear later on. But although these disappearances were obviously the *raison d'être* of the House, they played no more than a casual part in the picture—in the same way as people may sit for hours on the terrace of a café, taking only a sip of coffee or none at all. Abundance of opportunity has an automatically neutralising effect. In the adolescent's imagination the shared bed of marriage is a scene of permanent voluptuousness; the Anglo-Saxon idea of a Paris House was equally wide off the mark.

What was particularly relished in a House of solid reputation was to watch and listen to the conversation between a respectable *bourgeoise,* brought by her husband, and the girls of the establishment. The staid couple would walk in, sometimes arm in arm, respectfully greeted by the *gérante,* and be ushered to a table with the solicitousness displayed by the *maître d'hôtel* of a good restaurant. The husband, wearing his Sunday suit, would be in a difficult position; he has to

appear at his ease and show himself as a man of the world—
but also not too much at his ease or too familiar with the
locale; for the fiction must be maintained that he hasn't been
in such a place for the last twenty years, since his bachelor
days. The wife is flustered and flushed; her imposing bosom
heaves, and she tugs nervously at the feather boa round her
neck. They sit down and invite a girl to sit with them, for this
was agreed beforehand, 'to study life'. The conversation
which ensues is a marvel of French courtesy.

The *bourgeoise* is dressed up to her neck, the girl is nude
at least down to her navel; but she behaves demurely and
with perfect poise. She is offered brandy, or perhaps champagne, but chooses modestly a *crème de menthe*. 'You don't
like *les alcools,* Mademoiselle?' the *bourgeoise* asks.

'Ah, no, Madame. They give me the indigestion.'

'That is interesting. Me too. I don't mind a little *apéritif*
before dinner and a glass of wine, but when it comes to *les
alcools . . .*'

'I agree with you entirely, Madame. It is very bad for the
digestion. Once I remember . . .'

And so they are launched, talking about diets, livers and
congestions, exchanging cherished memories of illnesses and
operations. From here there is only one step to the rise in the
cost of living. The husband is left out and bored, as it should
be when there are two women present; when he tries to order
a second drink—the glasses of the women are still untouched
—he is firmly restrained: '*Ah, ces hommes . . .*' '*O là là,*
Madame, I could tell you stories . . .'

The heads of the woman and the girl move closer together.
The woman has lost all consciousness of the girl's bare bosom
which a moment ago she had surveyed with covert, envious
glances. The girl feels flattered by this intimacy with the
respectable *bourgeoise*; both are gratified by their revenge
on the husband, the poor brute. They giggle, and exchange
confidences which no male could listen to without blushing;

the *bourgeoise* is having the time of her life. At last the husband, with a demonstrative yawn, pulls out his watch and proposes that it is time to go to bed. To save his masculine pride, he accompanies the word 'bed' with a pathetically roguish twinkle; and the girl, polite to the end, remarks, with a giggle : 'Ah, for that you find yourself very happily situated, Monsieur—much happier than in this place.' And so they part in great spirits and perfect harmony.

The only difficulty of the situation, as far as the girl is concerned, is to find the opening gambit. If she does not succeed with her chatter in overcoming the initial deadlock, the *bourgeoise,* in her embarrassment, will almost inevitably blurt out the fatal question: 'Aren't you cold, Mademoiselle?'

The correct answer to this is : *'Ah, vous savez, Madame, on s'habitue,'* and then to continue with the abnormal weather and the poor harvest, which leads again, through a by-pass, to the cost of living, as above.

An anthropological survey which was never made, would have shown that the average 'serious' woman in a serious Paris House was twenty-five years old; healthy, thanks to regular medical inspection and preventive care; that she had one child boarded out in the country; that she counted on working as a prostitute for five years and then buying with her savings a shop or a café in a small provincial town, marrying a substantial widower and living happily and respectably ever after. Each week she had her fixed day off; on that day she put on a neat tailored suit, a slightly dowdy hat, conservative make-up and a mangy fox around her neck, and spent the day in the country with relatives, or with the child and its foster parents. The relatives or the foster parents had no idea what her profession was, and nothing about her dress or behaviour would distinguish her from the salesgirl in a department store or seamstress in a *maison de couture,* which she pretended to be. Nor, once her life's ambition was realised, would there be the slightest sign to distinguish her from the other owners of millinery shops or cafés in the small town, married to other substantial widowers. Except, perhaps, that she would have more understanding of her husband's foibles and whims, and of human nature in general. Among the black-clad, high-bosomed, cosy and energetic women behind the tinkling cash-registers of France there are thousands of ex-prostitutes, and the country is none the worse off for them. Some of them, I am sure, became heroines of the Resistance.

Since the Paris Houses were closed in 1946, they are rapidly becoming a legend. Should the reader detect between these lines a certain nostalgia for them, I plead guilty without embarrassment. For the Houses were an essential part of the Paris landscape, of French life and letters. As regards morality, all the hackneyed but nevertheless valid arguments were on their side : that prostitution is as old as our civilisation; that it will persist as long as sex remains determined by biological, marriage by social and economic conditions; that the main effect of legal prohibition—as in the case of the prohibition of liquor—was to force prostitution underground and to produce all the concomitant symptoms of crime, squalor and corruption. The Paris Houses, while they were legal, were neither Sodom nor the idyllic places described in some novels; they were orderly, commercial establishments where sex, deprived of its mystery, was traded as a commodity. The sale of any human faculty as a commodity is obviously a degrading process; but it is equally obvious that the difference between trading one's embraces and other forms of prostitution—political, literary, artistic— is merely one in degree, not in kind. If we are more repelled by the former, it is a sign that we take the body more seriously than the spirit. It is absurd to expect that in a mercantile society the most potent human urge should escape the process of commercialisation. And once trading in sex is recognised as inevitable, a legal, regulated trade is preferable to the squalor of the black market.

The necessity to repeat such truisms seems to me more embarrassing than to come out in defence of legal prostitution. But the cowardice in such matters is so general that mention of these honest platitudes seems justified. The more so, as the incident which led to the closing of the Paris Houses is itself a grotesque apotheosis of hypocrisy. The heroine of the tragicomedy was one of the famous spies of World War I, Mme Marthe Richard.

Marthe Richard, alias Marthe Richer, née Betenfeld, and later known as Marthe Crompton, was born in 1889 in Lorraine. She was one of the first women to obtain a pilot's licence in 1913. In 1914 she created public sensation by wanting to become a fighter pilot and proposing that the Ministry of War should to this end create a woman's air force—a proposal which the Ministry wisely refused. In 1915 her husband, a rich industrialist, was killed on the field of battle, and Mme Richer decided to avenge his death by becoming a spy. The Chief of French Espionage, Captain Cadoux, sent her to neutral Spain, where she succeeded in entering into relations with Corvette Captain Baron von Krohn, head of the German espionage services. She was decorated with the Legion of Honour in 1933 and subsequently published three autobiographical books.

During the last war Marthe Richard could no longer satisfy her craving for publicity. Her moment came after the liberation of Paris. She was elected a member of the Municipal Council; at the first public meeting of the new Council in December 1945, Mme Richard found a startlingly simple means to immortalise herself in the annals of Paris. She made a flaming speech against the brothels, and moved a formal vote for their closing down.

The galleries applauded. The Councillors were embarrassed. To know that brothels are a necessary evil is one thing; to get up at a public meeting and defend them is another. It would have meant disgracing one's party, providing opponents with cheap ammunition and, moreover, the certainty that one would be accused of being on the payroll of the *tauliers*—the rich and powerful organisation of brothel-keepers. So, one after the other the city fathers of the Christian M.R.P., of the Communists, the Socialists and the Radical Socialists got up to prove that they were all on the side of the angels. The vote was taken in public, and in the general confusion sixty-seven out of sixty-eight Councillors voted death to the Houses. The one heroic dissenter ought to be buried in the Pantheon, though otherwise little else is known about him.

Since the closing of the Houses, the rate of criminality and venereal disease has of course been on the increase, and there are more prostitutes in Paris than ever before. Most Parisians privately agree that the reopening of the Houses would be a boon. But none of the existentialists, postsurrealists, defenders of the philosophy of the absurd, flayers of hypocrisy, anarchists and libertines, whose books describe every vice in the alphabet with detached neutrality or implicit approval, had the guts to speak his opinion in public on this matter of social hygiene. Their excuse was that they would endanger their political reputations, or be accused of being in the pay of the brothel-keepers. The story has a curious sequel. The same category of progressive intellectuals also refused to protest against the Russian slave-labour camps—in this case they were afraid of the accusation of 'being in the pay of Wall Street', or of 'making common cause with the forces of reaction'. Which goes to show that the Left intelligentsia of our day have become as cowardly and hypocritical in their own way as the Babbits whom they despise.

To paraphrase an earlier remark : where sex is traded as a commodity, it ceases to be a mystery. The Houses were not an edifying spectacle, but they spelt death to homosexuality, impotence, neurosis, to the stammer and blush, to sexual crime. They helped to keep the nation spiritually sane.

Psycho-analysis arrived in France with a delay of twenty years, and French psycho-analysts still have a hard time to make a living. In England and the United States, the majority of the people I know have consulted psychiatrists on one occasion or another; in France, not a single one. There is not even a proper French word for 'neurotic'; *névrosé* is used in a much more specific, clinical sense. The same is true of words such as 'hysterical', 'morbid', and 'inhibited'.

The un-neurotic attitude of the French towards sex is the result of the wisdom and maturity of an old civilisation which has achieved a unique synthesis between Mediterranean hedonism and Nordic, urban diligence; which has married Eros to Logos, keeping Thanatos at bay—a civilisation where the cults of Descartes and of Rabelais coexist in harmony. The offspring of the marriage of Eros and Logos is tolerance, and the knowledge that the stability of society depends on its system of safety valves. To keep prostitution legal, since it cannot be abolished, was part of this wisdom; it is a symbolical fact that the Houses of France were called *maisons de tolérance*.

One of the cheapest among them was in the Rue de Fourcy, in the *Quartier Saint Paul*—the dismal slums between the Hôtel de Ville and the Bastille. It was frequented by factory workers, garage hands, Algerian carpet pedlars, post office clerks and navvies. On Friday evenings, with their week's pay in their pockets, the men formed a long queue on the narrow sidewalk of the little street. They looked like people peacefully waiting for seats in a movie, except that the queue comprised only men. They were smoking, chatting, reading the sports page of *Paris Soir*, chewing *cacahouettes* and sunflower seeds. From time to

time the *gérante* put her head out of the door and asked
whether there were any clients present for Mademoiselle
Josette; and then a man would tranquilly detach himself
from the queue and enter the House. The tariff in this
House in 1929 was Frs. 4.50 (*serviette comprise*) or the
price of a cheap *prix fixe* meal. Here sex was reduced to its
lowest common denominator, to the erotic equivalent of the
Salvation Army soup. It sounds revolting, but it was merely
pathetic; and the scene still had considerably more dignity
than that of an American strip-tease show. At least the men
knew that they would not be cheated, that their hunger
would be satisfied; and for them the House in the Rue de
Fourcy with its cheap glitter had even an aura of romance.
It was their version of the rich man's night-club; in the
name of what moral principle were these carpet pedlars
and inmates of the doss-houses deprived of their *prix fixe*
paradise?

One of the girls who worked in the Rue de Fourcy was
really called Josette. She was young, dark and pretty, born of
Italian parents near Marseilles. She reckoned that after
another two years she would be in the clear and marry her
boy friend—who was in the army and would be discharged
at about that time. With her savings they hoped to open a
service station somewhere in Provence; and of course he
would never know by what means her dowry had been
earned. Her working day ended at 4 a.m.; then she would
walk in her trim, neat, tailored suit and low-heeled shoes to
the vicinity of the Gare de Lyon, where she lived. On her way
home she was frequently accosted by late prowlers who took
her for a respectable woman. She mostly refused their invitations, though often she was offered ten or twenty times the
amount which was the tariff of the House. She did this partly
because she was too tired, and partly because keeping up
pretences bored and disgusted her.

'I shall never be good at that kind of thing,' she explained. 'The comedy, the fuss and the *chichis* disgust me. Here everything is straight and simple. But the moment I put a blouse on, and a skirt over my behind, my price goes up ten times and I become a *femme fatale*. You know why? Because the moment I put my blouse on, this here' (she slapped her pretty bare bosom) 'becomes a mystery. Some would pay a hundred francs for a peep down that blouse when here they can have everything for five francs, *serviette comprise*. And they tell me how clever I am, and how *spirituelle* I am, and that I am the woman they always dreamt of. Particularly the English and the Americans on their way home from the *Bal Musette* in the Rue de Lappe. They are so nice and blond and stupid that one feels pity for them. If they had Houses like this in their country they would learn that all the excitement is about nothing—so much noise for an omelette. They tell me half the English are impotent, or paederasts or *des mélancoliques*. It is because they see a mystery where there is only a corset with elastic panels. *O les pauvres malheureux. . . .*'

Now the House in the Rue de Fourcy has become a laundry, and there are no queues. The garage hands and navvies and the lonely post office clerks can no longer peacefully wait for their weekly ration of glamour and love; on pay day they must crawl around desolate street corners in search of a furtive tramp harassed by the police, and slowly acquire a guilt complex. The women can no longer remain 'serious'. They know that instead of the *bistro* in Provence, they must sooner or later land in the nearest equivalent of hell on earth, the women's jail called La Petite Roquette. Public morality is saved and the pimp rules supreme; like motor car tyres and dollar notes, love in post-war Paris has migrated to the black market.

When I had finished writing this chapter, a news item

appeared in *Time* magazine (of January 14, 1952) which said :

'. . . Last week Marthe Richard admitted she was wrong. She has just written a new book, *L'Appel des Sexes,* in which she now says: "The situation has become intolerable. We have to reopen the *maisons de tolérance.*" '

XXV. Drifting in a Magnetic Storm

A T 3.45 a.m. I would go to one of the all-night *bistros* between the *Bourse* and the *Halles* for a black coffee with a dash of rum and *croissant*. I stuck to this routine regardless of what I had eaten or drunk during the long hours of the night, because the eating of a regular breakfast symbolises the beginning of a working day. The only concession to the unusual hour was the dash of rum which, taken in scalding hot, pitch-black *espresso* coffee, has a sobering and stimulating effect.

These *bistros* were mostly frequented by newspaper delivery men from the adjacent Messageries Hachette, porters from the *Halles,* and garbage-disposal workers. Their customary breakfast was a glass of Pernod and a chunk of garlic sausage. Some of them were fascinating to watch as, still half asleep, they lifted the glass with the greenish-yellow liquid in a shaking hand. After the first sip, the shaking stopped abruptly and the whole man seemed to fill up with vigour, braced for the day. It was like magic. They took their real breakfast, coffee and *croissants,* an hour or two later.

The *Salle des Journalistes* in the airless basement was at this hour a place which, each time I entered it, made my stomach rise in my throat. Walter Mehring has feelingly described it as 'the underground Post Office below the Paris stock market, where the harmless vermin of the foreign Press had built their nests in six long-distance telephone booths'.[1] There were actually not six booths but nine; otherwise the

[1] *The Lost Library*, Walter Mehring (New York, 1951).

description is correct, because at 4 a.m. everybody condemned to live in that limbo looked as if he had undergone
Kafka's metamorphosis into a man-sized cockroach. There
was Monsieur Robert of the Agence Fournier who, having
lost his savings, looked every day more sunken and ghastly,
waiting for the heart attack which was to strike him down
at his desk. There was Monsieur Roquefort of the *Petit
Marocain*, a huge man in a knitted cardigan which was too
small for him and which, according to the old-timers, he had
worn night after night for the last twenty years. His unique
occupation was to erase with neat, punctilious strokes of his
pen the prepositions and conjunctions from the agency news-
sheets and, thus transformed into French cablese, paste them
on to telegram forms, and hand them to the sleepy cockroach
behind the Post Office grille. Needless to say, Monsieur
Robert and Monsieur Roquefort and the man behind the
grille all had the little ribbon of the *Légion d'Honneur*. Then
there was T. of the *Praguer Presse,* mostly tight; the tighter
he was the livelier the stories and the more incisive the political comments which he dictated ex tempore over the telephone. I envied him for being permitted to file without a
written text; my own messages had to be typed out and
passed on to the Chief the following morning, so that he
would know exactly what had gone through.

At five or ten minutes past four, a messenger from
Hachettes brought in the more important morning papers,
fresh from the rotaries, sixteen of them in all. I had approximately fifty minutes in which to read them, digest, mark and
clip them; then approximately the same time to prepare my
first nine-minute call to Berlin which came through at 5.45
a.m. and which had to contain not less than a thousand
words. It was a rather acrobatic feat, for the thousand-word
message had to represent an all-round survey of political
developments and trends among the French Parties, both
with regard to foreign and internal policy. These trends,

with their nuances and oscillations, were reflected in the
editorials and political columns of the sixteen morning
papers; but to learn to read between the lines one had to
develop a kind of seismographic ear. This is a mixed metaphor—which doesn't matter, as on a rush job of this kind
the essential organ of perception was neither eye nor ear, but
the thumb.

'Reading with one's thumb' is an expression which is to be
taken almost literally : by running one's thumb down an
editorial column one learns to absorb whole paragraphs at a
glance, by their *Gestalt* as it were. In a miraculous manner,
by sub- or pre-conscious perception, one's thumb stops automatically at the one relevant passage in the long rigmarole
where the cat is let out of the bag. Again automatically the
blue pencil darts out from the groove between your ear and
skull, leaves, guided by your left hand, a somewhat shaky
mark on the margin, while your right thumb continues to
glide down the column until it comes to a relieved halt under
the name at the bottom—Jules Sauerwein, in *Le Matin*, St.
Brice, in *Le Journal*, Pertinax in *L'Echo de Paris*, Gene-
viève Tabois in *L'Oeuvre*, André Viollis in *Le Petit Journal*,
Léon Blum in *Le Populaire*, Charles Maurras in *L'Action
Française*, Vaillant Couturier in *L'Humanité*, and so on.
The result of the computation is a paragraph somewhat like
this :

The first sign of a probable softening in the hitherto
unrelenting French attitude at the second conference at
The Hague concerning German reparation payments
came today from the usually inspired pen of M. Jules
Sauerwein in *Le Matin*. In a seemingly casual remark Mr.
Sauerwein intimates that the rate of reparation payments
after the first twenty years, that is, starting with 1950, to
be effected by the German Reich may be fixed at a ratio
between industrial and currency reparations more favour-

able to German interests than the somewhat unrealistic demands voiced up to now by France's die-hard Minister of Finance, Monsieur André Chéron.

In German, of course, when the verb comes at the end of the phrase, this would sound a little more involved; but for the purposes of the good old *Vossische Zeitung*, the involveder the better. *Es ist mehr gediegen—ça fait plus sérieux*. At 5.45 a.m., my thousand words of *politische Gediegenheit* went over to Berlin—a stodgy pudding squeezed at high pressure through the slender telephone line. The pudding was processed at the headquarters of the Ullsteins' News Service in Berlin; between 6.30 and 8 a.m., it lay on the desk of the various foreign editors in Bucharest, Budapest, Sofia, Prague, Frankfurt and Stockholm; and by 6 p.m., the French evening papers published the first reactions of the Berlin, Prague, Bucharest, etc., papers to Monsieur Sauerwein's article on the second Hague Conference. The knowledge of being such an important link in world events made me swell like a bull-frog.

I only committed one serious blunder, which caused a minor diplomatic scandal. One morning in October, 1929, when I was particularly sleepy and relied too much on my somnambulistic faculties of reading between the lines, my thumb stopped on a short item in small type according to which M. Anthériou, Minister of Pensions in the Government headed by Aristide Briand, had tendered his resignation to the Prime Minister. My thumb quivered knowingly. The exciting thing was not that M. Anthériou had resigned, but that the news had been hidden in small print at the bottom of the third page. The conclusion was obvious. The Government was tottering—I always had a feeling that the Government was tottering, and, as the country was France, the feeling was mostly right—so Monsieur Anthériou was leaving the sinking ship, and the pro-Government Press was trying to hush it up. I accordingly commented : 'Briand's Government seriously threatened.'

At twelve noon I turned up at the office in the Rue Pasquier where the Chief received me with a face like thunder. He had just read my morning despatch and declared that he had rarely seen anything so irresponsible. Monsieur Anthériou had recently been defeated at the elections to the Senate—which I ought to have known—and had tendered his resignation according to the custom in such cases. It was a matter of pure parliamentary routine with no political implications whatsoever.

I was duly contrite, but it was too late. At 1 p.m. the Berlin *B.Z. Am Mittag* came out with a full-page, front-page banner-head : 'Fall of French Cabinet Imminent.'

At 7 p.m. Monsieur Briand's Cabinet, unexpectedly defeated on a vote of confidence, fell.

At 9 p.m. the Quai d'Orsay summoned my unhappy Chief : how could he explain that Berlin knew about the impending fall of the French Government before Paris knew about it? There were rumours and allegations about a sinister conspiracy of left-wing Franco-German circles to bring the Government to fall. Stahl could, of course, explain the matter satisfactorily, and the incident was soon forgotten —but not without increasing the already existing tension between the Chief and me.

It was one of the few occasions when I had been right for the wrong reasons—a more cheering experience than to be wrong for the right reasons, as I mostly seem to be.

At 6.45 a.m. I had to dictate another seven hundred words over the telephone—this time mostly straight news and miscellaneous titbits. At 7.30 a.m. came the third and last morning call to Berlin, and this one was of a confidential nature. It was not addressed to the Ullstein News Service but to the German Socialist News Agency. For secretly the whole

staff of the liberal-capitalistic Ullstein Press in Paris func-
tioned also as correspondents of the Social Democratic
Party's News Agency. It was, however, merely a secret to the
outside world and to the readers; both the Ullsteins and the
Socialist Party knew of this curious arrangement. So, between
6.45 and 7.30 a.m. I changed from a *bourgeois* to a Socialist
reporter and filed an abridged and slanted version of my
previous messages to the *Sozialistischer Pressedienst*.

In itself it is neither considered unusual nor dishonourable
for a foreign correspondent to work for several papers with
slightly different political orientations—so long, of course, as
they do not clash directly. The reason for such arrangements
is that few newspapers can afford to have independent full-
time correspondents at all important centres. But in the case
under discussion—and that is the reason why I mention it—
the poor relative in the partnership, whom we looked after
in a somewhat offhand manner, was the German Socialists—
that is, the still strongest political party in the Reich. It
seems fantastic that they should have been unable to afford
a Paris correspondent of their own; yet this paradox is typical of Socialist parties all over the world and intimately connected with the reasons for their decline.

At various times during the last thirty years the German,
Austrian, French and British Social-Democrats wielded
power, with an absolute parliamentary majority or as
partners in a coalition; but not one of them was ever capable
of producing a really first-rate daily newspaper with a mass
circulation. The British *Daily Herald,* the French *Populaire,*
the German *Vorwärts* have always remained dreary, provincial Party rags, unable to compete with the newspapers of
their political opponents, even at times when their competitors were a beaten minority. The reason, I believe, was
lack of imagination and, even more, lack of a human
approach to the people. For 'the People' are regarded
through the Socialist bureaucracy's eyes as a target for propa-

ganda, not as a living reality whose interests, tastes and foibles must be understood and shared if you wish to change the face of the world. The Socialist party bosses, or most of them, came from the people but were not of the people; they tried to control and manipulate man without identifying themselves with him. Their voice was the voice of the pamphlet, of the lecturer at the evening school; not the voice of a new humanity. The *Daily Herald,* the *Vorwärts* and the *Populaire* never outgrew that deadly tradition. The Socialist parties could change a few laws and institutions; they could not change the human climate, the spiritual outlook of the people whom they governed—and that failure sealed the fate of Socialism as a historic movement.

I understood little of this at the time when I hung, half asleep, on the wire which connected me with the Socialist Press Headquarters in Berlin. But I could not take this part of my duties seriously. Not even the Chief insisted on a written record of the material sent to the poor relatives. I was equally unable to take seriously a party which had so little self-respect, or respect for the minds of the people whom it governed. It had not learnt that a popular press is a popular power; it did not care what second-hand trash its newspapers fed to the people as long as the Party slogans appeared in full on the front page. I had no clear intellectual conception of the relative merits of Socialism and Communism; but working as a correspondent for the Socialist Party, I felt the staleness and apathy which slowly led to its doom.

On the whole our reporting was honest, true to the great Liberal tradition which the Ullsteins had carried on for nearly a century. I do not remember having ever written a conscious lie in an article or a news despatch. Though nearly every message emanating from the Paris office had a political and *weltanschaulich* slant, this slant too was of an entirely honourable, 'progressive' nature. In this respect perfect harmony reigned between Stahl and myself.

Curiously enough we never discussed politics. It was unnecessary, because our orientation was identical by instinct. In spite of twenty years' difference in age, we were the product of the same epoch and *milieu*. We were Central Europeans, steeped in German culture, supporters of the Weimar democracy, yet immune against German chauvinism through a hereditary judeo-cosmopolitan touch. We were fervently anti-war, anti-militaristic, anti-reactionary. We were for 'Locarno' and for 'Rapallo', that is, for Franco-German and Russo-German collaboration. We were for the Kellogg Pact which outlawed war, and for the League of Nations which would punish every possible aggressor, and for Briand's Pan-Europa. Towards England we were cool because it had a Colonial Empire (the French had one too, but nobody took it seriously), and because it kept Europe divided by its 'Machiavellian balance-of-power policy'. We believed in national self-determination, and in freedom for the colonial people, and in social progress.

The later was embodied in 'the Left', which comprised Liberals, Socialists and Communists. These three differed with regard to 'progress' merely in degree, not in kind. The liberalism of the German Democratic Party, which the Ullsteins officially supported, was well-meaning but out-dated. The Socialists were nearest to us in their political programme, but they were Philistines, and we shrugged our shoulders at them with sympathetic contempt. The Communists in Germany and France were noisy and blustering, but their uncompromising radicalism was impressive—and behind them stood Russia, the Great Social Experiment, which had to be watched with a sympathetic and unprejudiced eye. In short, we were in every respect on the side of the angels.

We fought our honourable battles according to our lights. We fought for universal disarmament and for a European police force under the League of Nations. We fought against the senseless Reparation demands of the former Allies, and their harsh policy towards the young Weimar Republic—a policy which provided the fuel for the German Nationalists and seekers of revenge. We saw the folly of the victorious powers who still had the opportunity to build a new Europe —and who perpetuated instead the meaningless rivalries and suicidal feuds of the old. In short, we were very enlightened and reasonable. Only, we failed to see that the age of Reason and Enlightenment was drawing to a close.

Cosmic disturbances sometimes cause a magnetic storm on earth. Man has no organ to detect it, and seafarers often do not realise that their compass has gone haywire. We lived in the midst of such a magnetic storm, but we failed to notice the signs. We fought our battle of words and did not see that the familiar words had lost their bearing and pointed in the wrong directions. We said 'democracy' solemnly as in a prayer, and soon afterwards the greatest nation of Europe voted, by perfectly democratic methods, its assassins into power. We worshipped the will of The Masses, and their will turned out to be death and self-destruction. We regarded capitalism as an outworn system, and were willing to exchange it for a brand-new form of slavery. We preached broad-mindedness and tolerance, and the evil which we tolerated demoralised our civilisation. The social progress for which we fought became a progress towards the slave labour camp; our liberalism made us accomplices of tyrants and oppressors; our love for peace invited aggression and led to war.

At least we had an excuse; we did not know that we were living in a magnetic storm, that our verbal compasses, which had been such useful guides in the past, had become faulty.

As I am writing this, more than twenty years later, the storm is still on. The well-meaning 'progressives of the Left' persist in following their old, outworn concepts. As if under the spell of a destructive compulsion, they must repeat every single error of the past, draw the same faulty conclusions a second time, re-live the same situations, perform the same suicidal gestures. One can only watch in horror and despair, for this time there will be no pardon.

The Black Friday, 24th October, 1929, came soon after I had taken up my post in Paris. Its significance escaped us almost entirely. It took several months for its repercussions to make themselves felt in Europe. Once the first shock-waves of the depression arrived, events proceeded rapidly. Unemployment in Germany soared to the figure of seven million—one-third of the total number of wage-earners. The strength of the National Socialist Party increased at the same rate. The foundations were shaken, Europe ready for the collapse. Yet in our reports from Paris, the Wall Street crash played hardly any part. In the Rue Pasquier we thought that it was just another economic crisis; we did not notice that it was the crisis of humanity that had begun.

XXVI. Portrait of the Author at Twenty-five

IN between the strenuous office hours and night shifts, I wrote on an average two signed feature articles per month for the *Vossische Zeitung*. I wrote about surrealist films (Bunuel's classic *Le Chien Andalou* had just come out), and about the Pitoefs' theatre; about the fantastic scandals of the *Gazette du Franc* and the equally fantastic disappearance of the White Russian General Kutiepof (who had been kidnapped by the G.P.U.—a fact which, as a good Progressive, I refused to believe). I also wrote about the Piccolis' famous marionette theatre which for a while I frequented as a hobby; about Spring in Paris, the first French talkies, Maeterlinck's latest book, and the Duc de Broglie's theory of the nature of light which won him the Nobel Prize for Physics in 1929.

That last article had a decisive influence on my fortunes. I had called on de Broglie less than an hour after the newsflash from Stockholm had reached our office, and before he himself had received confirmation of the award. He was as happy as a schoolboy, made no effort to conceal it, and asked me twice : 'Are you quite sure that it is true and not a hoax?' One or two journalists had already telephoned and asked him idiotic questions about sun-spots and death-rays; so he was much relieved to discover that I had been a student of science and took a passionate interest in physics. We talked for three or four hours—de Broglie was then thirty-seven, and an exceptional combination of genius and charm —after which I worked through the night in a state of exaltation and wrote the article that I have mentioned. It was a popular exposé of the revolution in science and philosophy that the new de Broglie-Schroedinger theory of wave mechanics represented. It appeared a few days later in the *Vossische Zeitung,* and was read by Dr. Franz Ullstein, the senior partner in the firm, who decided that I had a special knack for popularising scientific subjects. Soon afterwards Franz Ullstein and his young wife (now Countess Waldeck) came to Paris. Dr. Ullstein took a paternal interest in me, and from that time on I was regarded as his special protégé.

Dr. Ullstein was then about sixty, a man of remarkable intelligence, wit and charm. None of these qualities was shared by his four brothers who for some time had been trying to oust him from the firm. Shortly after his visit to Paris, the conflict flared into one of the biggest scandals of the Weimar era. The brothers accused the new Mrs. Franz Ullstein of being an agent in the service of a foreign government. The accusation was eventually refuted in the course of a long and squalid lawsuit which split the whole firm, from editor to office boy, into two hostile camps : the 'Franciscans' who sided with Dr. Franz, and the 'Bernardines', so called after the editor of the *Vossische Zeitung*, Georg Bernhard. My own position became extremely precarious, for I was a 'Franciscan', my boss, Stahl, a 'Bernardine'; and for several months it was touch and go whether I would lose my job. It was a rather harrowing experience, which taught me the important lesson that in a polarised field of force neutrality is possible in theory but not in practice. In the end, Justice and the 'Franciscans' prevailed. The Science editor of Ullsteins, Professor Joel, was nearing retirement age, and at the demand of Franz, I was appointed his successor. I took up my new job in Berlin in September, 1930, a little over one year after my arrival in Paris.

Soon after my transfer to Berlin my professional career

progressed rapidly. I was now Science editor of Germany's most respected newspaper, and Science adviser to the huge Ullstein trust. A year later I became in addition to this, Foreign editor of the *B.Z. am Mittag*. My income was approaching the two thousand mark a month level—it had increased tenfold in four years and was not far from the maximum that a German journalist could earn.

In spite of all this, at twenty-five I still looked and felt like an adolescent, and what is worse, was treated like one. My shyness and insecurity were inadequately camouflaged by the dashing manner which I paraded; it did not fit, and it produced a jarring tone which set people's teeth on edge. I was disliked by most of my colleagues as I had been disliked at school, and had no social contacts with them.

The few friends whom I made were sorry for this state of affairs. When I relaxed in their company, I became a person so completely different from the tense, arrogant and aggressive youth that I appeared to be, that some of them seriously suspected me of schizophrenia. They argued loyally in my defence and tried to have me accepted by their friends and cliques, but without much success. Some twenty years later one of my colleagues of that period confessed: 'When you first came to my office you were not human—you were a machine-gun.'

I disliked myself more for this than anybody else did, but I could not help it. A successful journalist is supposed to be a tough, hard-boiled, sceptical type, and as I was lacking in all these qualities, I had to produce them synthetically, until the phoney personality overgrew the real one without ever fitting it. The trouble was not that I wore a mask, but that the mask did not fit.

In one of the illuminating flashes which pierce from time to time the tedium of his journals, André Gide remarks that he never got rid of his fundamental naïveté. The remark is a variation of Goethe's dictum about the 'perpetual adolescence of the artist'. It would be a comforting excuse to fall back on this formula, if I could claim that my immaturity and confusions of that period were part of the artist's emotional make-up. But at twenty-five I was not an artist and had no serious aspirations to become one. I had written my last poem and my last short story at eighteen. The four or five friends to whom I had shown them had been unanimously discouraging. I had accepted their verdict that I lacked the talent for being a writer the more readily as I had little faith in myself and set little store on those experiments.

Journalism, however, I took seriously. It was hard work but infinitely varied and stimulating. One day it carried you to the court of Arab kings, the next into a Paris brothel; one day you chased after a vanished Russian general, the next you became absorbed in space-travel and the structure of atoms. It seemed to me a full life and an exciting life. My new job in Berlin held infinite possibilities. I would bridge the gap between science and the people. A score of magazines and newspapers were at my disposal as channels of enlightenment. There was a mission waiting for me; gradually I would shift the emphasis in popular education from stale humanities to a lively comprehension of the mysteries of the universe and life. If I could not catch the arrow in its flight, at least I could impress its flashing image on the minds of people, and make them conscious of its message : the eternal and the infinite.

Thus my naïveté was not that of the creative artist but of the adolescent dreamer. That I was competent in my work does not alter this fact. In spite of my outward success, nobody took me really seriously, not even my colleagues. Franz Ullstein was my protector, not my friend; he treated me as an infant prodigy, not as a grown-up member of his staff. My colleagues felt that there was something false and basically unsound about me. They did not ask me to their houses, nor did I frequent their Clubs and Associations; I would have felt like an intruder. It seemed as if Har-Even's prophecy had come true: I would remain a fugitive and runaway; regardless of the pose I assumed, people always smelt the vagabond underneath it.

It is strange how little influence experience has on a psychological pattern of this kind. At twenty-five I had accumulated enough experience to make me into an old and wise man. I had sung 'God bless the Magyar' and had seen the defeat of my country; I had cheered Károlyi's Democratic Republic and had seen it collapse; I had identified myself with the Commune of the Hundred Days and seen it swept away. I had lived in a communal settlement, and sold lemonade and operated a press agency; I had been a tramp and had half-starved to death. I had seen my father become the victim of a spectacular act of injustice, and my family go to the dogs. I had run off to help build the New Jerusalem and had come back disillusioned. I had spent countless nights in the company of whores and in brothels; and had gained sufficient insight into French politics to disgust me with politics for ever. Yet all this had seemingly not brought me an inch nearer to maturity. I again had gained in experience but not in wisdom. Emotionally I was still nearly as unbalanced, naïve, unsure of myself, ready to fly off at a tangent, as at sixteen. I sat behind an important desk, had a secretary, two telephones, several mistresses and was called *Herr Redaktör,* but it was as if I were still surrounded by the taboo-forest of polar-bear rugs and potted palms in the parental flat. My colleagues were merely transmutations of the hostile Triumvirate at the boarding-school; my superiors of Bertha, the tyrannical maid. The more successful I became, the more of a fraud I felt; and somewhere in the background Dr. S., in his striped trousers, was waiting with his black bag, hiding the knife which would cut my tummy open. Ahor was dormant, but there were signs that it would not be long before it caught up with me again.

Intellectually, this was a period of stagnation. My spiritual development had been at a standstill ever since, at twenty-two, I had begun 'to make good' and to climb the ladder leading to a busy and successful career. The days when I had been tormented by the image of the split arrow, by the dilemma between action and contemplation, were in the past and in the future. My life in Paris and during the first year in Berlin, was full of nervous excitement but spiritually empty. It resolved around two poles: furious work, and a hectic chase after women.

I wish our cultural climate would permit one to approach the second subject as objectively as the first, or else to pass the whole question of sex in silence. But that would mean suppressing what was an essential, and at times the most essential, part of one's life: in my own case a phantom chase that lasted some twenty years. That it was a phantom chase and not a pleasure hunt as I believed it to be, I discovered, together with some other obvious facts about myself, only in my forties.

The phantom that I was after is as old as man: victory over loneliness through the perfect physical and spiritual union. Surely a modest aim? And certainly not an original one. Yet the pattern of one's life depends to a large extent on the manner in which one organises one's own particular phantom chase. It is all a matter of character alchemy. Mix in a mortar an acute sense of loneliness with an obsessive thirst for absolute values; add to this an aggressive temperament, sensuality, and a feeling of basic insecurity that needs constant reassurance through token victories: the result will be a fairly toxic potion.

> *'A bellyful of this witches' brew*
> *And every wench is Helena to you,'*

as Mephisto remarks, who is after all the most understanding and sympathetic character in Goethe.

Most men are promiscuous by instinct; to what extent they are so in practice depends on the intensity of the drive and on the nature of its incentives. Mere lecherousness, for instance, is a poor incentive. The lecher is nearly always frustrated in his aims, because emotionally he is a miser, unwilling to make any substantial outlay in passion. The real menace to maidenhood is not the cynic but the fool with the witches' potion in his belly. Somebody, I think Plekhanov, said about Lenin : If you talk revolution, think revolution, dream revolution for thirty years, no power can prevent you from making a revolution. The Lenin of the sex war is Flaubert's Julien Sorel, determined to spend all his time, energy, money and enthusiasm, on the conquest of Madame Renaud. Above all, he has an almost inexhaustible fund of illusions. How could a woman resist a pair of goggling eyes in which her reflection is transformed into Helena's?

To be sure, the reflection is merely a phantom. But while the magic of the projection lasts, the effect is bliss and ecstasy. The trouble in my own case was that it never lasted for long. An hour, a week, rarely a few months. When it wore off, the phantom-quest started anew. The emotional outlay was enormous. Yet this kind of outlay does not make one poorer; nor does it cause regret or disillusionment. For the illusion, while it lasts, is a reality in its own right. The distinction between true and false applies to ideas, not to emotions; an emotion can be cheap, but never untrue. Thus while it lasted, and regardless of how long it lasted, each involvement was authentic and sincere, and left no bitter after-taste.

As the number of experiences grew, it did not affect the power of the illusion. The illusion was merely withdrawn from one object and projected on another, carrying the same luminosity. Sometimes this happened suddenly; sometimes by imperceptible degrees; I had as little power over the process as over the revolving beam of a lighthouse, that holds up each object that it touches in a unique and singular light.

There seems to exist, in the sphere of emotions, a law of undiminishing returns for a certain category of people during a certain period of their lives. During that period, the capacity to generate illusion, the Helena-producing faculty so to speak, maintains itself on the same level, unaffected and untarnished by any previous experience. Judged by the freshness and toxic naïveté of the illusion, each episode is indeed the first. The reason for this is—always speaking of a certain type of person—that the creation of the illusion responds to a need as deep and inexhaustible and recurrent as the addict's craving for his drug.

This need, like all genuine instincts, has its own chastity; the type in question never shares a woman's pillow, not even a prostitute's, without believing himself in love with her. By that he means the sensation and conviction of experiencing something unique, set apart from all similar experiences past and future, of others' and one's own; which, in short, bears the stamp of the absolute in a world of relatives. This sensation of apparent uniqueness is the essence of the whole problem; falling in love restores one's virginity. No matter how often it happens, the thirst for the fresh water of a spring is always a virginal thirst, and the pillow next to one's own is always Helena's pillow. When it ceases to be, chastity goes down the bath-drain and it is time to be moving elsewhere, or for resignation; but not for confusing the latter with virtue.

It all boils down to the same *leit-motif,* the same obsession. All my life I have had emotional measles: the quest for the secret of the arrow was followed by the search for the knowing shaman, then by the pursuit of Utopia. The longing to embrace the perfect cause turned me into a Casanova of Causes; the phantom chase after Helena followed the same pattern. The form of the rash changed, but the disease remained the same; a glandular condition called absolutitis.

My friendships with men were, with a few exceptions, as

intense and short-lived as my love affairs; and for a similar reason. During the first few meetings with stimulating new acquaintances, I was liable to become intellectually infatuated with them; the phantom of Helena was here paralleled by the phantom of the true, real 'knowing one' whom I seemed to have met at last. Similarly, in a newly begun *camaraderie* with fellow-vagabonds, with dining-and-wining companions, the spook of the missed playmate would appear and make me hectic and eager. These honeymoons of friendship were regularly followed by a second phase, during which illusion faded and the new asset was devalued like inflated currency. It may have been a writer or a scholar, chess-partner, or bistro-acquaintance; the process was the same. Growing familiarity has the deadly effect of enabling one to predict the other person's responses; and when that happens, the stimulating quality and creative tension of a relationship are finished. Once the new friend's opinions on Stendhal versus Flaubert, on the meaning of causality, on Freud versus Adler, or Moselle versus Hock were either known or predictable, curiosity faded and weariness set in— together with the urge to move to another pillow of the mind, to the true shaman, the real playmate, who was surely just waiting round the next corner. The process of devaluation was free from hostility, but accompanied by a growing reluctance against further mental intercourse—which henceforth would become repetitive, stale, and thereby repulsive.

In relation to women, this process acted on the physical level. As the novelty of the relationship wore off and the illusion of uniqueness faded, the normal, neutralising effect of habituation would make itself felt at a sometimes frightening speed—as in those documentary films which telescope a span of several months into a single hour. The fatal predictability of response produced a mood of detached observation, a destructive awareness of detail; and to be actor and observer at the same time is the end of innocence. Helena, deprived

K

of her magic and mystery, became depressingly familiar; a sister, fondly liked, and tabooed by the senses—and that, for her, is the ultimate indignity. When that stage was reached, flight remained the only honourable solution.

> *I fled in vain; everywhere I found the Law.*
> *I must give in; Gate, admit the host.*
> *Trembling heart, submit to the master—*
> *To him in me who is more than myself.*

I found these lines, by Claudel, the Catholic, quoted in an essay by Gilbert Murray on 'The Religion of Rousseau.' Of all memoire writers of the past, I feel farthest removed from Cellini and, in one respect, nearest to Rousseau. If his 'whole life had been an attempt to be himself and nothing else besides' so was mine; like him I found this task more difficult than any other; like him I had to submit, in middle age, to that something 'that is more than myself'; and my nearest formulation of that something is again Rousseau's : 'It is to our souls what our soul is to our body.'

At forty-six, the number of people with whom I am able to shed the protective crust of false personality is about half of those I know; in another ten years I hope to be at last 'myself and nothing else besides'. But at twenty-five, the period that I am discussing, I could only be myself with women whom I loved. To the psychiatrist, the phantom chase is merely a neurotic symptom, yet on a different level it had a different meaning, for each meeting with Helena's image brought out what was best in me. The face I loved was my contemplative truth; in Helena's womb, as in Utopia, as in the Perfect Cause, the torment ceased, the arrow came to rest. In her presence shyness and insecurity vanished, the pose and the smirk and the cramp dissolved; I became relaxed, myself, and nothing else besides. These were perhaps my only moments of maturity—procured by a series of immature illusions. But that is how these things work.

The reason why I started to write fiction so late is intimately connected with this subject. A phantom chase of this nature is nearly a full-time job. It absorbed the brief hours of leisure left by my exacting profession; often I did not even read a book for weeks on end. But lack of time is always a poor excuse; it is perhaps nearer the truth to say that I did no creative writing from the age of eighteen to thirty because all the resources of my imagination were spent on that obsessive quest of creating illusion for myself, of transforming the raw material of experience into the image I wanted to see. Lichtenberg has described the works of the mystic Jacob Boehme as 'a picnic where the author provides the words and the readers provide the meaning'. If one is out on a permanent picnic of the fantasy, one has no time to do one's own cooking. Emotion and intuition, dialogue and analysis of character, were all spent in lived relationships. By the time they had become dead relationships I felt no urge to record them; the experience had been too completely consummated and burnt out. The Russian writer Vera Imber says somewhere that 'each calory produced by the soul can only be used either to live or to create'. The involvements of those years were so many and so intense that they deadened the creative urge. The calories I spent on them would have sufficed for writing half a dozen novels. But they would have been bad novels, and they made good living.

To this day—as the critics often tell me—women are the poorest characters in my books. The reason is that I like dining with women, talking, listening and making love to women—but to write about them bores me.

Part Five

THE ROAD TO MARX

1930 – 1931

'*Our goal is the total recasting of man*'
TROTSKY
Literature and Revolution

XXVII. Liberal Götterdämmerung

I ARRIVED in Berlin on the day of the fateful Reichstag elections, September 14th, 1930.

It was the third turning point in my adult career, and each of the three was marked by a symbolic date. I had left the home of my parents and set out for Palestine on April Fools' Day, 1926. I had arrived in Paris on the day which commemorates the beginning of the French Revolution : on Bastille Day, July 14th, 1929. And I arrived in Berlin on the day which heralded the end of the Weimar Republic and the beginning of the age of barbarism in Europe.

Up to September 14th, the National Socialist Party had twelve seats in the German Parliament. After that day, one hundred and seven. The parties of the Centre were crushed. The Democratic Party had all but vanished. The Socialists had lost nine of their seats. The Communists had increased their vote by 40 per cent, the Nazis by 800 per cent. The final show-down was approaching. It came thirty months later.

The day after the elections, I took up my new job in the imposing building in the Kochstrasse. Everybody there was still dazed. I had to pay courtesy calls on the editors of the four daily papers and of a dozen weeklies and monthlies, all housed on the second and third floors of that one labyrinthine building. They shook hands limply, with absent looks. One or two of them said with a wry smile : 'Why on earth didn't you stay on in Paris?' The arrival of a new Science editor at that particular moment struck everybody as exceedingly funny.

After a few days the panic subsided and the people in the Kochstrasse, as everywhere else in Germany, settled down to carry on business as usual in a country that had become a minefield. The ticking of the time-fuses was sometimes more audible, sometimes less. One soon became accustomed to it, and there were still thirty months to go. (It is just the same now, as I am writing this, in the summer of 1951. The time-fuse is ticking, but we hardly hear it any longer. Maybe thirty months, maybe more, maybe less ...)

More than half the people in the Kochstrasse building were Jews. The other half did not fare much better later on. The Ullstein crowd was Dr. Goebbels's *bête noire*. We stood for everything that he hated: 'rootless cosmopolitanism', 'judeo-pacifism', 'pluto-democracy', 'Western decadence', 'gutter literature'. *Mutatis mutandis.* ...

Individuals reacted to the approaching apocalypse according to their varied temperaments. There were the professional optimists, and the constitutional optimists. The former fooled their readers; the latter fooled themselves. There were those who said: 'They can't be as bad as all that.' And those who said: 'They are too weak, they can't start anything.' And those who said: 'They are too strong, we must appease them.' And those who said: 'You are frightened of a bogey, you've got a persecution mania, you are hysterical.' And those who said: 'Hatred doesn't lead anywhere, one must meet them with sympathy and understanding.' And those who said simply: 'I refuse to believe it.'

Thirty months is a long time. There were ups and downs. Elections followed each other at an increasingly feverish rhythm. The Nazis' votes increased by leaps and bounds, but in between they suffered minor setbacks and everybody breathed a little more freely. There was the great purge in the Party which brought the end of Gregor Strasser and which was said to have weakened them to such an extent that they were incapable of action. There was a time when the democratic parties seemed to have awakened from their complacency and the Prussian police actually arrested several Brownshirts. And there was also a minor electoral defeat of Hitler in November, '32, which caused a last surge of euphoria just before the end came.

After the event, people asked themselves : How could we have been such fools to twiddle our thumbs when the outcome was so obvious? The answer is that there were ups and downs and that it took thirty months, and that, owing to the inertia of human imagination, to most people it wasn't obvious at all.

I did not wait for the end. I left Germany for Russia in July, 1932, a few days after the Social Democratic Government of Prussia was chased out of office by one lieutenant and eight men acting on von Papen's orders. So I only witnessed twenty-two out of the thirty months of agony. In my memory this period appears telescoped into a continuous sequence of events: the oscillations of the curve between hope and despair are no longer distinguishable, only the steady descent into the abyss—gradual at first, then gathering momentum, and ending in rapid, headlong fall.

Every phase of this process of decomposition was reflected in the public-opinion factory where I worked. The tone of our papers changed by perceptible degrees. A regular column began to appear in the *Vossische Zeitung*, devoted to news about German ethnic minorities outside the Reich. Quite a number of us heard for the first time the word 'Sudeten-German'. It sounded so funny and backwoodsish that it became a standing joke in the feature department of the *Vossische* to say : 'You are a typical Sudeten-German.' But that new column was not meant as a joke. It was the symbol of a half-conscious shift of emphasis from a cosmopolitan to a Pan-Germanistic orientation.

The attitude of the paper towards the Western powers stiffened. We had always been critical of the Versailles Treaty; now balanced criticism yielded to pompous self-righteousness. The editorials became stuffy, patriotic and provincial. It was not necessary to instruct editors and foreign correspondents to change their course. Once the tone was set, they followed suit—automatically and by instinct. If one had accused them of having changed their convictions they would have sincerely and indignantly denied it.

For years the Ullstein papers had waged a vigorous campaign against capital punishment. While a correspondent in the Middle East, I had gone to great trouble to procure for them snapshots of hangings because it was part of the campaign to show the appalling reality behind the academic discussion. Owing to the strong current against capital punishment in the Liberal strata of the public, no executions had been carried out in Weimar Germany for some years. Now, in 1931, a series of murders were committed by a homosexual killer called Harman. He was sentenced to death, and the public controversy about capital punishment assumed a new urgency; after a long period of rest for the hangman, the Harman affair became a test case.

Matters of policy in the House were decided by the so-called *Fürstenrat*. The 'Council of the Princes' was a weekly conference of the heads of the firm, the Editors-in-Chief and seconds in command of the four daily papers, presided over by one of the Ullstein brothers. I was at that time Assistant Editor of the *B.Z. Am Mittag,* and participated in the conference which decided to abandon the campaign against the execution of Harman. It was a swift and smooth conference. The Managing Director informed us that Harman was a disgusting character, and that to ask for commutation of his sentence would antagonise public opinion, 'which we could not afford to do in these times'. Already most of the editors felt so insecure in their posts that no protest was voiced. I remember that I mumbled something about few murderers being attractive characters—it was my first or second appearance at the 'Council of the Princes' and my muttering was passed over in polite and complete silence. Thus was abandoned, within an hour, a campaign which we had been waging with fervent conviction over a number of years. It was merely one in a series of capitulations, but all the more striking as it had no direct bearing on political issues. We capitulated before the rapidly increasing brutalisation of the masses. In the futile hope of gaining public favour, we sacrificed, on the spur of the moment, our whole social philosophy which held that the function of justice was not punishment but the protection of society. Because there was a question of basic values involved here, the incident shocked me more than a direct political betrayal. It frightened me to discover that the 'Princes', who were the embodiment of democratic public opinion *par excellence,* had neither courage nor convictions.

Long before the thirty months had run their course, our *Vossische,* the Bible of German Liberalism, had little more than its name in common with its former self. Some departmental heads fought a valiant rearguard battle, but they were the exceptions. New faces appeared in the house and old members of the staff vanished. Georg Bernhard, the dynamic editor of the *Vossische,* known all over Europe as one of the outstanding spokesmen of Weimar democracy, became involved in a lawsuit between the Ullstein brothers, and was fired. His post fell late in 1932 to some stalwart nationalist. But not even that saved the old dishonoured paper.

The cold purge dragged on through 1932. Though the Ullsteins were Jews, they tried to Aryanise the firm by degrees, in an indirect way. The victims of the purge were, as far as I can remember, all Jews; the newly hired members of the staff all Aryans. Similarly, though the Ullsteins had radically progressive tendencies, the victims were all radicals, the new acquisitions sturdy nationalists. Stefan Grossmann, one of the most respected Liberal essayists, was among the first victims; then came Heinz Pohl, the brilliant movie critic of the *Vossische*; then Franz Hoellering, Editor-in-Chief of the *B.Z.* I took Hoellering's place for a while until my own turn came; but at least for my dismissal there was a valid reason.

The building in the Kochstrasse became a place of fear and insecurity which again reflected the fear and insecurity of the country in general. We still walked the long sound-proof corridors with the important air of cabinet ministers but we covertly watched each other, wondering whose turn would come next. In some cases the colleagues of a man knew that he was due for the axe while the victim himself was still strutting among them ignorant of his fate. The situation was summed up in a gruesome joke which at that time circulated through all editorial rooms. It is the only Chinese joke I know, and it is worth telling, for it is symbolic of the atmosphere of the German Republic during its last months.

Under the reign of the second Emperor of the Ming Dynasty there lived an executioner by the name of Wang Lun. He was a master of his art and his fame spread through all the provinces of the Empire. There were many executions in those days, and sometimes there were as many as fifteen or twenty men to be beheaded at one session. Wang Lun's habit was to stand at the foot of the scaffold with an engaging smile, hiding his curved sword behind his back, and while whistling a pleasant tune, to behead his victim with a swift movement as he walked up the scaffold.

Now this Wang Lun had one secret ambition in his life, but it took him fifty years of strenuous effort to realise it. His ambition was to be able to behead a person with a stroke so swift that, in accordance with the law of inertia, the victim's head would remain poised on his trunk, in the same manner as a plate remains undisturbed on the table if the tablecloth is pulled out under it with a sudden jerk.

Wang Lun's great moment came in the seventy-eighth year of his life. On that memorable day he had to despatch sixteen clients from this world of shadows to their ancestors. He stood as usual at the foot of the scaffold, and eleven shaven heads had already rolled into the dust after his inimitable master-stroke. His triumph came with the twelfth man. When this man began to ascend the steps of the scaffold, Wang Lun's sword flashed with such lightning speed across his neck that the man's head remained where it had been before, and he continued to walk up the steps without knowing what had happened. When he reached the top of the scaffold, the man addressed Wang Lun as follows :

'O cruel Wang Lun, why do you prolong my agony of waiting when you dealt with the others with such merciful and amiable speed?'

When he heard these words, Wang Lun knew that the work of his life had been accomplished. A serene smile appeared on his features; then he said with exquisite courtesy to the waiting man :

'Just kindly nod, please.'

We walked along the hushed corridors of our citadel of German democracy, greeting each other with a grinning 'Kindly nod, please.' And we fingered the back of our necks to make sure that the head was still solidly attached to it.

The Weimar Republic was doomed. German Liberalism had betrayed its convictions and dishonoured itself without improving its chances of survival. To expect salvation from this side was absurd.

Nor was there more to be hoped from the Socialists. Their record for the preceding quarter-century was one of un-principled opportunism and spineless compromise. In 1912 they had solemnly pledged themselves to make it impossible for their government to go to war; two years later they enthusiastically supported Kaiser Wilhelm's war of conquest. In 1918, when military defeat carried them into power, they missed their historic chance to transform Germany into a truly democratic country. In order to do so it would have been an elementary necessity to break the power of the Ruhr magnates, of the Prussian Junkers, of the Reichswehr *camarilla*. They did not dare to touch any of them. They never had a constructive policy; instead of boldly advancing, they manœuvred. In the 1932 presidential elections, their candidate was doddering old Field Marshal Hindenburg, the Pétain of Germany. They got him elected, and six months later he called Adolf Hitler into power.

Their only firm and uncompromising stand was taken against the Communists. It was inspired not so much by questions of principle as by jealousy of the rival who had dared to challenge the Socialist monopoly in representing the working class. In the early years of the Republic when the German Communists were still a genuine, *bona fide* revolutionary party, the Socialists crushed the workers' risings on the Ruhr and in Saxony with a ruthlessness that betrayed their fratricidal hatred. It was at that time that the Socialist Minister of National Defence, Noske, made his famous pronouncement: 'If the Party needs a bloodhound, I'll be it.' He lived up to his promise. Karl Liebknecht and Rosa Luxemburg, heroes of the working class, were arrested and murdered by their escorts in cold blood. The counter-revolutionary 'Black' corps of former officers was called into action against the socialist Spartacus Bund, forerunner of the Communist Party. The betrayal was so overt and complete that even the staid *Encyclopædia Britannica* remarks ironically: 'Thus only a few weeks after the Revolution, officers of the former army were appearing as saviours of society against Socialists.'

The rift between the two working-class parties never healed. On May Day, 1929, the Berlin police, commanded by the Socialist Zörrgiebel, opened fire against a Communist demonstration. The incident led to street-fighting in the capital which lasted several days, and claimed over a hundred dead. It was the last time that the workers of Berlin fought on the barricades. When the Nazis came to power there were no barricades. They were able to carry out their *coup d'état* on 5th March, 1933, without firing a single shot. By that time the German working class as a political power was dead.

If the social-democratic idea ever had a chance of becoming reality, it was after the collapse of the German and Austrian empires in 1918. The old order had vanished; the people in the defeated countries were ripe for a complete change; it was a unique historical opportunity. The Socialists not only failed to seize it, but each major act of their policy was a further step towards the suicide of their young Republics. To listen to their booming, complacent voices made one feel sick with despair and exasperation. This feeling was so strong that it still reverberates in my memory—and with much greater intensity than my feeling about the Nazis at the time. I must dwell for a moment on this psychological difference for it is typical of left-wing politics in general, and throws a sidelight on one of the factors in Europe's decline.

I feared and hated, of course, Hitler's legions; but it was a cold hatred, without the emotional glow which only intimacy with the hated object can provide. For hatred, like love, can only flourish where there is some common ground, where a common denominator exists.

The Socialists, on the other hand, subscribed to the same principles in which I believed. I had regarded them as the legitimate heirs and trustees of the Judeo-Christian tradition —of the Hebrew prophets and the Sermon on the Mount; of the Kantian Imperative; of Liberty, Equality and Frater-

nity. The Nazis were savages who remained true to themselves; the Socialists were my own kin who had betrayed their
trust. You cannot hate a tiger for being a tiger; but the
irresponsible keeper who exposes people to the beast's claws
you would like to shoot on the spot—even before you shoot
the tiger. It is an emotional attitude deeply rooted in the
political psyche. Few generals hate their opponents; but they
grow ulcers and throw fits of apoplexy because of their allies.
The Church tries to convert the pagans, but burns her
heretics. It seems to be a general law in politics that hatred
increases in proportion to the amount of shared convictions
and interests. Accordingly, on the eve of Hitler's victory, the
Socialist and Communist leaders concentrated their main
efforts on fighting each other.

At this point it is important to bear in mind the date of
the events under discussion. In 1930, the progressive intellectuals of Germany were only too familiar with the sad record
of the Socialist Party, but as yet few unfavourable facts about
Soviet Communism had become public knowledge. Trotsky,
leader of the Opposition, had been exiled; but as revolutions
go, exile is a relatively mild punishment. No prominent
Soviet politician had been tried in public, no member of the
Opposition had been executed. Those were comparatively
idyllic days; the purges, the show trials and the Terror only
started four years later, after the assassination of Kirov, in
December, 1934.

Forced collectivisation of the peasants' land had only just
begun. The mass deportations of 'Kulaks', the famine and
partial depopulation of the countryside were still a matter of
the future. The first Five Year Plan had been undertaken in
1929; it was in its second year. It was a gigantic enterprise
of truly historic significance. Russia was still regarded as 'the
great experiment'; one could have reservations about the
régime and be critical of it, but there was no *prima facie* case
for rejecting it out of hand. Only the Conservatives and

reactionaries did that—while at the same time they displayed a benevolent neutrality towards the Italian and German variants of Fascism. There were a few isolated voices among progressive intellectuals—Bertrand Russell and H. G. Wells for instance—who from the beginning had uncompromisingly opposed the Soviet régime; but they were few, and were not listened to.

Thus, in 1930, Russia was still an asset for the German Communist Party, whereas today it has become rather a liability to the Communists of Western Europe. The Socialists had no such asset, only their dismal reputation of having stifled the German Revolution and made a mess of their Republic. Since 1918, each time they were faced with the choice between allying themselves to the *bourgeois* parties or the radical wing of the working class they had opted for the former; and however controversial the details, this basic fact weighed heavily against them.

By contrast, the record of the Communist Party of Germany was, in appearance, a relatively honourable one. There had been waverings in the Party line, and parallel changes in Trade Union policy. But these were matters for the expert in revolutionary politics; that Moscow had played any part in them was only known to the initiates; from the outsider's point of view, the Communists had followed a fairly consistent policy during the whole period from 1918 to 1930. Their tactics were sometimes obscure and slightly bewildering; but the period of sudden and total reversals of policy had not yet come. When, in 1931, the Communist Party joined hands with the Nazis in initiating a referendum against the Prussian Socialist government; and when, in November, 1932, it again made common cause with them in the Berlin transport workers' strike, I was already so immersed in Marxist thought that I found these stratagems 'dialectically correct'.

One may arrive at a decision by a positive impulse, or by elimination of other possible solutions. After the elections of September, 1930, I had seen the Liberal middle class betray its convictions and throw all its principles overboard. Active resistance against the Nazis seemed only possible by throwing in one's lot either with the Socialists or the Communists. A comparison of their past records, their vigour and determination eliminated the first, and favoured the second.

I was not alone to arrive at this conclusion. The trend towards polarisation between the two extremist movements was evident; it bore all the signs of inexorable fatality. The title of H. R. Knickerbocker's famous best-seller of that time, *Germany—Fascist or Soviet?* was an exact summing up of the situation. There was no 'third force' and no third choice.

XXVIII. The Psychology of Conversion

AGAINST this background I now began to study Communist literature in earnest.

'By the time I had finished with Engels' *Feuerbach* and Lenin's *State and Revolution,* something had clicked in my brain and I was shaken by a mental explosion. To say that one had "seen the light" is a poor description of the intellectual rapture which only the convert knows (regardless to what faith he has been converted). The new light seems to pour from all directions across the skull; the whole universe falls into pattern like the stray pieces in a jigsaw puzzle assembled by magic at one stroke. There is now an answer to every question; doubts and conflicts are a matter of the tortured past—a past already remote, when one had lived in dismal ignorance in the tasteless, colourless world of those who *don't know*. Nothing henceforth can disturb the convert's inner peace and serenity—except the occasional fear of losing faith again, losing thereby what alone makes life worth living, and falling back into the outer darkness, where there is wailing and gnashing of teeth.'

The preceding paragraph is quoted from my contribution to *The God That Failed,* a book in which six men (Louis Fischer, André Gide, Ignazio Silone, Stephen Spender, Richard Wright and myself), who formerly believed in the tenets of Communism, have described the reasons why they became converted to the new faith. After rereading the book, it seems to me that none of us succeeded in giving a complete answer to this crucial question of our time, which has split the planet into two camps and may well cause the downfall of our civilisation. The pages which follow are a further attempt to analyse the mental lure of the Marxist-Leninist-Stalinist creed.

The first, and decisive, effect which the study of Marxism had on me I can only describe by saying that, without my being aware of it, I had stepped from an intellectually open into an intellectually closed world. Marxism, like orthodox Freudianism, like Catholicism, is a closed system. By a 'closed system' I mean, firstly, a universal method of thought which claims to explain all phenomena under the sun and to have a cure for all that ails man. It is, further, a system that refuses to be modified by newly observed facts but has sufficiently elastic defences to neutralise their impact—that is, to make them fit the required pattern by a highly developed technique of casuistry. It is, thirdly, a system which once you have stepped inside its magic circle, deprives your critical faculties of any ground to stand on.

The last point is perhaps the most important. Within the closed system of Freudian thought you cannot, for instance, argue that for certain reasons you doubt the existence of the so-called castration complex. The immediate answer will be that your arguments are rationalisations of an unconscious resistance which betrays that you yourself have such a complex. You are caught in a vicious circle from which there is no logical escape. Similarly, if you are a Marxist and if you claim that Lenin's order to march on Warsaw in 1920 was a mistake, it will be explained to you that you ought not to trust your own judgment because it is distorted by vestiges of your former *petit-bourgeois* class-consciousness. In short, the closed system excludes the possibility of objective argument by two related proceedings : (*a*) facts are deprived of their value as evidence by scholastic processing; (*b*) objections are invalidated by shifting the argument to the psychological motive behind the objection. This procedure is legitimate according to the closed system's rules of the game which, however absurd they seem to the outsider, have a great coherence and inner consistency.

The atmosphere inside the closed system is highly charged; it is an emotional hothouse. The absence of objectivity in debate is many times compensated by its fervour. The disciple receives a thorough indoctrination, and an equally thorough training in the system's particular method of reasoning. As a result of this training, he acquires a technique of argumentation which is mostly superior to that of any opponent from outside. He is thoroughly acquainted with the great debates of the past between the apostles and the unbelievers; he is acquainted with the history of heresies and schisms; he knows the classic controversies between Jansenites and Jesuits, between Freud and Jung, between Lenin and Kautsky. Thus he recognises at once the type and attitude of his opponent, is able to classify the latter's objections according to familiar categories; knows the questions and answers as though they were the opening variants of a chess game. The trained, 'closed-minded' theologian, psychoanalyst, or Marxist can at any time make mincemeat of his 'open-minded' adversary and thus prove the superiority of his system to the world and to himself.

This superiority enables the initiate of the closed system to display a patient tolerance towards the outsider. In discussion with pagans, patients, and *bourgeois* reactionaries, he is calm, paternal and impressive. His superiority, his self-assurance, the radiance of his sincere belief, create a peculiar relationship between the initiate and the potential convert. It is the relationship between the *guru* and the pupil, between confessor and penitent, analyst and patient, between the militant Party member and the fascinated sympathiser, the admiring fellow-traveller.

This 'transference situation' is an essential phase in the process of conversion which has been curiously neglected in the literature on the subject. I believe that no man has become a convert without going through the phase of admiring devotion, of a rationalised *Schwämerei* for the person who does the converting, and serves as master and example. In the case of converts to Catholicism and Freud-ianism—to cite again the two most obvious parallels—the importance of the spiritual guide, or of the analyst, is overtly emphasised. In the case of the Communist convert, however, this phase is slurred over in the convert's memory, because the system categorically denies the importance of individual relationships. Yet in the history of the Marxist movement, personal, emotional relationships have always played an overwhelming part. Marx the prophet tolerated no equals, only disciples—who, in most cases, started by worshipping and ended by rejecting him. Freud's relations with his disciples followed a startlingly similar pattern; he, too, was constantly 'abandoned' and 'betrayed' by them—for dis-agreements which in the normal world are settled by argu-ment, become in the all-or-nothing atmosphere of the closed system acts of treason, heresy and schism. Jung and Adler are to Freud what Lassalle and Bakunin are to Marx.

Every closed system must of necessity develop an apostolic hierarchy. The original Master, whose word is revelation, delegates his spiritual and secular authority to his select inner caucus—the Apostles; the bearers of Freud's 'seven rings'; the tried disciples of a 'Central Committee' or 'Politburo'. Each member of the inner caucus in his turn radiates some of this apostolic authority and delegates some of its magic substance to his followers on the next lower level of the hier-archy; and so on, down to the periphery. Even the member on the lowest level of the hierarchy feels that he is the bearer of a torch whose flame has been passed down to him from the Holy of Holies. Thus every 'militant Party member' who undertakes an outsider's conversion is invested with the prestige of an esoteric order. He is not an ordinary proselytiser but a messenger from a different and fascinating world, surrounded by a halo; a purer, more dedicated, more admirable being, whose example one would like to imitate if only such dedication were within one's power.

Part of the proselytising Communist's attraction resides in the secrecy which surrounds his person. He is only known by his first name, or by an alias. He has no address and can only be reached through intermediaries or 'contacts'. This is true not only of members of the 'Apparat' but of militant Communists in general, regardless whether their Party is 'legal' or 'underground' in the country and at the time in question. The conspiratorial tradition originated in Czarist Russia and has become the rigid etiquette of Communist Parties all over the world. Even a superficial contact will make the innocent outsider feel that members of the Party lead a life apart from society, steeped in mystery, danger and constant sacrifice. The thrill of being in touch with this secret world is considerable even for people with an adult and otherwise unromantic mentality. Still stronger is the flattering effect of being found worthy of a certain amount of trust, of being permitted to perform minor services for the harassed men who live in such constant danger. Lionel Trilling, in *The Middle of the Journey*, has written an excellent psychological study of the relations between the militant apostle and the fascinated, hesitating sympathiser. This type of relationship explains in part the astonishing conversions of cool-headed State Department careerists like Alger Hiss; of Public School-bred Foreign Office diplomats like Guy Burgess and Donald Maclean; of neurotic millionaires like Frederick Vanderbilt Field; of sober scientists like Bernal, Fuchs and Joliot Curie. Only in part, of course, for the mixture and dosage of this and other psychological factors differ from case to case.

The tradition of 'conspiratorial secrecy' in Communist circles has grown into a cult with specific rites, mannerisms, and a jargon of its own. After a few years in this atmosphere, most members of the Party begin to display symptoms of what one might call 'conspirativitis'—a mental condition often indistinguishable from paranoia. In a later section I shall describe the case of a girl comrade who developed acute persecution mania before my eyes. But even this pathological tendency has a strange lure for the outsider, as the following episode may show.

One of the two *gurus* who played a prominent part in my conversion was a young man whom I first knew by the name of Otto. At the time I knew neither his profession, nor anything about him except that he was 'an important comrade on the cultural front'. A few weeks later I learnt that he wrote literary essays for Marxist papers under the pen-name of Paul Berlin; and also that he played a leading part in the German 'League of Proletarian Revolutionary Writers'— the Communist writers' caucus directly affiliated to the Comintern.

That was in 1931. In 1934 we met again, after Hitler had come to power, as exiles in Paris. We became intimate friends and collaborators in a Party office, and a while later we became in-laws by my first marriage. In this way I learnt— after four years of close friendship—that his real name was neither Otto nor Paul, but Peter Maros. However, I still did not know the name that was on his passport—though I understood, from one or two casual hints, that it was, of course, again a different one.

Otto, alias Paul Berlin, alias Peter Maros, had a very impressive personality. He was spare, lean, wiry. The expression of his face captivated you at first glance. It radiated a quiet, ascetic saintliness. He had thin lips, a high forehead and unnaturally large pupils whose luminous gaze outstared you, without being aggressive, with their radiance of sheer brotherly love. Later I found out that this extraordinary effect was due to a slight disfunction of the thyroid gland, related to Basedow's disease. But its effect, and that of Peter's whole personality, was irresistible when brought to bear on sympathetic *bourgeois*. And during those days of the Popular Front, the Party was going all out for *bourgeois* support. I saw Peter in action visiting French university professors, authors and bankers, to enlist their support for some 'anti-Fascist' committee, to collect money, signatures, letters of recommendation, and character testimonials. The unanimous reaction of these good people may be summed up in one formula : 'If the Communist Party consists of such men, then nothing much can be wrong with it.'

Apart from his direct Party activities, Peter continued to write literary essays and anti-Nazi articles for German émigré papers under two or three different pen-names. I sometimes wondered why this extreme caution was necessary since, from the point of view of the French authorities, the articles were quite harmless. However, he gave me to understand that he had special reasons for acting as he did, and it would have been an unpardonable breach of Party etiquette, even among in-laws, to ask further questions.

Among our sympathisers in French academic and literary circles Peter soon became a legend. Everybody knew him, and everybody by a different name; but as his striking personality could easily be identified by description, his namelessness further nourished the legend. When some professor at the Sorbonne or a progressive *député* asked what name he should put in a letter of recommendation, Peter would say with his brave, resigned smile :

'Just put any name you like. Or simply say "A Friend" . . .' So he was usually referred to as 'Our Friend—you know who I mean,' in a respectfully hushed voice.

It took years of intimate friendship before I began to suspect that Peter might be a phoney; but to what extent he was a phoney I cannot decide to this day. He lived with his wife in austere poverty, never sought any personal advantage, and occupied a modest but respected position in the Party hierarchy. His was a pronounced case of 'conspirativitis'. Yet, though his conspiratorial antics brought him no material benefits, they enormously enhanced his prestige, and thereby the Party's prestige, among the Philistines. This circumstance he must have vaguely sensed and half-consciously exploited *pro gloria dei*—like the juggler in the mediæval legend who, having no other gift to offer, performs his somersaults and sleights-of-hand before the altar of the Virgin.

The *dénouement,* as far as I am concerned, came after I had known Peter for five years. In 1935, I was staying with the widow of the German actor, Eugen Kloepfer, in her house on the Lago di Lugano. Maria Kloepfer was a rich, middle-aged woman, devoted in equal parts to Buddhism, Communism and psycho-analysis, and a predestined victim of apostles like Peter. She gave large sums to various Front organisations of the Party, and acted as a Maecenas to Communist writers by letting them live and work in her house; Ludwig Renn and Johannes R. Becher were among those who had enjoyed her hospitality. I met her through Peter, who had been her guest on previous occasions; she was, of course, devoted to him and completely under his sway. One day, after dinner in her house, she told me about a mysterious journey of Peter's to Zurich. In spite of his usual discretion, she had gathered from a hint or two that the purpose of the trip was to collect a new forged passport under a new name, the old one being no longer safe. She had asked him how many different passports he had had in his life, and he had answered that he had forgotten their number. Then she had asked teasingly : 'I wish I knew your real name.' And Peter had answered, with his resigned smile : 'I have almost forgotten it myself.'

I could not refrain from telling Maria that I was one of

the select few who *did* know Peter's real name. This nettled her, and provoked her to remark that though she did not know his *real* name, she did know the alias he had used on his latest passport—one day he had left the passport lying in his room and she had not been able to resist the temptation to peep at it. We were both slightly tight and very excited about the subject. So, breaking the sacred rules of conspiracy, I wrote down Peter's real name on a piece of paper, and Maria wrote down the alias which was on his passport; then, with a guilty feeling, we exchanged the two papers. On mine was the name PETER MAROS. On Maria's was the name PETER MAROS. Honest Peter had never had a false passport in his life. He was the Marxist equivalent of Oscar Wilde's 'Sphinx without a secret'.

A few years later, during the Spanish Civil War, Peter became one of the organisers of the famous anti-Fascist Writers' Congress in Madrid, which Stephen Spender has described with such caustic humour in his memoirs. I lost sight of him when I left the Party in 1938; but I heard later on that at the outbreak of the war he had managed to get back to his native country, Yugo-Slavia.

In 1950, at a luncheon in the house of a State Department official in Washington, I sat next to one of the members of the Titoist delegation to U.N. He was of course a member of the Yugo-Slav Communist Party, though of a later vintage than mine : I had left the Party in '38, he had joined in '39. I asked him whether he had ever come across my friend Peter Maros. His face lit up. He explained to me that Peter was one of the most wonderful people he knew : pure, brave and dedicated, practically a saint. He was now the editor of a leading Communist literary magazine in Yugo-Slavia; and I gathered from my neighbour's enthusiastic comments, that once again Peter had acted as a *guru* in this particular conversion.

Peter Maros is, of course, not his real name either. I have

had to alter it for this text, because I have no reason for getting him into trouble with Marshal Tito's régime. So he has to appear under still another alias—conspiracy is endemic in our times.

My second *guru* was of an entirely different type. He, too, must appear in these pages under an alias for he lives in a country where even a dead and buried Communist past might still mean trouble for a foreigner. Karl was a former plumber's apprentice who, by attending Marxist evening classes and dogged night reading, had become a fairly well-known political writer. He knew his Marx and Lenin forward and backward, but his outstanding quality was physical courage. He made a sport of going to local meetings of the Nazis and making speeches against them which usually ended by his being beaten up and thrown out. But he was also capable of waking me up at six o'clock in the morning and taking me for a walk to the Zoo to study 'conditioned behaviour patterns of servility through the example of oppressed chimpanzees'.

In later years Karl wrote scripts for the Soviet movie industry; won a sensational libel suit against one of the biggest industrial concerns of Central Europe whose labour policy he had attacked in a pamphlet; and tried to sell a no less sensational Russian invention through my father to a group of Hungarian financiers. The invention consisted in transforming whole live pigs into salt pork. The pig was anaesthetised with laughing gas; then the blood was pumped out through a tapped vein while simultaneously a saline solution was pumped in through its main artery. Thus the pig was salted from inside and under its own steam as it were, before its blood could clot as in the normal process of slaughtering. The invention was entirely in keeping with my father's other ventures, and like the others, it came to naught —at least in so far as Hungary is concerned. Whether the process is actually used in Russia or anywhere else, I do not know.

In every conversion to the Communist faith, some *guru* plays an important part. He makes his appearance in most memoirs of former Party members—sometimes as an 'unselfish nurse' as in the case of the former Comintern agent Elisabeth Bentley; sometimes as a fascinatingly clever intellectual like Gerhart Eisler in the case of Hete Massing; and sometimes as a simple, honest proletarian, as in the case of many of my friends. In all novels by authors who at one time were close to the Communist Party, one finds a key character who reflects the writer's infatuation with the person, or type of person, who attracted him to the movement. In Malraux's *Man's Fate* it is the Russian, Borodin; in Steinbeck's *In Dubious Battle* it is Mac; in Hemingway's *To Have or Have Not* it is Captain Morgan; in Sartre's *The Age of Reason* it is Bruneau. An interesting exception is Silone's hero, Peter Spina, who is a self-portrait; for Silone, the son of poor Abruzzi peasants, was perhaps the only one among us who was not a convert but a 'natural' Communist. At the opposite end of the scale is Sartre, the middle-class professor of philosophy; his *guru*—honest, hard-fisted Bruneau in *The Age of Reason*—is the archetype of the 'ideal Proletarian' who exerts such a strong fascination on intellectuals. Worship of the proletarian appears at first sight as a typically Marxist phenomenon, but is in fact merely a new variant of romantic shepherd cults, peasant cults, noble-savage cults of the past. That, however, did not prevent Communist writers in the nineteen-thirties from feeling for workers in an automobile factory the same kind of emotion which Proust felt for his duchesses.

XXIX. Rebellion and Faith: Rebellion

To the convert, his conversion appears as a single and indivisible act, a spiritual rebirth in which emotion and reason, the perennial duellists, are for once in complete harmony.

In retrospect, however, the unitary act can be analysed into its various components. In the preceding sections I have tried to retrace some of these. I have briefly discussed the process of elimination which, after the disappearance of the progressive middle-of-the-road Parties in Central Europe and the spineless opportunism displayed by the Socialists, left the Communists as sole apparent champions of anti-Fascism; the intellectual comfort and relief found in escaping from a tragic predicament into a 'closed system' of beliefs that left no room for hesitation or doubt; the lure of a militant Order of modern saints and martyrs with its ritual of secrecy and its apostolic hierarchy; finally, the psychological bond, or transference-situation, which occurs when proselytising members of the Order act as the potential convert's spiritual guide.

My childhood and early youth bore a markedly individualistic stamp; on the other hand, my progress towards the Communist Party followed a typical, almost conventional pattern of that time. It seemed to confirm the Marxian dictum that man is a product of social conditions, and his mentality a reflection of them. Regardless of the individual crotchets of my mind, my political progress was essentially determined by these conditions; and those who shared the same social and cultural background, however different their psychological make-up, went by and large the same way. It was a mass migration of the sons and daughters of the European *bourgeoisie* trying to escape from the collapsing world of their parents. The inflation years which had followed the First World War were the beginning of Europe's decline; the depression years which came a decade later accelerated the process; the Second World War completed it. The economic and moral disintegration of the middle strata of society led to the fatal process of polarisation which is continuing to this day, from the Channel ports to South East Asia. The active element among the pauperised *bourgeois* became rebels of the Right or of the Left; Fascists and Communists shared about equally the benefits of the social migration. The remainder, who found no consolation in hatred, lived on pointlessly 'like a swarm of tired winter flies crawling over the dim windows of Europe, members of a class displaced by History'.

East of the Rhine, in 1930, there was no escape from the choice between Fascism and Communism. Western Europeans have never completely understood the compulsory character of that dilemma, and the historical fatality behind it. Like iron-filings between two magnetic poles, the peoples of Germany and of the countries to the South and East aligned themselves according to their position in the field of forces.

Yet these are once again judgments after the event. At the time when the decision to join the Communist Party was maturing in me, neither the process of elimination, nor the process of polarisation in which I was caught, was clearly in focus in my mind. Social pressures were working on me; I was carried by the tide; my impulses and decisions were a reflection of those pressures, but not a conscious reflection. In so far as a 'class-consciousness' exists—that is, a mental attitude conforming to social circumstance—it is not begotten on a conscious level. The average human mind does not say : 'I am a bus conductor; therefore a wage-earner; therefore a member of the exploited proletariat; therefore I must join the revolutionary movement.' Nor did I compute in my mind the decline of the European middle class, plus social polarisation, plus selective elimination of other possible courses of action in the tidy order in which I have set them down on these pages. That computation was carried out by an erratic, partly unconscious, piecemeal kind of reasoning, until the final conclusion was suddenly present in my mind —like the result which appears on the dial of electronic calculators.

The conscious experiences of which, during that period, I was aware, were of a different order and predominantly not of a logical, but of an emotional nature. They can be summed up in two words : rebellion and faith.

'A faith is not acquired by reasoning. One does not fall in love with a woman, or enter the womb of a church, as a result of logical persuasion. Reason may defend an act of faith—but only after the act has been committed, and the man committed to the act. . . .'

'Devotion to pure Utopia, and revolt against a polluted society, are the two poles which provide the tension of all militant creeds. To ask which of the two makes the current flow—attraction by the ideal or repulsion by the social environment—is to ask the old question about the hen and the egg. . . .'

It did not require much persuasion to make me into a rebel. Since my childhood I seem to have lived in a state of Chronic Indignation. When this state reached its peak, I joined the Communist Party.

Rousseau remarks somewhere that he, too, suffered from this affliction, and explains it as an after-effect of the ignominies and sufferings which he had endured in his childhood. Here he seems, for once, to be unjust to himself, for early suffering may sensitivise or thwart a person in many different ways without turning him into an indignant rebel. This type seems to depend on a specific quality : the gift of projective imagination, or empathy, which compels one to regard an injustice inflicted on others as an indignity to oneself; and vice versa, to perceive an injustice to oneself as part and symbol of a general evil in society. The chronically indignant person is not necessarily quarrelsome, but always a rebel. His incessant campaigns to obtain justice for himself, for one Cause or another, for his friends and protégés (for he always has a large clientèle of protégés to whom he causes more embarrassment than relief) occupy most of his time and make him into a kind of admirable bore—I am talking of course of myself. Whether he appears more admirable or more of a bore, depends to a lesser extent on himself, and to a greater extent on the constellation of events. The difference in qualification for statesmanship between Garry Davis and Harry Truman is incomparably smaller than the hazard of circumstances makes it appear.

What distinguishes the chronically indignant rebel from the earnest revolutionary is that the former is capable of changing causes, the latter not. The rebel turns his indignation now against this injustice, now against another; the revolutionary is a consistent hater who has invested all his powers of hatred in one object. The rebel always has a touch of the quixotic; the revolutionary is a bureaucrat of Utopia. The rebel is an enthusiast; the revolutionary, a fanatic. Robespierre, Marx, Lenin were revolutionaries; Danton, Bakunin, Trotsky were rebels. It is mostly the revolutionaries who alter the material course of history; but some rebels leave a subtler and yet more lasting imprint on it. At any rate, the rebel, for all his tiresome fulminations and enthusiasms, is a more attractive type than the revolutionary—I am again speaking *pro domo,* of course.

L

I have mentioned how the ignominies of the colonial administration in Palestine changed me from a romantic into an active Zionist. The event that roused my indignation to a pitch never reached before was the American policy of destroying food stocks to keep agricultural prices up during the depression years—at a time when millions of unemployed lived in misery and near starvation. In retrospect, the economic policy which led to these measures is a subject for academic controversy; but in 1931 and '32, its effect on Europeans was that of a crude and indeed terrifying shock which destroyed what little faith they still had in the existing social order. By 1932, there were seven million unemployed in Germany—which means that one out of every three wage-earners lived on the dole. In Austria, Hungary and the surrounding countries the situation was similar or worse. Meat, coffee, fruit had become unobtainable luxuries for large sections of the population, even the bread on the table was measured out in thin slices; yet the newspapers spoke laconically of millions of tons of coffee being dumped into the sea, of wheat being burned, pigs being cremated, oranges doused with kerosene 'to ease conditions on the market'. It was a grotesque and incomprehensible paradox—incomprehensible to the simple-minded among its victims, and to the socially conscious a sign of the total breakdown and decomposition of the economic system. Had not Marx foretold that Capitalism would perish through its internal contradictions; that the cycle of prosperous periods ending in a crisis would repeat itself in an accelerated rhythm and each crisis be worse—until the last would bring the capitalist system to its end? Clearly, the prophecy was on the point of being fulfilled. When people starve and food is destroyed before their eyes so that their fat exploiters may grow even fatter, then the last judgment must be at hand.

Woe to the shepherds who feed themselves but feed not their flocks! Indignation glowed inside me like a furnace. At times I thought that I was choking from its fumes; at other times I felt like hitting out, and shooting from a barricade or throwing sticks of dynamite. At whom? It was an impersonal fury, directed at no individual or group in particular. I did not hate the police, or the factory owners, or the rich— I had at that time a very comfortable income myself. I found the Brownshirts repellent, but they belonged to a strange and absurd world. I disliked the ostensibly rich—but not because of their riches, only because they used their wealth frivolously and behaved as if they were dumb and blind. My seething indignation had no personal target; it was directed at the System in general, at the oily hypocrisy and suicidal stupidity which were driving us all to perdition. In my rage-fantasies no people were killed but huge buildings burst open and their walls came tumbling down as if in an earthquake— Ministries, editorial offices, radio stations, the whole *Sieges Allee* with its hideous statues of princes and field marshals. . . .

> *To wipe out the past for ever*
> *O army of slaves, follow us.*
> *We shall lift the globe from its axis. . . .*

Echoes of the hundred days of the Hungarian Commune; echoes of the indignant wrath of the Hebrew prophets, and of the forthcoming Apocalypse according to St. Marx; the memory of my father's bankruptcy, the sound of the hunger-marchers' broken-down boots on the pavement and the smell of fresh wheat being burnt in the fields—all these ingredients fused into one emotional explosion. My political latency period had come to an end.

Though the mixture which set off the explosion varied from case to case, the reaction was the same for a large number of writers and intellectuals the world over: Barbusse, Romain Rolland, Gide, Malraux in France; Piscator, Becher, Seghers, Brecht in Germany; Auden, Isherwood,

Spender, Day Lewis in England; Sinclair, Dos Passos, Stein-beck, Caldwell in the U.S.A.—to mention only a few. In the nineteen-thirties conversion to the Communist faith was not a fashion or craze—it was a sincere and spontaneous expression of an optimism born of despair : an abortive revolution of the spirit, a misfired Renaissance, a false dawn of history. To be attracted to the new faith was, I still believe, an honourable error. We were wrong for the right reasons; and I still feel that, with a few exceptions—I have already mentioned Bertrand Russell and H. G. Wells—those who derided the Russian Revolution from the beginning, did so mostly for reasons that were less honourable than our error. There is a world of difference between a disenchanted lover and those incapable of love.

Looking at my individual case through the psychological microscope, after having deliberately laid myself open to such examination, it can, of course, be argued that my conversion was caused not by a 'genuine' social conscience but by a neurotic disposition. But I doubt whether a highly developed social conscience is ever 'genuine' in the sense of being completely detached from private experiences in the individual's past. 'Whether they spoke of the necessity of political liberty, or the plight of the peasant or the socialist future society, it was always their own plight which really moved them. And their plight was not primarily due to material need: it was spiritual.' The quotation is from Borkenau's *The Communist International* and refers to the Russian revolutionary intelligentsia of the nineteenth century. But it could be equally applied to the French Encyclo-pedists, the Liberals of 1848, and the champions of any other progressive movement.

In short, behind the achievements of reformers, rebels, explorers, and innovators who keep the world moving, there is always some intimate motivation—and it mostly contains a strong element of frustration, anxiety or guilt. The happy are rarely curious; those who are smugly tucked into the social hierarchy have no reason to destroy the conventional system of values, nor to build new ones. The contempt of the hale and healthy for the neurotic is justified so long as the latter's obsessions remain sterile and find no constructive outlet. But there is another type of neurotic who labours under the curse of experiencing a collective predicament in terms of personal pain, and has the simultaneous gift of transforming individual pain into social or artistic achievement. In the evaluation of that achievement the intimate motives behind it ought to play no part.

Thus the Historian and the Psychiatrist, each in his own terms, arrive at completely different judgments of value regarding the same action. 'To the psychiatrist, both the craving for Utopia and the rebellion against the status quo are symptoms of social maladjustment. To the social reformer, both are symptoms of a progressive, rational attitude. The psychiatrist is apt to forget that adjustment to a deformed society creates deformed individuals. The reformer is apt to forget that hatred, even of the objectively hateful, cannot beget a happy society. Hence each of the two attitudes reflects a half-truth. It is true that the case histories of most rebels reveal a neurotic conflict with family and society —but this only proves, to paraphrase Marx, that a moribund society creates its own morbid grave-diggers. It is also true that in the presence of revolting injustice the only honourable attitude is revolt—but if one compares the noble ideals in the name of which revolutions were started with the sorry end to which they came, one realises that a polluted society pollutes even its revolutionary offspring.

'In fitting together the two half-truths, the psychiatrist's and the social reformer's, one must conclude that if, on the one hand, oversensitivity to social injustice and obsessive cravings for Utopia are signs of a neurotic disposition, society may, on the other hand, reach an impasse where the neurotic rebel creates more rejoicing in heaven than the sane administrator who orders food destroyed under the eyes of starving men. And that, precisely, was the impasse reached by our civilisation in 1931.'[1]

[1] *The God That Failed*

XXX. Rebellion and Faith: Faith

I HAVE tried to describe some of the reasons which, in the nineteen-thirties, turned millions of Europeans, including myself, into rebels. The new faith that emerged from this rebellion was, and to a large extent still is, based on Soviet mythology.

The Soviet myth—as distinct from Soviet reality—acts on its victims both on the rational and the irrational level. The two are, of course, so intimately tangled up in experience that it is difficult to reconstruct the various stages of becoming a myth-addict in their proper sequence.

I remember, however, the first stage with especial clarity, as it appeared to me as a purely rational, and eminently reasonable one. Every comparison between the state of affairs in Russia and in the Western world seemed to speak eloquently in favour of the former. In the West, there was mass unemployment; in Russia, a shortage of manpower. In the West, chronic strikes and social unrest which, in some countries, were threatening to lead to civil war; in Russia, where all factories belonged to the people, the workers vied in socialist competitions for higher production outputs. In the West, the anarchy of *laissez faire* was drowning the capitalist system in chaos and depression; in Russia, the First Five Year Plan was transforming, by a series of giant strokes, the most backward into the most advanced country of Europe. If History herself were a fellow-traveller, she could not have arranged a more clever timing of events than this coincidence of the gravest crisis of the Western world with the initial phase of Russia's industrial revolution. The contrast between the downward trend of capitalism and the simultaneous steep rise of planned Soviet economy was so striking and obvious that it led to the equally obvious conclusion : They are the future—we, the past. In so far as Eastern Europe is concerned, the prediction has, in an unexpected and terrible way, come true.

The next stage was my falling in love with the Five Year Plan. On one-sixth of our sick planet, the most gigantic constructive effort of all times had begun; there Utopia was being built in steel and concrete. Steeped in the Soviet literature of the period whose one and only subject was the building of factories, power stations, tractors, silos and the fulfilment of the Plan, I half-seriously considered writing a modern version of the Song of Songs :

'The eyes of my beloved shine like blast furnaces in the steppe; her lips are boldly drawn like the White Sea Canal; her shoulder is slenderly curved like the Dnieper Dam; her spine is long and straight, like the Turkestan-Siberia railway . . .' And the foxes, the little foxes that spoilt the vine, were the counter-revolutionary fascist saboteurs.

It is not easy to recapture that mood today. Irony keeps intruding; the bitterness of later experience is always present. We can add to our knowledge, but we cannot at will substract from it; no brain surgeon can restore the virginity of an illusion.

In *The Age of Longing* I have tried to revive the lost illusion through the eyes of a Russian boy of fifteen, whose father had died as a martyr of the revolution :

'The announcement of the First Five Year Plan came like the sudden roar of thunder which shook the country and whose echo reverberated throughout the world. The ship of the Revolution had been becalmed; now it shot forward as under a whip, with cracking masts and sails stretched to bursting. . . . Discipline in school became stricter; each class, the teacher explained, was to regard itself as a shock battalion in the battle for the future. Fedya's head buzzed with the figures of the Plan, learned by rote : so many million tons of pig iron after the first year, so many million kilowatt hours, so many million illiterates turned into cultured members of society. The sound of all these millions of riches, produced by the people for the people, was intoxicating. The kilowatt hours, the tons, bushels, gallons and kilometres became characters in a heroic saga. . . .'

When I said that I fell in love with the First Five Year Plan, this was hardly an exaggeration. At twenty-five, I still regarded happiness as a problem in social engineering. Russia had undertaken the greatest engineering experiment in history—at a time when the remaining five-sixths of the world were visibly falling to pieces. Marxist theory and Soviet practice were the admirable and ultimate fulfilment of the nineteenth century's ideal of Progress, to which I owed allegiance. The greatest electric power dam in the world must surely bring the greatest happiness to the greatest number.

Five years earlier I had left home to help the building of the New Jerusalem. To resurrect the Jewish State after two thousand years appeared to me not only as a romantic undertaking, but at the same time as a kind of miracle cure for a sick race. I had been disappointed by the provincial chauvinism of Palestine; now a new Zion was in sight, on an infinitely larger, all-embracing scale. It again promised a magic cure—not only for a small ethnic group, but for the whole of mankind. And, just as the new Jewish State was meant to bring back the ancient age of the Prophets, so the Classless Society, according to Marx, would be a revival, at the end of the evolutionary spiral, of the primitive communistic society of a past golden age.

A short time before I actually joined the Party, I planned to throw up my job and to go, for a year or two, as a tractor driver to Russia. The Soviet State needed skilled tractor-men and I was an engineer; so the plan seemed logical. But the Party officials who took me in hand explained that it was a 'typically *petit-bourgeois* romantic idea', so I had to abandon it. I mention this project because it aimed at an exact, though unconscious repetition of my setting out for *Kvutsa* Heftsebā to become 'a drawer of water and a hewer of wood'. This time, however, I was past twenty-five, a veteran foreign correspondent and hard-boiled journalist. My readiness to repeat the same pattern of action proves that in my emotional life I was still an adolescent—but also it proves that, living in a disintegrating society, I was thirsting for faith, thirsting for an opportunity to build, create and construct.

To create, build, connect and construct . . . that was the lure of the New Faith. The world revolution was merely an inevitable formality which had to be accomplished before the Classless Society could be built, just as the Last Judgment had to precede the establishment of the Kingdom of Heaven on earth. The rule of the *bourgeoisie* had of course to be abolished, and its values, codes, taboos and mores thrown on the rubbish heap—in the same way as the *bourgeois* revolution of 1789 had done away with Feudalism, Aristocracy, the *jus primae noctis*, and all that nonsense. This could not be accomplished without some fighting and bloodshed—but that part of the programme left me rather indifferent. I was only interested in what was to come afterwards; in the building of that Communist society which meant the ultimate fulfilment of man's destiny. It would liberate his immense creative potentialities, now smothered and thwarted by the economic yoke. 'The average citizen of the classless society,' wrote Trotsky, 'will be raised to the level of an Aristotle, a Goethe, a Marx.' Once the yoke was shattered, man's Promethean energies would pour forth like lava after a volcanic eruption. They

would 'lift the earth from its axis', and tie it to the arrow
in the blue. . . .

It was a powerful belief, and its loss is a lasting impoverish-
ment. The majority of my comrades were moved by similar
notions; at least during the initial stages of their Party
career, the Promethean vision dominated the destructive
tendency. In later years I saw them change, one by one, as
the End receded from their vision, and the Means alone
remained. But that we could not foresee when, like the cap-
tive Tribe, we set out on our journey leaving the fleshpots
of Egypt behind. We did not yet know the desert; we knew
only that there was a Promised Land—and that the plagues
were descending on Pharaoh according to plan.

In one sense we were in a privileged position. Unlike other
revolutionary movements, from Christianity to the Socialists,
whose programmes were purely theoretical blueprints of the
future, our Utopia was already incarnated in a real country
with real people. Its inaccessibility and remoteness were an
additional advantage—it allowed free rein to one's imagination, stimulated by the picturesque costumes and nostalgic
songs of the steppes. Progress, Justice, Socialism were abstract
words that provided no food for dreams, no opportunity for
worship, love and identification. But now the homeless, dis-
persed socialist movement had gained a country, a flag, a
sense of power and self-confidence; and even a genuinely
beloved father-image in the silhouette of Lenin with the
shrewd Mongolian look in his twinkling, humorous eyes. The
epic struggle of a great people, fighting its battles of freedom
and playing the balalaika in between, satisfied our romantic
yearnings and filled us with a new sense of patriotism.

Our fragmentary knowledge of what was happening in
Russia assumed the character of a Homeric legend:

The People had come to power on one-sixth of the
earth. Private ownership, the greed for power, social dis-

tinctions, sexual taboos, had been abolished at one stroke. There were no longer rich and poor, masters and servants, officers and other ranks. The history of homo sapiens had started again from scratch. There was thunder behind each of these new decrees, like the voice from Sinai giving the Ten Commandments. Those who listened felt that a rigid crust inside them, the parched crust of scepticism, frustration, and resigned common sense had suddenly burst. They felt an emotional surge of which they had no longer thought themselves capable. A faith had been released in them, so deeply repressed that they had been unaware of its existence; a hope so deeply buried, that they had forgotten it....

The passage that I have quoted (from *The Yogi and the Commissar*) refers to the first years of the Russian Revolution. But in 1930 the Soviet régime was still in its early 'teens; the reality behind the myth was still difficult to discover for outsiders; besides, the effectiveness of Russia's appeal had been manifoldly increased because of the economic crisis and the threat of Fascism in Europe. Gentle Liberals, who disliked Marx and abhorred violence, came back from guided tours in Russia with a changed, friendly attitude towards 'the great Soviet experiment'. Worried industrialists and bankers admitted that, after all, 'there may be something in it'. The various 'Societies for promoting Cultural Relations with the U.S.S.R.' had on their Committees everybody from duchesses to dentists. And the unforgettable Russian films of that epoch received an enthusiastic welcome from critics and public, regardless of their political views.

When I remember films like 'Storm over Asia' or 'Potemkin', I still believe that they were among the most powerful emotional experiences of my past. To a lesser degree this is also true of the performances of Tairoff's and Meyerhold's theatres in Europe; and of the books of the new Soviet novelists—of Leonof's *The Thief*, Sholokhov's *Silent Don*, Serafimovich's *The Iron Flood*, and of Isaac Babel's stories of the Civil War. I don't know, and I do not want to know, how I would respond to them today; at the time it looked as if Soviet Russia were on its way to a fresh and radiant culture which in due time—probably at the end of the Second Five Year Plan—would equal the glories of the Renaissance and of the Golden-age of Greece.

And to think that the masterpieces of Eisenstein and Pudovkin were produced by the State; that Stanislavsky and Meyerhold and Wachtangof were employees of the State; that all literature, poetry and prose, was published by the State—that is, by the sovereign People, the workers and peasants, the greatest and most original patron of the Arts ever seen! A régime capable of such achievements could inspire only love and admiration, and a new faith in humanity.

It also seemed to me that Communist Russia continued where the Liberal Ullsteins had left off. That super-trust which I had served for the last five years in the Middle East, in Paris and Berlin, and to which I had become intimately attached, had represented in my eyes the embodiment of progressive Liberalism and of a bold *avant-guardism*. The revolutionary writers and poets of Germany had always been warmly acclaimed on our literary pages. There was in my eyes no break, but a logical continuity between the modernism of Weimar and the new Soviet culture, which seemed destined to become its heir.

This feeling of continuity also extended to the sphere of social problems. I have spoken of my dismay when the Ullsteins gave up their campaign against capital punishment. It was the Communist and fellow-travelling Press of Germany which continued the campaign, by setting up Russia's new penal code as an example. The same happened to other

social crusades which the Liberal press abandoned for fear
of the Nazis. I particularly remember our campaigns for a
reform of the laws concerning homosexuality and abortion.
Both were urgent problems in Germany. Homosexuality
was rampant; because of the legal ban on abortion, around
500,000 women of the poorer classes were taken to hospital
every year with sepsis or hæmorrhage, due to illegal operations performed by quacks or by themselves. In both cases
imprisonment was neither a deterrent nor a remedy. In both
cases the Liberal press, cowed by the accusation of promoting
immorality, dropped the campaign for legal reform; again
it was the Communist Party who took it up.

Wherever I looked, in every field of social and cultural
activity, the Communist movement appeared as the logical
extension of the progressive humanistic trend. It was the
continuation and fulfilment of the great Judeo-Christian
tradition—a new, fresh branch on the tree of Europe's progress through Renaissance and Reformation, through the
French Revolution and the Liberalism of the nineteenth
century, towards the socialist millennium.

How could this conception of historic continuity, of the
Communist Party as the respectful heir of a venerable cultural legacy, be reconciled with its other aspect of destructive
hatred, its avowed intention 'to abolish the past' completely
and for ever? The contradiction did not occur to me until
several years later; when it did, my newly acquired training
in dialectics took care of it. It explained that the seemingly
self-contradictory dual aspect of all social phenomena was
the very essence of evolution, which proceeded through the
negation of negations. Thus at the present stage Capitalist
Civilisation must be regarded as the thesis, the Proletarian
Revolution as its anti-thesis; the Classless Communist Society
of the future as the synthesis, in which the culture of the past
was negated, but its negation also negated. So all was well
and there was nothing to worry about.

This double-faced, Jekyll and Hyde character of the Communist movement was to become a decisive international factor during the next twenty years. Gentle, bedside-mannered Dr. Jekyll was in evidence during the years 1934–39 and 1941–45; he was a freedom-loving, peace-loving, anti-fascist, Popular Front-democrat with a polite and respectable vocabulary from which ugly words like 'class-struggle', 'revolution', and even the distinction between *bourgeois* and proletarians, was completely absent. Comrade Hyde, on the other hand, who dominated the scene in 1929–34 and 1939–41, declared that democracy was a sham and merely a disguised form of capitalist rule, of which Fascism was a more open variant, so that there was nothing to choose between the two; his rude manners and inflammatory speeches were in complete contrast to courteous Dr. Jekyll's. Since 1945, Dr. Jekyll and Comrade Hyde appear on the scene in quick alternation, and sometimes even at the same time—standing back to back and addressing different parts of the audience in opposite terms.

Though I am anticipating, this is the place to mention a curious psychological fact. The self-contradictory, split pattern of communist propaganda induces an equally split, schizophrenic mentality in those who are exposed to it. They only see, according to their bias, one of the twin aspects, and deny the existence of the other. The radically inclined believe in Comrade Hyde's revolutionary promises, regardless of the diplomatic deals, the compromises and betrayals of Dr. Jekyll; into this category enter the millions of economically distressed, politically naïve, C.P. voters in Europe and Asia. Confused Liberals, on the other hand, dismiss the existence of Comrade Hyde as a bogey invented by reactionary witch-hunters. This category includes a number of statesmen (from the late President Roosevelt down), politicians, scientists and artists in the West.

Such confusions and illusions were, however, more excusable in 1930 than in 1951. After the purges, the show trials, the Stalin-Hitler pact and so on, it required a larger and larger blind spot on the retina not to see the obvious. Hence the odd phenomenon, that among ex-Communists a certain importance is attached to the date or 'vintage' of one's one-time Party membership. This may sound like a new form of snobbery; but obviously there is a difference between the mentality of people who joined the movement in the nineteen-twenties when there was still hope, and those who joined after the liquidation of the Old Guard and the deification of Joseph Djugashwili.

My loyalty was put to a first test even before I had formally enlisted in the Party. As already mentioned, in March, 1931, the German Communists made common cause with the Nazis in initiating a referendum aimed at removing the Socialist government of Prussia from office. The dialectical arguments by which the Party leadership endeavoured to justify this absurd and suicidal move are too tedious to relate; the remarkable fact is that in spite of my critical faculties and my thorough training in practical politics, I accepted them. I had stepped inside the 'closed system', and tasted of that new witches' brew, which made the absurd logical to you.

With that step began a mental evolution which in retrospect appears to me as an attack of progressive insanity, lasting several years—a state of 'controlled schizophrenia' to quote Professor Klaus Fuchs who, out of sheer idealism, became an atom spy for the U.S.S.R. It was a mental process that worked simultaneously in two opposite directions.

On the one hand, the study of Marx, Engels and Lenin (nobody in the Party ever took Stalin seriously as a philosopher) opened genuinely new vistas on History, on past and present social relations; it provided a methodical approach to social phenomena more precise and 'concrete' than that of *bourgeois* sociologists; it served as a kind of compass which, in the presence of any problem in any walk of life, pointed, if not to its solution, at least to the direction from which it should be tackled. Although today I reject the End-justifies-the-Means ethics of Marxism; its rigid economic determinism; its dogma of the irreconcilable hostility between the classes; the rudimentary character of its mass-psychology, and, in fact, most of its basic tenets—I have nevertheless retained a residue of the Marxian method of approach as a valuable asset. I also still believe that the elimination of Marx and Engels from the history of human thought would leave a gap almost as large as the elimination of Darwin. However, during the last hundred years both sociology and genetics have covered new ground; so that to be an 'orthodox Marxist' today is as much of an anachronism as it would be for a biologist to call himself an 'orthodox Darwinist'.

While my Marxist training thus enriched my mental outlook and sharpened my critical faculties, it imposed on them at the same time a tendency towards an abstract, schematic, and oversimplified way of thinking which, for all the clever scholastics involved, was often staggeringly naïve. The danger of such logical short-circuits from sophistication to simplicity is inherent in all closed systems. Leaving for once the obvious parallels of the Freudian and Catholic churches aside, we find a recent and striking example in the conclusions drawn by Professor Toynbee from his monumental *A Study of History*. According to that eminent historian each vanishing civilisation leaves a new religion behind it which becomes the chrysalis of the next civilisation, except in our case—because Christianity is the last and ultimate religion. Though Professor Toynbee's system is not strictly a 'closed' one, and is immensely stimulating when viewed from a sceptical distance, *qua* system it has the fatal quality of setting mountains of facts in motion to produce a mouse of a conclusion.

The Marxist schema, for all its inner coherence, substituted for the portrait of man an X-ray photograph of his economic skeleton. You could diagnose with its help a fracture, or a softening of the bones, but nothing more. Hence, while the schema was extremely useful as far as it went, predictions of human behaviour based on it proved invariably wrong. A minimum of psychological insight into the mentality of the Russian peasant as it really was, and not as it ought to have been according to the schema, would have made it possible to foresee that the enforced collectivisation of 1930–31 would lead to disaster. And a more realistic approach to the phenomenon of Fascism would at least have prevented the Communists from making the absurd prediction that 'the year 1932 would see the final triumph of the communist revolution in Germany'.

Another consequence of applying the Marxist X-ray method to a complex situation was that colours and nuances vanished from the picture, and reality was represented in black and white. The analytical studies published in 1930 in the official periodicals of the Comintern were able to show with considerable precision the causes of the economic crisis, or the political ties between the National Socialist movement and the Ruhr industrialists, the Prussian Junkers, and so on. They also correctly predicted that, despite all contrary assertions, the leaders of the Reichswehr would submit to Hitler *en bloc*, and that the Socialists would offer no serious resistance. These studies were as a rule shrewd, concise, and documented in considerable detail—yet they were at the same time completely valueless as guides for political action because, applying the black-and-white schema, they lumped together 'Hitler-fascists', 'Social-fascists' (i.e. the Socialist Party), 'Bruening-fascists' (i.e. the Catholic Centre Party), and the 'imperialistic semi-fascist régimes'—meaning the

Governments of England, France and the United States.

The above is an example of what I meant when referring to the mentality that I had adopted as one of progressive schizophrenia—a method of thinking which, while in itself coherent and even ingenious, has lost touch with reality, or produces an absurd distortion of it.

One of the principal methods of distortion in Communist thought is what one might term 'arbitrary polarisations'. An example of an arbitrary polarisation is the statement: 'There are two categories of people: (a) the good ones who travel by train, and (b) the bad ones who travel by air.' With a little casuistry it can then be shown that people who travel by sea are (a) good, because they don't fly, and (b) bad, because they don't run on rails. For Communists, the world was at various times successively polarised in the following manner:

1930—Soviet Russia plus the international working class *versus* the capitalist world, which was a fascist world, because 'fascism is the inevitable last phase of capitalism'.

1940—The peace-loving Russian and German people *versus* the pluto-democratic imperialist aggressors: England and France.

1941—The bestial German fascist aggressors *versus* the united democratic nations: Russia, England, France and America.

1950—The criminal imperialist warmongers: England, France and America *versus* the peace-loving People's Democracies in the East.

Every one of these arbitrary polarisations was represented to the faithful as an eternal dualism like good and evil, darkness and light, and justified with all the persuasive ingenuity of closed-system logics. And each time there were millions who, thanks to the spontaneous amnesia which is one of the features of the schizophrenic mind, promptly forgot the last alignment and believed the present one to be the eternal truth.

When I ask myself with the melancholy wisdom that comes after the event, how I could have lived for years in this mental trance, I find some comfort in the thought that mediæval scholasticism and Aristotelian exegesis lasted for a much longer period, and completely befuddled the best brains of that time; and furthermore, that even in our day many approve of the idea that ninety per cent of their contemporaries are designated for an eternal super-Auschwitz by their loving Father in Heaven.

In fine, the mentality of a person who lives inside a closed system of thought, Communist or other, can be summed up in a single formula : He can prove everything he believes, and he believes everything he can prove. The closed system sharpens the faculties of the mind, like an over-efficient grindstone, to a brittle edge; it produces a scholastic, Talmudic, hair-splitting brand of cleverness which affords no protection against committing the crudest imbecilities. People with this mentality are found particularly often among the intelligentsia. I like to call them the 'clever imbeciles'—an expression which I don't consider offensive, as I was one of them.

XXXI. The Exploding Universe

IN spite of my premonition that doomsday was approaching, or rather independently of it, I threw myself with enthusiasm into my new job. It was an ideal job, with unlimited possibilities for roaming through the domains of science and fantasy, from the electron to the spiral nebulæ, from experiments in telepathy to the quest for the lost Atlantis. To be a science editor sounds like a rather dull occupation; I found it incomparably more exciting than that of a foreign correspondent or a war reporter. After four years of travel I had begun to tire of living in a whirl of colourful but undigested impressions, and of the superficiality of the type of journalism in which I had been engaged. I felt that during all this rush and bustle my mind had been free-wheeling; now, parallel to the reawakening of political interest, the questing, contemplative mood also reappeared. My new job made me turn back to my first youthful passion, to Science as a key to the ultimate mystery:

> Astrophysics is a science which should be pursued in the following manner. Drink some vodka on a clear, cold night, wrap your feet in a warm blanket, sit down on your balcony and stare into the sky. Preferred localities are mountainous regions with a faint thunder of avalanches in the distance; preferred time, the hours of melancholy. If this prescription is not followed, the science in question will appear as a petrified forest of numbers and equations; but he who observes the prescription will

experience a curious state of trance. The algebraic signs will change into violin clefs, X and Y will ring and boom like soprano and bass, and out of the bizarre equations will emerge the symphony of the rise and decline of the universe. . . .

This was the romantic preamble to an article on Professor Picard's famous balloon ascent into the stratosphere. Another piece, on the cultivation *in vitro* of living tissues—which, under proper conditions, are potentially immortal—began:

Philosophy is the gaseous state of thought, Science its liquid state, Religion its rigid state. In all three states doubts are expressed regarding the necessity, and even the possibility, of absolute death. We shall discuss this doubt only in its liquid state. . . .

The more I became engrossed in historical materialism, and in the dry schema of a world governed by the class struggles of Economic Man, the more romantic became, by a kind of backstroke process, my approach to science. This, however, was not a purely subjective reaction. Just at that time science itself was in the throes of a revolutionary crisis which was rapidly demolishing all familiar assumptions of thought, and replacing our traditional concepts of reality by a new, wildly futuristic picture of the world. The arrow in the blue no longer pursued its flight in a straight line through infinity; it followed an elliptical path through the curved space of a finite universe, and would eventually return to its point of origin from the opposite direction like a traveller on the earth always heading due east. It had even become possible to foretell how long the arrow would take to return to the hills of Buda, whence it had started its flight past the moon, the sun, the galaxies and spiral nebulæ, on a summer afternoon during the school holidays of 1919. Provided it flew with the speed of light, it would take approximately 10^{11}, that is no more than a hundred thousand million years. In the new Relativistic cosmology, the universe had lost its attribute of infinity, as the earth had lost it some centuries ago; and from the average density of the material which it contained, it had become possible to calculate that its 'diameter' amounted to between ten and a hundred thousand million light-years.

Even more startling was the discovery that this finite world of ours was expanding at a terrific speed, like, to quote Einstein, 'an exploding grenade'. This conclusion was reached by direct observation of the distant nebulæ, whose spectra indicated that they were all running away from us; the farther away they were, the quicker they went. So we were living, both in the political and in the physical sense, in an exploding world. From the speed of flight of the nebulæ, and the average density of matter in space, it could also be calculated when the explosion had started. The answer was: approximately 10^{10} to 10^{11} years ago. On the other hand, the solid crust of the earth was only about 10^{9} years old. From this it seemed to follow that the whole universe was only ten to a hundred times as old as the earth. So either the Old Testament was vindicated, or something had gone wrong with interpreting the data. I obtained an exclusive interview with Einstein on his return from his visit to Mount Wilson Observatory in 1931, and got my comments straight from the horse's mouth, as it were. Einstein was not in the least disturbed by the fact that our universe was exploding:

'If you just simply take the findings of General Relativity,' he explained in his gentle and cosy manner, 'and put beside them the empirical findings about the expansion of cosmic matter, then you arrive straight at a solution which shows that the relation between the rate of expansion and the mean density of matter agree quite nicely with what you would expect. . . .' So far so good. '. . . But,' Einstein continued, 'the speed of this expansion is, according to recent observations, simply dreadful (*'fürchterlich gross'*) . . .' He agreed that the idea of a universe only about ten times older than the earth was 'not nice at all'; but was confident that 'if we keep our eyes open, something will turn up to get us round this difficulty'.

This interview, incidentally, was one of the two occasions in my journalist years on which I employed unfair means. Einstein was so fed up with the sensational reports in the American Press during his trip, that after his return he refused to see any newspapermen. So I rang him up and, taking advantage of his good-natured, simple ways, induced him to talk shop over the telephone—with a stenographer posted on another extension. (My second breach of journalistic etiquette was committed years later, during the Spanish Civil War, when I obtained access to Rebel territory by pretending to be a Hungarian fascist.)

During my science editorship, not only was the universe exploding, but the microcosmos, the inside of the atom, was in even worse fermentation. Work on the splitting of the atomic nucleus was making rapid strides. One of the most adventurous efforts in this field was an experiment by three young Berlin physicists—Brasch, Lange and Urban—to smash atoms with lightning from the sky—quite literally. The cyclotron and synchroton were not yet invented; and to split atoms effectively in those days, tensions of several million volts were needed. To obtain these, the three enterprising young physicists built a laboratory 5,000 feet high in the Italian Alps, on Monte Generoso, and obtained discharges up to fifteen million volts by flying a kite in the thunderclouds over the peaks. Such a Promethean challenge to the gods could not remain unpunished; one of the three, Kurt Urban, fell off a rock and was killed.

One of my first science articles in the *Vossische Zeitung* discussed the future of atom splitting; it occupied an entire page, under the melodious heading : *'Millionen wohnen in den Atomen . . .'* and brought in a shower of protests from German academic circles because it was so 'fantastic and utopian' :

> . . . If our reading of these phenomena is correct, then we are on the eve of a new era in the history of man, and the technological progress of the last hundred years, which has so radically changed the face of the earth, will be regarded by the future Historian as a mere fumbling prelude to the performances of a utopian society . . . It is characteristic that the signs of the coming new technological age should appear in these times of social and political confusion, of a chaotic malaise . . .

There followed some optimistic speculation about the peaceful uses of atomic energy, and some anxious speculation about destructive chain-reactions which might transform the nucleus

> . . . into a Pandora's box charged with lightning bolts. Is there no Faustian Earth-Spirit to guard the entrance of the microcosmos, where Nature's most secret forces dance their electronic rounds?

No wonder the Herr Professors didn't like it. . . . About the same time Chadwick at Cambridge published experimental proof of the existence of the neutron, while Hahn and Meitner at Dahlem were working on radio-active fission. The contents of Pandora's box were rapidly being assembled. By a special fluke of history, the hydrogen isotope No. 2 (heavy water) was discovered in the course of the same few months—which sent German atom bomb research off on the wrong track.

Even more important than this twin-revolution in the realms of the infinitely large and the infinitely small, was the philosophical upheaval which accompanied them, and which became known as 'the crisis of causality'. Absolute space and absolute time had already gone overboard; the third pillar of our traditional view of the world, the law of causal determination, now followed suit. The so-called Laws of Nature lost their solid character; they could no longer be regarded as expressing certainties, merely statistical proba-bilities. The rigid causal connections between 'cause' and 'effect' were loosened, softened up as it were; the physicist found himself living in a world where it was no longer possible for him to say: 'Under such and such conditions this and that will happen'; he could merely say: 'This and that is *likely* to happen.' What he had regarded as universal laws now turned out to be mere rules of the thumb, whose validity was limited to medium-sized phenomena; on the sub-atomic level determinism itself dissolved in a kind of blurred fringe, and all certainty had vanished from the universe.

This crisis had been brewing in the physicists' laboratories since the beginning of the century; but its full philosophical implications only became apparent around 1930. The law of Rutherford and Soddy, published in 1903, had already implied that the collapse of radio-active atoms was 'spon-taneous', that is, independent of the atom's physical state, position and environment; and that the most complete description of the atom's present condition in physical terms permitted no predictions regarding its future. Its destiny, in the words of Sir James Jeans, seemed determined 'from inside and not from outside'. The individual atom seemed to experience freedom at least in the sense that no explanation of its behaviour was possible in the language of physics. In 1917 Einstein showed that the right to 'spontaneous' col-lapse had to be accorded *all* atoms. Then, between 1927 and '32, a series of swift blows put an end to the age-old illusion of a solid, rigid, causally determined world. Schroedinger's wave-mechanics implied that the exact whereabouts of an electron travelling through space could only be expressed in terms of probabilities; Heisenberg's 'Uncertainty Relation' seemed to prove that the same ambiguity reigned with regard to electrons inside the atom, and moreover, that an exact determination of the position and momentum of such electrons was not only practically impossible but also theoretically *unthinkable*. Within a certain, though very narrow margin—Planck's quantum 'h'—the data as such became blurred, events were undeterminable, and 'measurement' was a meaningless term. At about the same time Dirac published his matrix mechanics which assumed that all phenomena in space and time arise from a sub-stratum which is not in space and time and is entirely beyond measurable grasp. By 1932 the tidy Newtonian view of the universe had been replaced by a kind of expressionistic portrait full of such horrors as 'negative energies', 'holes in space', and electrons 'moving in the opposite sense of time'.

This upheaval, which I witnessed so closely, had a profound influence on my spiritual development; but once again the lesson was slow to sink in, and its assimilation was not a conscious process. At sixteen, I had lived in a neatly arranged, comprehensible clockwork-universe whose last mystery was just about to be solved. At twenty-six I saw the arrogant self-confidence of the nineteenth century scientist collapse, and the commandment 'Thou shalt not make unto thee any graven image' acquire a new meaning with regard to curved space, electrons, wave-packets and a universe in permanent explosion. Since the Renaissance, the Ultimate Cause had gradually shifted from the heavens to the atomic nucleus, from the super-human to the sub-human level. But now it became clear that the working of this 'destiny from below' was just as unfathomable in terms of man's spatio-temporal experience as 'destiny from above' had been. I learnt a decisive lesson in intellectual modesty which, without my noticing it, counterbalanced the 'total explanations' offered by Marxist philosophy.

In still another way my return to Science acted as a corrective to the Marxian 'closed system'. In that system the course of History appears rigidly determined by economic forces; individual responsibility has no place in it. Historical materialism is a typical product of the nineteenth century, in keeping with the mechanical clockwork-universe of its physics—a clockwork which, once it has somehow been wound up, will unrelentingly follow its preordained course. But this rigid schema was no longer in keeping with the twentieth century's conceptions of the physical world, of biological processes, psychological motivations. The philosophical part of the Marxian doctrine was, by the time I became acquainted with it, already an anachronism. But this a disciple of the 'closed system' could not admit, even to himself. So, I modified and adapted the doctrine, in the process of absorbing it, for my private use. (Later on I discovered that some of my intellectual comrades, too, had arrived at their private brand of Marxism which, for fear of being accused of heresy, they kept to themselves. There also existed small, secret factions in the Communist movement who adhered to some esoteric version of the official doctrine.)

The problem that particularly worried me was that of individual responsibility in politics, and the related question of ethical values. The tentative solution which science offered was that the movements of History were determined by laws not of a rigidly causal, but of a statistical nature, comparable to the physical laws of probability :

A great mass of people exposed for a long time to certain pressures and stimuli—climatic, economic, and so on —will sooner or later react in certain roughly predictable ways. But the emphasis is on 'sooner or later' and on 'roughly'; they provide a margin of unpredictability, and

within that margin the 'subjective factors' of chance and
leadership exert their influence. If we survey History in big
time-units, in centuries instead of decades, the importance
of this 'subjective factor' becomes negligible, and statistical
probabilities become certainties. Thus we may confidently
predict that the increased speed of communications will
inevitably lead to a unified Europe; if Hitler did not
succeed in doing it Stalin may, and if Stalin doesn't, somebody else will, within a century or two. History resembles
a river, and the 'subjective factor' a boulder thrown into
its bed. A mile farther down the water will flow in its
broad bed, determined by the general structure of the
terrain, as if the boulder had never existed. But for a
short stretch of, say, a hundred yards or years, the shape
of the boulder does make a considerable difference.

Now politics do not count in units of centuries, but of
years, thus leaving a margin of freedom and subjective
responsibility to the leaders. It is not an abstract responsibility to History, but an ethical responsibility to their contemporaries. *Historically* it would make little difference
whether Hitler unified Europe or some future figure. For
within a century or two from now, the rough edges of
Nazism would have been polished down, Jew-baiting
would have shrunk to an episode of the past, and the lasting result would have been a unified Europe which, round
about A.D. 2500, would have displayed much the same
general features as the one which Hitler's successor will
create. But *politically*, that is, counted in short time-units,
the difference is enormous—both with regard to the
amount of human suffering involved, and the painful
detour forced upon the river's course. . . .[1]

Thus the two decisive years, 1930–32, which I spent in
Berlin, stood again under the sign of the split arrow, the dual

[1] *The Yogi and the Commissar,* 1944.

temperament which drove me in two opposite directions:
into the fanatical ranks of the Communist Party and towards
detached scientific contemplation. At that time, however,
there was as yet no practical conflict between the two; that
conflict, with its incertitudes, torments and self-contradic-
tions came much later. At twenty-five, the crusade for
Utopia and the quest for Truth, the dubious battles of the
day and the vista of eternity, seemed to complement each
other.

The reason for this is not only that I was then twenty
years younger. In 1931 we lived under the fascist threat, but
we saw an inspiring alternative in Russia. In 1951 we live
under the Russian threat, but there is no inspiring alternative in sight; we are forced to fall back on the threadbare
values of the past. In the 'thirties, there existed a specious
hope; in the 'fifties, only an uneasy resignation. Not I alone
—the whole century has grown middle-aged.

XXXII. Of Charlatans and Cranks

IN one unexpected sense the arrow in the blue was becoming material reality : rocket-propulsion brought space travel to planets and stars within the reach of technological possibility. In America, Science Fiction was already flourishing in pulp magazines; in the Europe of 1930, the general public was still unaware of the fantastic vista of astronautics. From the point of view of the science editor, this was virgin territory, and I applied myself with enthusiasm to its cultivation. Next to atom-splitting, interplanetary travel became my main journalistic hobby.

In one field, or rather borderland of science, my journalistic efforts remained completely unsuccessful : occultism. Some time in 1931 I put the following advertisement in all four Ullstein dailies :

CREDO QUIA ABSURDUM

Scientist is looking for authentic reports on occult experiences—telepathy, clairvoyance, levitation, etc. Reports will be suitably paid for provided that they can be verified beyond any reasonable doubt through independent trustworthy witnesses; otherwise they will not be taken into consideration.

I was afraid of being snowed under by thousands of letters. Actually, I only received between thirty and forty—the last sentence in the advertisement, or the Latin headline, had evidently put people off. Not a single one of the communications lent itself to verification in a form which would satisfy the requirements of scientific evidence.

I tried a second experiment whose result was equally negative in an objective sense, but amusing from a psychological point of view. In those days a charlatan named Eric Jan Hanussen enjoyed a great vogue in Europe, and particularly in Germany. Hanussen was a cheap modern version of the Count of Cagliostro. He was a good hypnotist, and did the usual tricks—lining up volunteers from his audience on the stage, putting them into a trance, and making them perform ludicrous actions on command. In addition, his repertory included routine experiments in the finding of hidden objects, 'thought-reading' stunts, the deciphering of messages in sealed envelopes, and the rest. None of this was particularly remarkable by the usual standards in this field, but Hanussen had a special knack for publicity which explains his swift rise to fame and his lurid end. When a newspaper accused him of bamboozling his audiences, he sued for libel, turned the courtroom into a variety show under pretext of providing evidence of his occult faculties, and completely dazed the poor members of the jury. He was the confidant of one of the Nazi leaders, Count Helldorf, who later became Chief of the Berlin Police. In Count Helldorf's villa on the Wannsee, Hanussen acted as master of ceremonies at nocturnal orgies, in the course of which he put pretty actresses into hypnotic trances and made them display the emotions experienced in a fictitious lover's embrace.

When the Nazis took power, Hanussen became their Court magician and astrologer—until the Gestapo discovered that his real name was not Eric Jan Hanussen but Herman Steinschneider, and that instead of being a Danish Baron as he pretended to be, he was the son of a Jewish merchant from Prossnitz, Bohemia. A few days later his body, riddled with bullets, was found in the woods on the outskirts of Berlin.

I met Hanussen some time in 1931. He was a short, squat, swarthy man with quick movements and an extremely dynamic personality, which was not lacking in charm. My purpose was not to test his alleged occult powers—that would have required a technical apparatus beyond my means —but to test the reliability of observers who believe themselves to be objective, when exposed to a personality of this type. The procedure which I devised was as follows. Two journalists—a lady considered an expert in occultism and myself—were to make Hanussen perform a certain experiment in our presence. We were not to exchange our observations, nor to comment on the experiment to each other, but to write down independently what each of us thought he or she had seen. Then we would compare the reports and see what journalistic use we could make of them.

The experiment itself was a simple test in so-called psychometry—the divining of events associated with an inanimate object or with the owner of the object. The owner of the object to be psychometrised had, of course, to be a third person and a reliable, honest soul. We agreed on Herr Apfel, the trusty head-porter of the house of Ullstein, who had occupied that post for some thirty years—a model of Prussian efficiency, correctness and pedantry.

At the appointed hour the three of us presented ourselves at Hanussen's sumptuous villa, which was decorated in what one might call the lacquer-Japanese, functional Neo-Gothic Al Capone style. We were offered liquors, cigars, and a choice of preliminary warming-up experiments, all of which we sternly refused. No conversation was permitted between Hanussen and Herr Apfel, so as not to allow the magician to form an opinion of the psychological lie of the land. Somewhat dismayed by this puritan procedure, Hanussen came at last, somewhat reluctantly, to the point. He turned briskly to Apfel and told him : 'Give me that bunch of keys in your left-hand trouser-pocket !'

M

Herr Apfel was not impressed. According to his instructions he listened to everything that Hanussen said without nodding consent or shaking his head in denial, and thus gave Hanussen no lead whatsoever. Hanussen clutched the keys in one hand, pressed the other against his forehead, occasionally closed his eyes and told us in a trailing, trancelike voice that the keys spoke to him of severe illness and recovery; of an act of violence; of the delivery of a healthy child after much anguish; of a long-expected inheritance; of somebody afflicted with a feeling of liverishness or chronic constipation, and of a burglary—which, however, may have been committed in the neighbourhood. When he had finished, we all looked expectantly at Herr Apfel.

'Well,' said Herr Apfel, calmly recovering his keys, 'to tell the truth no event of the kind described by the gentleman has occurred since I got these keys, which was thirty years ago. Except,' he added thoughtfully, 'I did feel liverish around last Christmas.'

We went home and wrote our reports. The next day the lady journalist, whose name I have forgotten, showed me hers. It ran something like this :

'I had entertained grave doubts regarding the mediumistic faculties of Eric Jan Hanussen. These doubts have been entirely dispelled by the spectacular experiment in psychometry which Hanussen performed yesterday in the presence of two reliable witnesses, Herr Apfel and Herr Koestler, in his tastefully furnished villa in the Tiergarten. Using a bunch of keys belonging to Herr Apfel as a contact-object, he produced the following psychometric associations. . . .' (Here followed an enumeration of all that Hanussen had said, from 'severe illness' to 'burglary in the neighbourhood'.) 'I can solemnly testify and prove that all the events listed by Hanussen have in fact happened in the course of the last year; however, these events have happened not to Herr Apfel, but to me. My explanation of this phenomenon is that in the taxi which took us to Hanussen's villa, I was sitting close to Herr Apfel on the side on which he carries his keys; this physical contact with the test object has evidently caused Hanussen to establish the subconscious psychometric nexus with me, while believing that it was Herr Apfel. . . .'

Out of kindness to the lady, the story of the Hanussen experiment was never published.

Thus life as a science editor was full of variety and excitement. I could pick my theme according to mood and taste, from space travel to a new type of vacuum cleaner, from genetics to diesel engines—for applied research and technology also belonged to my department. The four daily papers, the dozen or so of weeklies and monthlies published by the Ullsteins provided a practically unlimited outlet. The relatively high level of scientific education in German schools made the task of vulgarisation much easier than it is in Western Europe and the Anglo-Saxon countries. I was given an entirely free hand by my various editors, and this independence was an inestimable boon after the severe regimentation in the Paris office. At the same time I was obliged to read a score or more of scientific and technical journals to keep abreast of new developments, and though I soon forgot all specialised details, the general residue of this drudgery was a broad over-all view of the methods, achievements and trends in contemporary science and philosophy.

For the average newspaper reader it is difficult to form an idea of the versatility which a person engaged on a job of this kind is compelled to develop. To illustrate this point, here is an incomplete list of the subjects on which I wrote articles for the *Vossische* during my first few months in Berlin :

The atom-smashers on Monte Generoso—What is the Raman Effect? (The Hindu, Raman, was awarded the

Nobel Prize for 1930)—A new type of movie camera for amateurs—The outbreak of the Volcano Merapi in Java— The crisis of causality—The death-fog in the Valley of the Maas (in that Belgian valley around 100 persons were killed in 1930 by a mysterious black fog)—Problems in Heredity —Results of the dissection of Lenin's brain, and problems of brain-physiology in general—More about heredity and eugenics—New directions in cancer research—New burglar-warning devices, electronic compasses and other inventions —The uses of radio-activity in geology, metallurgy, medicine, etc.—The exploding universe—How does one become a Doctor of Agronomy?—Thyxotrophy and other news in colloidal chemistry—Life rays and death rays—and so on, and so on.

A fascinating part of this work was the investigation of crank inventors and of eccentrics, working on the border-lands of science, who might be swindlers or unknown geniuses. I spent two days examining a conventional type of electric generator with a new arrangement of the armature coil, constructed by a Berlin engineer named Paul Hoffman, which seemed to yield an energy output ten per cent higher than ordinary machines. If the claim was correct, this would mean a technological revolution. A number of experts— including engineers employed by the Siemens research laboratory and several technological advisers to German courts —had testified that the claim *was* correct. So I wrote a cautious report on Hoffman's 'Wonder-Dynamo', and nearly lost my job because of it. The article was quoted by other papers in Germany and abroad; reporters came flocking to Hoffman—who thereupon, in a sudden fit of emotional unbalance or insanity, put forward the claim that his machine had an efficiency quotient of over a hundred per cent. Now an 'efficiency' (the word is used here in its technological sense) of over a hundred per cent means that the machine is generating energy out of itself, in other words that it is functioning as a so-called '*perpetuum mobile* of the first type'; and an engineer who puts forward such a claim is either a charlatan or a lunatic. Protests came flooding into the editorial offices of the *Vossische*; I had to write a second piece in which I repeated the experts' testimonies already quoted in the first, and at the same time disclaimed any responsibility for the extravagant statements made in the meantime by Hoffman himself. There the matter ought to have ended, but it didn't. A few days later I was summoned into the presence of one of the Ullstein brothers—the one with the notoriously lowest I.Q. of the five.

'I have here a letter,' he said, with his habitual worried look, 'which I would like you to read.' The letter was from a German professor of physics with an international reputation. It asked in a peremptory tone for the dismissal of 'that ignoramus of a science editor, who in the respected columns of your paper voices the insane claim of an obvious charlatan who pretends without blushing that he has invented a machine with a *Wirkungsgrad* (efficiency) of over 100%.' I explained to Herr Ullstein that the professor must have misread my article, and that I had never pretended that the machine worked over the hundred-per-cent level.

'Why shouldn't it work over one hundred per cent?' my employer asked musingly.

I explained that this was impossible according to the Second Law of Thermodynamics—known as the 'Law of the Conservation of Energy'.

'But why are you so sure that this law is correct? Laws come and go. You shouldn't be such a doctrinaire. I like my editors to have an open mind. . . .' And he produced a second letter, obviously written by a crank, who protested against my having said that the machine could *not* work over the hundred-per-cent limit.

I tried to explain that the two charges were mutually contradictory. Was I accused of attacking the Second Law of

Thermodynamics—which I hadn't done—or of defending it?

'How do you expect me to know about the Second Law of Thermodynamics?' retorted Herr U. 'But *you* ought to know what you are talking about.'

Fortunately, he left it at that; but from that day on Herr U. took a profound dislike to me.

In a special category with a certain historic interest are inventions which are scientifically and technologically sound, and yet, for economic or other reasons, never quite make the grade. For example, there was the 'Zeppelin on Rails'—an aerodynamically streamlined rail-car, shaped in the typical cigar-form of the Zeppelin, and driven by an air-propeller at the back. After a few successful test-runs in the summer of 1931 between Hamburg and Berlin—a distance of a hundred and sixty miles, which the vehicle negotiated in an hour and a half, thus averaging over 100 m.p.h., and reaching a top speed of 151 m.p.h.—the 'rail-Zepp', as it was affectionately called, became the craze of Germany—only to be completely forgotten a few months later. The test runs were sponsored by the German State Railways, and the inventor—a gentle little man with a black, pointed beard called Dr. Kruckenberg—seemed to be one of the few inventors destined to see his dreams materialise. I met him one morning at 5 o'clock in July, 1932, at the Berlin-Spandau station, as he climbed out of his fantastic and yet aesthetically perfect vehicle after the completion of the first trial run from Hamburg (the trials had of course to be conducted at night when the rails could be freed of other traffic). His wife, a timid provincial woman, had been with him on the test; both were slightly shaky and radiant with happiness. It seemed not at all crankish when Kruckenberg explained that this hour would mark the beginning of a new epoch in human communications—rail-traffic would be revolutionised and gain the upper hand over its competitors, aeroplane and motor car, both much less safe and more expensive.

Similar technologically sound revolutions which came off nearly, but not quite, during my time, were Flettner's rotor ship, driven by an upright revolving cylinder instead of propeller, mast or sails; the wind-turbines of Engineer Honeff, based on a similar principle, which promised the tapping of the energy of atmospheric movements on a much larger scale than hydro-electric power-stations could tap the energy of river movements; the various machines designed to exploit the energy of the tides and the temperature differences of various oceanic depths (Claude's 'Ocean-Turbine'); finally, hydroponics—the art of growing vegetables and grains without soil, in water-tanks impregnated with chemicals (in this field, at least, experimentation is still continuing).

As far as a science editor can have a policy, mine was a definite bias towards a 'naturalistic' trend in technology—that is to say towards '. . . inventions which tend to exploit natural sources of energy in a clean, direct and elegant manner, by-passing the archaic drudgery of coal-mining, and the wasteful, unhygienic and air-poisoning methods of low-grade combustion. In the visions of a naturalistic technology there is no place for such purgatoria as the stokehold of a steamship, or a mining-shaft; nor for such pariah occupations as the dustman's or the chimney sweep's. The energy supply of the future must come from sources purer, closer to nature, and incomparably more powerful than those now used; from solar radiations concentrated by giant parabolic mirrors and stored in tidy heat accumulators; from turbines which suckle energy direct from the great mother of organic life, the ocean; from power-stations fed by the natural movements of rain, river and wind; from the very same radioactive transformations of matter into energy which govern the rise and fall of stars, galaxies and spiral nebulæ. In other words, technology will be integrated into the natural processes on which all organic life is based, with only this difference that machines are capable of feeding on cosmic energies in a more concentrated form and of transforming them more effectively than organic beings.'

Another invention, or rather a whole series of inventions, which had reached maturity yet failed to graduate for production, were electric musical instruments. Without Hitler and the war, they might have revolutionised the leisure habits of the civilised world and put an end to the juke-box and related horrors of canned music.

Some of these instruments I heard demonstrated at the 'Eleventh Congress of Radio Music', in Munich, in the summer of 1931. Among them was an electronic Bechstein baby grand, designed by Professor Nernst, one of the world's leading physicists, and made jointly by the firms of Bechstein and Siemens. It had of course nothing in common with the dreadful 'electrical pianos', pianolas, or whatever they are called. These are ordinary pianos operated, in lieu of human hands, by electrically driven punch tapes, like barrel organs. The Bechstein-Siemens baby grand worked by an entirely new method. It had a keyboard which you used like that of any other piano and it had strings; but it had no sounding board. The vibrations of the strings—which, in the absence of a sounding board are too faint to be heard—were transformed into electrical impulses and translated into music by an amplifier. The same principle was applied by Vierling to his electrical violin. The violin was played like any other with a bow on four strings; but it had no resonant body.

Now the difference between a Stradivarius and a cheap fiddle is in the body—its shape, the quality of the wood and varnish, the glue, the exact fitting together of the parts. The function of the body is to amplify the strings' vibrations, which are too faint to be audible of themselves. But in doing so, the resonant body adds to the desired tone a number of undesired overtones and mars the purity of its timbre. The whole art of body-making aims at keeping down these parasitic overtones. By eliminating the body altogether, and replacing it by an electronic amplifier, desirable harmonics could be added at will, undesirable parasites kept away—in other words, it became theoretically possible to produce cheap instruments of the quality of a Stradivarius or a Bluethner.

Naturally, the quality of the performance would still depend on the skill of the performer. But the availability of near-perfect instruments at a cheap price might well have caused a revolution in the public's attitude towards music. Musical taste develops automatically by learning to play an instrument. A cook hates eating canned soup; a person who plays the violin, however modestly, becomes allergic to the musical ketchup poured out by the ton by the radio stations. The reason why our culture is in danger of being drowned in a flood of acoustic and visual slush is that the rotary press, radio and television make the masses passive receivers of 'art', and condition their taste to the lowest level. Folk music in any country could never sink so low, because it is based on the active participation of the people, and is performed on instruments within the people's reach.

While the Bechstein-Siemens piano and the Vierling violin were aimed at the perfecting of conventional musical instruments, there was in the same period a crop of inventions designed to create a new type of futuristic music. At the Munich Congress Hindemith conducted the first performance of his 'Concert for Trautonium and Strings'. The Trautonium was an electronic instrument invented by a certain Trautwein. It was played by moving one's hand along a metal rod, and produced eerie sounds of a curiously exciting

M*

quality. The Frenchman Martenot invented an equally uncanny contraption which was meant to reproduce the 'music
of the spheres', while the Russian Teremin specialised in
'Aether music'—which was produced by simply moving
one's hand in graceful curves in front of an electrically
charged panel, as a conductor gesticulates in front of his
orchestra.

I mention these curiosities because the contours, if not the
content, of a civilisation are determined by its technological
features, and it often depends on small hazards whether a
certain feature will become prominent or not develop at all.
There are inventions and techniques which are given a
tremendous impetus by war—like aviation, atomic piles,
rockets, brain surgery; and others which, in the absence of
such tragic catalisers, fizzle out or are actualised much later,
though potentially they could alter the whole profile of our
culture. It is strange and exciting to observe how much that
everchanging profile is shaped by the 'subjective factor' of
history, generally regarded as accidental.

There is one particular kind of inventor, half-way between
genius and crank, who seems to be fated for pathetic failure,
and whose life is a permanent tragi-comedy. Inventors of
this type mostly have original ideas and the elements of
technical know-how; but they regard considerations of
production-cost and industrial economy with a lofty disdain,
and thus produce machines which work 'in principle' and
are yet technical monstrosities. Poor Professor Nathan, who
sold my father his giant envelope-opening contraption,
belonged to this type; in Berlin I was to meet quite a number
of others.

One day, I drove an automobile which, incredible as it
sounds, used for fuel nothing but air and water. . . . It
worked, after a fashion, and its inventor, one Erich Graichen
from the village of Altenburg in Thuringia, had put all his

hopes in it. If you could run a car on nothing but air and water, and it worked, were you not entitled to foresee the end of General Motors and Standard Oil, and yourself in the role of a new Henry Ford?

Graichen's car developed $\frac{1}{2}$ h.p.; in other words, it had the strength of one half horse. He was a little man who had built the model with his own hands. It carried one person, its body consisted mainly of cardboard reinforced by a packing crate, and upholstered with two cushions from the family sofa; its brakes were operated by shoe-strings. But it ran. It ran at a maximum speed of twenty-five miles per hour, had been duly licensed by the Thuringian Motor Transport Office, taxed by the Revenue Department, patented by the German *Reichs-Patent Amt*. It took three years to build; when it was finished Graichen, a modern Ulysses, set out from Altenburg in Thuringia for the metropolis, Berlin.

For the benefit of the technically minded, here is how this fantastic vehicle worked. It had a battery, which acted through an electro-magnet on the back axle, as in the pre-First World War electrical automobiles. Now a battery has to be recharged at frequent intervals, and that is where the innovation came in. To recharge his battery *en route* Graichen used the following method. Firstly, the battery was connected with an electromotor which, when the car drove uphill, acted as a dynamo and helped to turn the wheels; when the car rolled downhill, it acted as a generator and helped to charge the battery. Secondly, additional current for recharging was provided by a cylinder containing compressed air, which via air-pump drove the aforementioned generator. Thirdly, to make compressed air, there were a number of small air-pumps activated by the vibrations of the chassis and by the action of the brakes. Fourthly, additional energy for the air-compressor was gained by transforming water through electrolysis into oxyhydrogen gas and exploding it! In other words, all that Graichen had gained was that he had to recharge his battery at less frequent intervals.

Graichen started on his great journey to Berlin on a Tuesday morning—November 3, 1931, at 6 o'clock. As his car had only room for one, Graichen's wife, his friend Ferdinand Frühauf, a mechanic named Ewald Ihle, and an assortment of spare parts followed him in a taxi-cab, as a lifeboat follows a Channel swimmer. The taxi-cab belonged to one Paul Müller of Altenburg.

Leipzig was reached on the same morning without incident. On the way out of Leipzig, the car broke down. It took two days to repair it. On Thursday evening, November 5, the journey was resumed.

On the Düben Moors the rear axle broke. It was welded together, and the journey continued the next day.

On Sunday, November 8, our travellers reached the town of Wittenberg, seat of an ancient university. Here they partook of a hearty meal, and as they were about to leave Wittenberg discovered that some practical joker had stolen several essential working parts of the machine. Undaunted, Graichen attached his car by a rope to the taxicab and was towed into the borough of Treunbrietzen. In Treunbrietzen, the missing parts were replaced by spares, and on Monday, November 9, at 4 a.m. the caravan made its triumphant entry into Berlin.

On the following Wednesday, at 4 p.m., I talked to Graichen and tried his car. Two hours later he rang me up at the office to say that while he and his wife had been sitting in a coffee-house, the most expensive part of the car, the electro-magnet, had vanished; and with it Müller, the taxi-driver, Ihle, the mechanic, a camera, and all the documents from the Patent Office.

Poor Graichen. . . . His story was typical of the grotesque tragedies which inevitably befall the crank inventor. I felt such sympathy for him that, disregarding the qualms of my professional conscience, I gave him a big write-up in the paper, hoping that somebody would take an interest in his patent, or offer him a job. But a few days later he vanished from Berlin, and I never heard of him again.

Less interesting than the crank inventor is the crank scientist who discovers that the earth is not convex but a hollow sphere, with sun, moon, and stars circling not outside but inside it; or that all inter-stellar space consists of solid ice; or that the earth stopped spinning in 1500 B.C. after a near-collision with Venus. The crank inventor usually produces at least a model of sorts, however absurd; the crank scientist is mostly a monomaniac, if not outright insane. In two years at the science desk I met more cranks than during seven years among revolutionary intellectuals—and that means saying a lot. Among them was a man who had invented a new alphabet consisting only of symmetrical letters which—like the letter O—looked the same when read upside down or sideways. By adopting this symmetrical alphabet, he explained, one book or newspaper could be read by four people at the same time—from the North, South, East and West. And he proved to me with great enthusiasm, how many billion marks of national income could be saved annually in this way.

Only in rare cases is there occasion for doubt as to whether the prophet of some new theory is a crank, charlatan or genius; or possibly a mixture of the three. Such a case was a Russian named George Lhakovsky, in Paris. He claimed that every body-cell was an electric resonator, the nuclear chromosomes acting as vibration-circuits surrounded by a faint electro-magnetic field of a specific frequency. Any disturbance in the chromosomes or in the surrounding medium would alter this natural frequency of the cell and manifest itself as illness. The 'tuning' of the circuit could be altered by such factors as improper mineral balance; the presence of virus and bacteria; abnormal fluctuations in solar and cosmic radiations and the secondary radiations caused by them. (That is, of course, where the sun-spots came in.) Hence, to keep the body protected against harmful radiations, Lhakovsky invented a belt consisting of an insulated, open copper spiral, to be worn round the waist or as a necklace, armlet, ankle-band, etcetera. For a while these contraptions (a modern version of the charms against the evil eye) sold like hot cakes in Paris and—thanks to an enterprising export firm—in Budapest. Needless to say, thousands of people swore that since they wore the Lhakovsky belt they felt 'as if reborn'.

All this could have been dismissed as simple charlatanry. However, the possibility that 'there might be something in it after all' was warranted by the fact that Lhakovsky's work had been presented to the French Academy of Sciences, with a very warm recommendation, by Professor Arsène d'Arsonval, an eminent scholar and past president of that academy. Professor d'Arsonval testified i.a. that geranium plants infected with tumour and treated by Lhakovsky had not only recovered completely, but had grown to five feet in height, several times their normal size. . . . There were also alleged reports from the cancer ward of the San Spirito Hospital near Rome, according to which Lhakovsky's cure had been tried on human patients with promising results. Though I had never heard of a new cancer cure which did not produce some initial results, all this sounded sufficiently intriguing to warrant a special trip to Paris to interview Lhakovsky. I met a man as charming as he was ambiguous, who showed me his laboratory, and repeated orally all that he had claimed before in print. I returned convinced that half of his claims were phoney, and none the wiser with regard to the other half. Since then, Lhakovsky seems to have vanished from the scene. I still feel that some day official science may discover that there was 'something in it, after all', just as modern chemistry discovered that there was, after all, something worth salvaging in the Alchemists' jumble; and meanwhile I have found comfort in a memorable phrases from Professor d'Arsonval's introduction to Lhakovsky's book :

'What distinguishes the ideas of a fool from those of a scientific genius is that experiment refutes the former and confirms the latter. . . .'

One day in 1931, shortly after poor crank Graichen's half-powered Odyssey, my father unexpectedly turned up in Berlin. He was beaming, secretive and full of sanguine optimism about the future—an ominous sign that he had embarked on some new 'colossal' project like the radioactive soap or the self-heating bricks. The bricks (surrounded by wiring like self-heating blankets) were another venture he had launched in recent years. But this time it was worse than that—it was everlasting electric light bulbs. I felt a wrench in my heart when, on the second day of his visit, he came out with it, for electric wonder bulbs (cheaper, brighter, ever-lasting) were the classic hunting-ground of charlatans and cranks. Sure enough, he had the bulb in his suitcase, wrapped in cotton-wool. He screwed it with a mysterious air into the socket of my bedside lamp. 'You see—it burns,' he exclaimed, radiant like Father Christmas.

And so we were back again, after some twenty years, at the memorable scene when Professor Nathan, hunch-backed and bearded, had demonstrated his envelope-cutting machine and blown all the fuses in the apartment. But this time the situation was even more painful, for my father expected me to co-operate on the project, by giving it a 'colossal' write-up in my papers. The inventor—this one's name was Professor Marcus—had come along with him from Budapest and was staying in a cheap hotel; my father was in touch with a German syndicate which showed a colossal interest in the matter; only a little Press publicity was needed and the deal would be clinched, and my father would take my mother on a stupendous Mediterranean cruise.

I took that cursed bulb, after having promised my father that I wouldn't drop it, to a laboratory and had it tested. It consumed twenty-five per cent more current than the average commercial article, and had half its life expectancy. Then I rang up the morgue at the office and asked them whether they had any clippings on one Professor Marcus, inventor. They had : Julius Marcus, alias Professor Marko alias Mark, sentenced to two years' imprisonment for fraudulently obtaining money by posing as an inventor; two previous condemnations for fraud and confidence tricks. There was even a photograph on one of the clippings. I borrowed it from the morgue and went home. In the flat I found my father in conference with two stiff, starched Prussian industrialists from the syndicate. My father, who had never ceased regarding me as an infant prodigy, proudly presented me to the Prussians :

'This is my son, the famous journalist about whom I have talked to you. And these gentlemen, my son, are my future business partners.'

The Prussians shook hands a little sourly; they were not accustomed to mixing business with family idylls. I asked to have a word with my father in private, and took him to the other room. When I had shown him the clipping with the photograph, he looked for a moment twenty years older; but only for a moment. Then he shrugged slowly, and said : 'Well, we shall have to postpone that cruise once more—and I shall have to borrow from you my fare back to Budapest.' I saw in my mind's eye my mother going cluck-cluck with her nervous tick as he arrived back in their furnished room, once more beaten yet undefeated, and countering her I-told-

you-so by yet another colossal project which he had hatched
on the train.

We went back to the waiting Prussians. *'Meine Herren,'*
my father said, solemn but beaming, 'my son has some very,
very stupendous news for you.' From the tone of his voice
the Prussians must have thought I was about to tell them
that the bulb was a gold mine. Instead of which I read them
the text of the clipping. They listened with an expression
which in German is eloquently described as *Die Spucke
bleib ihnen Weg*—'the spittle froze on their tongues.'

'Unglaublich,' one of them said at last to my father.
'What on earth do you find to look so radiant about, Herr
K.?'

'But, *meine Herren,*' said my father, 'isn't it wonderful to
have such a clever son?'

XXXIII. Apprenticeship for the Arctic

IN the summer of 1931 the four biggest German banking firms closed down, and the Government of the Reich gave notice that it was no longer able to continue reparation payments. The depression had hit rock-bottom, and unemployment reached its peak; nobody was any longer safe in his job. In the middle of this crisis, the managing director of Ullstein's called me to his office.

'How old are you, Herr K. ?' he asked.

'Twenty-six.'

'Unmarried? No family or dependants?'

I was, figuratively speaking, rubbing the back of my neck, in remembrance of the story of Wang Lun's victim. The managing director, Dr. Wolff, a burly, shy and kindly Bavarian, seemed embarrassed.

'You have travelled quite a lot for your age—everywhere except to the North Pole, ha, ha,' he said.

'Ha, ha,' I said.

'Well, if you promise not to quarrel with the polar bears, ha, ha, we may send you to the North Pole,' said Dr. Wolff. 'We have bought the news monopoly for the Zeppelin's Arctic expedition at a bargain price, after that fool, Hearst, let it go....'

In 1930, a polar expedition still had the romantic aura of a boyhood dream; Captain Scott and Commander Peary, Amundsen and Nansen were among the heroes of my schooldays, as Charles Lindbergh and Lawrence of Arabia were to be for the next generation. I can still feel the wild rush of elation, the reddening of my face, the stammering, blissful helplessness which followed the managing director's announcement.

The Zeppelin Arctic expedition started some three weeks later, on July 26, 1931, and was on the whole one of the technically most successful ventures of its kind. It was also the climax of my career as a journalist. The Ullsteins held the news monopoly, and I was the only representative of the Press on board—about the most perfect assignment a newspaperman could pray for. During a non-stop flight of five days and four nights, the expedition accomplished a nearly complete geo-photographic survey of the Arctic land-masses between the fortieth and hundred-and-tenth degrees of longitude East (Franz Josef Land, Northern Land, etc.), discovered half a dozen islands, crossed others off the map, filled in one of the last remaining blank spots on the chart, and, in the words of the leader of the expedition, 'did in about ninety hours an amount of work which would have taken a combined sea-and-land expedition several years to accomplish without producing equally reliable results.' Some previous Arctic air expeditions had ended in disaster. Nobile's airship *Italia* had crashed; Amundsen, looking for the survivors, had for ever vanished together with his plane. The Zeppelin expedition marked the dividing line between the romantic and the scientific era in Arctic exploration. Therein, more than in its specific results, lay its historic significance.

However, the curious series of events which led up to this expedition was neither of a romantic nor of a scientific nature. It began with one of the most absurd plans for a newspaper stunt, conceived by the late William Randolph Hearst.

Anno domini 1900, a certain Professor Anschitz of Kiel had published a pamphlet in which he suggested that the North Pole could be conquered by a submarine making its way beneath the ice-pack. In 1929 the journalist and Arctic explorer Sir Hubert Wilkins announced his intention of carrying out that project. He approached the American Government which, very sensibly, refused to have anything to do with it. Wilkins then entered into negotiations with Hearst, who liked the idea and gave it an additional twist. A submarine under the North Pole would be a moderately attractive stunt; but a submarine under the North Pole, and the *Graf Zeppelin* over the North Pole, exchanging greetings through a hole in the pack would be the greatest stunt of all time. And now the project got going in earnest.

On June 3, 1930, the American Government agreed to let Sir Hubert Wilkins charter one of its obsolete submarines, the P.12. The P.12 was renamed *Nautilus* in memory of Captain Nemo's famous ship in Jules Verne's *Twenty Thousand Leagues Under the Sea*. In December, 1930, Commander Sloan Dawenhover, U.S. Navy, retired, journeyed to France to confer with Jules Verne's grandson, Jean Jules Verne, a lawyer in Rouen. Hearst asked him to baptise the *Nautilus* and to participate in the expedition; Verne accepted.

Next, the *Nautilus* was outfitted with a number of gadgets that would enable her to gauge the thickness of the ice overhead, to detect holes in the ice-cover and, in the absence of holes, to bore through the ice and emerge on the surface. This last feat was to be accomplished by means of an electric drill mounted on the submarine's prow. Technologically, this was about the craziest *Schnaps-Idee* that had ever sprung from an inebriated engineer's brain. When it became known, the leading German authority on submarines, Professor Flamm of the Berlin Polytechnic, wrote in horror :

'The whole conception is so absurd, and the details about the construction and fittings of the boat so fantastic, that it is hard to take the project seriously. In any case, it may be in order to issue an earnest warning against participation in this enterprise. . . .'

But no warning prevailed. In April, 1931, the *Nautilus,* alias P.12, set out for the great journey, which was to lead via Spitzbergen, and the Pole, to Alaska. The journey was a tragi-comedy, not unlike Graichen's Odyssey. In mid-Atlantic the engines broke down and the *Nautilus* had to be towed to Plymouth. After lengthy repairs she made Bergen, where she again broke down; after more repairs she reached Spitzbergen, where she broke down a third time. She was finally scuttled, to everybody's relief, in Bergen Fiord.

Now the Zeppelin, according to the original plan, was to start for the polar rendezvous after the *Nautilus* had crossed the 85th parallel. But the *Nautilus* never crossed the 85th parallel and Hearst was no longer interested. So the Ullsteins stepped in and bought the news and picture monopoly at the bargain price of 10,000 dollars. But this sum was far from sufficient to cover the cost of the expedition, and now the second part of the comedy began. The *Graf Zeppelin* was owned by a private firm, the Zeppelin G.m.b.H., of which it constituted the only asset. The managing director of that firm was the Zeppelin's famous skipper, Dr. Eckener. Eckener was at that time also President of the 'Aero-Arctic', an international society of Arctic explorers, founded in 1925 by Fridtjof Nansen.

The Aero-Arctic had many ambitious projects, but no money to carry them out. When Nansen died in 1930, the society made the shrewd move of electing Eckener as his successor, hoping that he would put his ship at their disposal. But Eckener, forewarned by Nobile's crash, showed little inclination to expose his Zeppelin—Germany's one and only —to the hazards of the Arctic skies. He preferred to run her as a luxury bus for pleasure cruises to the Orient and to South America. The *Graf Zeppelin* was probably the most expensive means of transportation of all time; a berth on one of those cruises cost several thousand dollars.

The Hearst project, which subsequently became the Ullstein project, tempted Eckener, and at last he agreed to take his bus to the North Pole.[1] The Ullsteins covered part of the costs; the Aero-Arctic took the expedition under its sponsorship and contributed some of the funds; more money was to be raised by a special collector's issue of 'Zeppelin North Pole Stamps'—about which more later. However, all this was still not enough. So an appeal was made to patriotic German manufacturers, asking them to provide the necessary equipment free of charge. They responded magnificently. Crates poured in at the Zeppelin base in Friedrichshafen containing watertight overalls, dried fish, biscuits, sledges for the eventuality of a forced march over the ice, tents, sleeping-bags, storm-lamps, harpoons to kill seals, lassos to catch polar bears, Rhine wine to keep the morale up, frost-proof fountain pens, and even plastic imitation cigarettes with a menthol flavour to keep the nicotine craving at bay—for in the Zeppelin smoking was forbidden. Only one item, the most essential, did not arrive : fur coats. Fur coats are too expensive to be given away *pro gloria polaris*. So we started out without warm coats—a fact which, in the event of a forced landing, would have meant certain death, and which reduced the sledges, harpoons and lassos that we carried to mere stage properties or Hopalong Cassidy equipment. This was one of the expedition's secrets about which, as its official chronicler, I was bidden to keep silent.

[1] In his memoirs Dr. Eckener describes the terms of his agreement with William Randolph Hearst as follows :

'If the airship and the submarine contrive to meet at the North Pole and to exchange passengers and mail there, Hearst will pay $150,000 for the monopoly on news reports from the airship. If the airship and the submarine merely succeed in meeting at the Pole, this sum will be reduced to $100,000. If they meet somewhere else in the Arctic, the sum will be $30,000.'

(Dr. Hugo Eckener, *Im Zeppelin über Länder und Meere*; Flensburg, 1949.)

A second, and even more depressing circumstance had also to be kept secret from the expectant public. We were not going to fly over the Pole itself. The original itinerary of the expedition, as mapped out by the Aero-Arctic, led from Leningrad via Archangel—Novaya Zemlya—Taimyr Peninsula—Northern Land—the Pole—to Kamchatka. As far as the Zeppelin's fuel-carrying capacities were concerned, the plan was perfectly feasible. But the planners had forgotten one important factor: the Insurance Companies. And the Insurance Companies turned out to have a horror of the North Pole. Up to the 80th degree of latitude, the premiums on the policies mounted in arithmetical progression; from the 80th degree upward they rose in geometrical progression. After some haggling with the insurance men, the 82nd degree was secretly agreed upon as the northern-most limit of our itinerary. During the flight, Eckener kept strictly to the letter of the agreement, to the despair of the other members of the expedition, and in spite of the perfect flying weather which, at one point, would have enabled us to reach the Pole in less than six hours and return to base with fuel for another thirty or more hours to spare. The Pole itself, whose mystic attraction has claimed so many victims, is of course merely a theoretical point of considerably smaller scientific interest than the territories which we surveyed. It was nevertheless galling when, the moment we reached Cape Fligely on the 82nd parallel, Eckener swung the nose of the ship through 90 degrees to eastward and continued for hours on this course, hugging the fateful 82nd as if he were skirting a wall—or rather, as if we were attached to a rubber string, whose other end was held by earnest businessmen in Berlin.

This seamy side of our expedition was by no means exceptional in the history of exploring ventures. From Columbus, who had to go begging for funds from court to court, to Captain Peary who, on his return from the Pole, had to give 168 lectures in 96 days to pay his debts, to Willy Ley's first

'Society for Space Travel', whose pioneering experiments depended upon the fortunes of a hat manufacturer in Moravia, it had always been the same tale of woe, carefully left out of the heroic accounts in boys' books. As I was preparing myself for the expedition, I read the story of polar conquests in a new light, and was amazed at the amount of squalor, cupidity, vainglory and spite among the rugged heroes of the Arctic.

In the three weeks between the Managing Director's announcement and the actual day of our departure I read so much about the Arctic that I got sick and tired of it. But a few days before the start, I had an inspiration which made me jump up from my desk and run, unannounced, straight to the head of the firm, Dr. Franz Ullstein. If *that* idea could be carried out—and there seemed to be no reason why it couldn't—it would create one of the most fantastic curiosa in History. The idea was, simply, to establish a colony of the future Jewish State in the Arctic.

It is common knowledge that if you plant a flag on a hitherto uncharted island or territory, you have staked a claim to that territory on behalf of the nation which the flag represents. Now at that time, in 1931, I still had a Palestinian passport and was a citizen by naturalisation of that country. Furthermore, it was certain that in the little-known waters around Nordland we would discover a number of unknown islands—as we actually did. So I only had to equip myself with a dozen or two of Zionist flags—blue and white with the shield of David in gold in the centre—weight them with lead, and drop one on an uncharted island. Then the future State of Israel would have a colony, or at least a health resort, near the North Pole. And who would appreciate that more than the citizens of that blazing desert land?

Dr. Ullstein considered this. 'Not a bad idea as ideas go,' he said after a while. 'It would certainly make some headline. . . .'

He called in a couple of his advisers for a conference. There was the usual hemming and hawing. The main argument against the proposal was that it would fan anti-Semitism in Germany. Germany's proud Zeppelin buzzing around to grab territories for the Jews. . . . I pointed out the symbolic value of the gesture; the tremendous-effect it would have in America at a time when the Reich was in dire need of credits; and that this was not a German, but an international expedition. 'But you are on the staff of a German firm,' I was told. I said I could, as a formality, resign from the staff and go as a Special Correspondent hired for his knowledge of scientific matters, even though a Palestinian. . . . I wish that conference had been recorded; rarely can earnest Prussian executives have grappled with a more surrealistic proposal. In the end, Dr. Ullstein, who had a great sense of humour, adjourned the meeting until he had consulted our expert on international law. The result of that consultation was sad. Our lawyer explained that all Arctic lands and islands to be discovered in the future between $32°—4'—35''$ east from Greenwich and $168°—49'—30''$ west from Greenwich belonged automatically to Russia, regardless of who discovered them.

So, after all, Israel has no colony at the North Pole, in spite of the fact that our expedition did discover several uncharted islands. They were named by the Soviet Government Samoilowich Island after the leader of the expedition; Eckener Island; Karolus Island after a German member of the group, and so on. I was rather hurt that no island was named after me; but the etiquette of voyage and discovery has its rules of precedence, and there were not enough islands to go round. Later on I found consolation in the thought that had I been awarded an island, it would have been renamed after my break with the Party, just as Kamenev Island and innumerable towns, streets and factories in Russia have been re-baptised after the men whose names they bore had been purged and shot. A Koestler Island, which later changed to Ehrenburg Island, would have been more galling than no island at all. I wonder, by the way, what the various Stalingrads, Stalinogorsks, Stalin Squares, Stalin Boulevards and Stalin Factories will be called twenty years from now. . . .

Once you see a thing from a grotesque angle, it is difficult to change your perspective; so every event until the actual start of the expedition seemed to have some absurd facet. There was, for instance, the matter of the 'Polar Stamps'. As I have said, the German Post Office had issued a special series of 'Zeppelin North Pole Stamps' : fifty cents for postcards, one dollar for letters. Though the airship had been stripped of every ounce of superfluous equipment to be able to carry more fuel, we carted with us round the Arctic some 75,000 letters and postcards weighing 300 kilos. The value of the stamps on them amounted to $50,000, which was split half and half between Dr. Eckener and the German Reich. A special post office had been installed inside the ship, under one of the crimson tents which we carried in case of a forced landing on the ice (minus warm overcoats). In that tent, during the flight, two men were busy day and night stamping the mail with the Zeppelin's special rubber stamp. At the 82nd degree of latitude we met the Russian ice-breaker *Malygin* (a kind of *Ersatz* rendezvous for the missed date with the *Nautilus*) and passed the mail bags on to her. Some three months later, after her return to Archangel, the *Malygin* delivered the bags to the regular Soviet mail service. By this ingenious method, a sentimental young man in Leipzig could write a 'Zeppelin-card' to his sweetheart in Dresden, put it into the mail-box, and lo, after a little detour via Friedrichshafen—Leningrad—Franz Josef Land—Archangel—Moscow Censorship Department—the card would be duly dropped, half a year or so later, into the letter-box of the young lady of Dresden. That fifty thousand dollars could be raised in this manner proves once and for all the romantic nature of the German temperament.

I cannot resist relating one more absurd little episode from my apprenticeship as an explorer. About a week before our start, I received a telegram from Dr. Kohl Larsen, the expedition's quartermaster in Friedrichshafen: would I please immediately wire my tailoring measurements, as all members of the expedition were to wear uniform polar suits, made to measure by a large firm of outfitters (at fifty per cent discount). The measurements were required within twenty-four hours.

When the telegram arrived I was just leaving with some friends by car for Munich, to attend the Radio-Music Congress in Munich that I have mentioned before. I could not postpone our departure, so I thought I would have my measurements taken somewhere en route. Our first stop was Nürnberg, where I set out in search of a tailor. It was late in the afternoon and most of the shops were closed, but finally I did find a tailor in one of Nürnberg's narrow, gabled mediæval streets. He was a wizened little man with steel-rimmed glasses, wielding an enormous pair of scissors and looking exactly like the tailor in an illustrated book of fairy tales. I asked him to take my measurements.

'What kind of a suit wishes *der Herr* to order?' he asked.

I explained that I did not wish to order a suit; I only wanted my measurements and would gladly pay for his trouble.

'But if *der Herr* does not wish to order a suit, what does he want the measurements for?'

So I had to explain that I needed the measurements for an outfitter—whose name I did not know—and who was to make me a special kind of suit by mail order. The little tailor became more and more suspicious. Did I live in Nürnberg? No, I was on my way from Berlin to Munich. And where did that outfitter live? I had not the faintest idea. During the conversation the tailor discreetly called in first his wife, then his son, a huge, moronic lout wearing a swastika badge. In despair, I started to explain the whole story : I needed the measurements for a Polar suit to be made by a special outfitter as I was preparing to join an Arctic expedition on board the *Graf Zeppelin*. . . . It sounded utterly incredible, even to me; all four of us were convinced that never had a bigger lie been told in Nürnberg. In the end I made a hasty retreat before they could call an ambulance and put me in a strait-jacket.

Fortunately I found a bookshop, and in it a booklet called 'Tailoring Self-Taught in 12 Easy Lessons', or something to that effect. With its help, my friends executed that compli-cated topological survey, left armpit to right kidney, collar-bone to hip-joint, which always baffles one when ordering a suit. Later on I wrote a little story about my Nürnberg adventures for one of the Ullstein dailies. But the German public doesn't like such objects of worship as its Zeppelin treated in a frivolous vein; so the story only brought in one fan letter. It was written by a woman in a Bavarian village who said that she had read my story with enormous interest; and would I please tell her where she could buy that book about becoming a tailor in twelve easy lessons.

XXXIV. Through the Polar Night on a Flying Whale

I N spite of these irreverent preliminaries, the flight itself was a majestic experience. No lesser adjective would fit both the landscape over which we hovered during four undistinguishable days and nights of midnight sun, and the airship which carried us.

Since the building of lighter-than-air ships was abandoned, the Zeppelin has come to rank as a historic curiosity, an obselete monster like the dinosaur. It represented, just like the dinosaur and for similar reasons, the ultimate product of a dead branch of evolution: it was too bulky, vulnerable and slow. But it was a monster of supreme beauty, the idol and fetish of a nation easily given to idolatry. Shaped like a giant goldfish, it measured from head to tail 260 yards—twice the maximum length of a soccer football field. It was 120 feet high—the height of a twelve-storey building or the steeple of a medium-sized church. Its smooth, glossy aluminium skin had a silvery sheen, and by its unbroken smoothness made it appear from a distance like a live animal: a good-natured, colossal Moby Dick of the air serenely swimming through the clouds.

The nacelle, or passengers' cabin (the Germans call it the 'gondola' which sounds more poetic), is attached underneath the main body, near the front. It houses the commander's bridge and the passengers' quarters, the latter equipped with all the luxury of a modern ocean liner. At the rear end of the nacelle is a little door, normally locked. It leads, through a dark passage, to the land of mysteries, into the belly of the whale. And that is indeed a most fantastic place.

That whole inner space, vaster in volume than a cathedral, but elongated to the shape of a 780-foot cigar, is filled with darkness, the smell of bitter almonds, and a dull, subdued sound as if invisible bats were lazily flapping their wings. The smell is caused by the presence of hydrocyanic gas and the sounds by the flutterings of the hydrogen-filled balloon-cells which are the vitals of the flying whale, its float-bladders, whose buoyancy carries the enormous structure through the air. These balloons are arranged in two rows down the length of the whole inner space, like giant pears suspended upside down, each some fifty feet across. Under normal air-pressure, when the ship rests on the ground, they hang limply, their skin wrinkled and slack, like old witches' pendulous breasts; but when the ship rises into rarefied air they fill up, become plump and taut, and fill the belly of the whale with sound, as with the cracking of a thousand whips. Between the rows of balloons runs a perilous, narrow catwalk, suspended in mid-air and obscurity, with only a vibrating cable for a hand-rail, and a drop of sixty feet underneath. From this catwalk are the balloon-cells serviced, by the light of Davy lamps as used in coal mines, because of the extreme danger of explosion.

Though nobody was permitted to enter this place except when accompanied by one of the ship's officers, I spent much time loitering on the dark, narrow catwalk; the thrill of it never wore off. In the surrounding obscurity amidst the drowsy bitter-almond smell, the shudderings of the ship, the flapping and cracking of the balloon-cells became magnified and reverberated with a hollow echo; I was surrounded by a labyrinth of girders, rafters, lattices, trusses and buttresses, a jungle of steel and aluminium, and a thousand feet below lay the uncharted white deserts of the north.

We started on July 24 from the Zeppelin base at Friedrichshafen, on Lake Constance. There were fifty-six men on board—the regular crew of forty and sixteen members of the expedition. Of the latter, four were Russians, including the expedition leader Professor Samoilowich; eight Germans, two Americans, including the Polar explorer Lincoln Ellsworth, one Swede, and one Hungarian-born Palestinian. As civilian clothing was barred to save cargo-weight for fuel, we all wore our clumsy Polar uniforms—at a temperature of 75°F., in the shade, and to the great merriment of the several thousand spectators on the airfield, who had come from all over Germany and Switzerland to watch the take-off.

The take-off of the colossus is a spectacular experience. When grounded, its gas content and ballast are so delicately balanced against each other that gravity just matches buoyancy, and the ship floats weightlessly in the air inside its hangar, its nose attached by a kind of press-button clutch to a mast. After we had all climbed inside, a ground crew of about a hundred men started to pull the floating whale out of the hangar by means of ropes dangling from the nacelle. From the window it looked as if they were all engaged in dragging some reluctant beast by its halter. Once outside, on the green field in front of the hangar, we began to spout water which serves as ballast, through a couple of hoses. A moment later, the ground crew performed a dramatic manoeuvre. At a command, the men let go of the guide ropes and grabbed instead two horizontal bars, attached on both sides along the bottom of the nacelle. At a second command, they lifted the whole, enormous whale of a ship over their heads and literally threw it up into the air. The ship gave a faint shudder and continued to soar vertically into the blue sky, at such speed that ground crew, hangar, airfield and streets shrank within a matter of seconds to the size of a toy town. Its buoyancy now being greater than its gravity, that initial, almost playful throw by the crew had been sufficient to set it free and to make it rise, like an air-bubble in a pond, through the atmosphere.

The experience of this swift, silent and effortless rising, or rather of falling upwards into the sky, is beautiful and intoxicating. It is entirely different from the alarming take-off of an aeroplane, at a flat angle, accompanied by the roar of the engines, followed by sickening tilts of the horizon. The lighter-than-air ship rises in complete silence, smoothly, peacefully, as if by its own will; it gives one the complete illusion of having escaped the bondage of the earth's gravity. One floats, suspended from a huge gas-bubble, in the sky.

Only at about a thousand feet up in the air did the engines start up, and the ship begin its horizontal flight. As the five engines with their propellers are mounted in separate 'cars' way out from the inflammable hulk, their sound is only heard in the nacelle as a distant, gentle hum. There are no vibrations and no bumps: air-pockets, minor gusts and squalls have no effect on the enormous floating mass. In an aeroplane, the propellers have to provide an air-stream which supports the wings, kite fashion, in space; the flying whale is supported by its own buoyancy, and the propellers merely serve to push it along through the air. It does not, in fact, fly—it swims. And if all five engines go dead, it will still keep on swimming in its good-natured, elephantine way. All these factors combine to give the passengers in the 'gondola' a feeling of safety and a relaxed, contemplative mood, otherwise so alien to air travel.

By 5 p.m. we were over Berlin, our first scheduled stop. Eckener, whose exceptional skill for navigation was only equalled by his gift for showmanship, circled for a full hour over the town to provide the Berliners with an opportunity for working up their Zeppelinomania to a new pitch. All

across Germany we had left a wake of howling factory
whistles, of traffic snarls with madly hooting cars, of waving
crowds and, presumably, an epidemic of stiff necks. Freud-
ians explained the German people's Zeppelin craze, which
lasted unabated for several years, by declaring the ship to
be a phallic symbol; the followers of Adler saw in it the over-
compensation of a national inferiority complex; in the
Marxist view it was an escapist pie in the sky, a cunning
diversion from the class struggle. However that may be, our
circus-display over Berlin had the desired effect : it started a
mass-migration to the aerodrome of Staaken where the ship
was to be on show overnight against an entrance fee shared
half and half by Eckener and the Municipality of Berlin.
(Incidentally, on our return flight from the Arctic, Eckener
refused to land in Berlin after an acrimonious exchange of
radio messages with the Mayor, Dr. Sahm, whom Eckener
asked for a guaranteed minimum of ten thousand marks
against gate receipts, whereas Sahm offered only five. At the
last minute, Sahm gave in. That was another expedition
secret, not to be divulged to the public.)

The take-off from Staaken was scheduled for 5 a.m., so
we were free for the evening and I took the two Americans—
Lincoln Ellsworth and Commander Smith, U.S. Navy—on
a special expedition to show them the night life of Berlin.
As we had nothing to wear but our Polar suits, and Berlin
was in the throes of the Zeppelin fever, we were recognised
in every *Lokal* and attentions were not lacking. Taxi-drivers
refused to accept pay, night club proprietors regaled us with
free champagne, the ladies at the bar swooned by just
glancing at us. It was a wonderful feeling to be a hero. We
arrived at the airfield just half an hour before the start,
under the disapproving eyes of the *Herren Professoren* on
board who had given us up for lost.

The second day took us across Sweden, Esthonia and Fin-

N

land to Leningrad. Though I only became a card-carrying member of the Communist Party five months later, I was already sufficiently advanced in that direction to look forward to my first contact with the Soviet land as the climax of the whole expedition. For the Berlin outing of the previous night I had originally invited Samoilowich and the other Russians; but they had politely declined, and during the whole night had not budged from the airfield. I had regarded this as an admirable example of monastic discipline, and, with a slightly guilty class-conscience, had fallen back on the Americans. During the flight to Leningrad another small incident occurred of which I was hardly conscious at the time. We had just crossed the coastline of Esthonia; I was standing next to the Russian wireless operator, Krenkel, both of us looking down through a window. I made some remark about the pleasant character of the landscape, and he answered with a derisive shrug: 'Esthonia? It is not an interesting country. In Russia we call it "the potato-republic." ' As I had to file my daily five thousand words of copy, and nothing of interest had happened so far, I put into one of my despatches a mention of 'Esthonia, referred to by Russians on board as "the potato-republic".' Krenkel saw this despatch in the wireless room. The next time I ran into him, he said quietly: 'Why did you want to make trouble for me?' I had no idea what he meant, until he explained in a halting, resigned sort of way that every remark that might disturb the friendly relations between the Soviet Union and its neighbours was to be regarded as a provocation. I said: 'But surely you can't get into trouble because of a harmless joke? I haven't even mentioned your name.' He said, in the same resigned tone: 'Harmless . . . ?' Then he turned his back, and during the whole flight never spoke to me again.

Later I got into difficulties with the other Russians too. In my first despatch I had mentioned, I do not remember in

what connection, that on the morning of our start Samoilowich had been seen shaving while the rest of us were having
breakfast. One of our evening papers built up this story into
an obvious, but quite harmless and good-humoured joke
about 'the absent-minded Professor who nearly missed the
start'. Samoilowich learned about this during our stop at
Leningrad. He remarked on it in an apparently offhand
manner—and that was about the last remark he ever
addressed to me.

As I have said, small incidents like this—and there were
of course more, between the Germans and the Russians on
board—had no meaning for me at the time. This is hardly
surprising, as one's perceptions are always influenced by
emotional bias. It is much more remarkable that such experiences, to which originally no conscious importance was
attached, are nevertheless registered and stored away.
Memory seems to consist of a series of delayed-action fuses
which may go pop years later, or never at all. Thus from my
very first contact with Soviet Russia and its citizens, a subtle
mechanism set to work which, like a sorting machine, made
all my perceptions fall into two distinct categories. Those
that were retained by the filter were consciously registered,
and added up to a picture that in itself was authentic and
genuine, though its authenticity was that of a mosaic with
all but the white stones taken out. The other experiences,
which fell like dust unnoticed through the meshes of the
filter, formed a kind of ash heap down in the pit of my consciousness. It took several years for the heap to grow so large
that it choked the filter and came oozing back to the surface.
And, lo, in the process of this painful regurgitation every
forgotten item reappeared, with its rank smell, and each had
been neatly catalogued down in the pit.

Two years after this first crossing of the Soviet border, I
wrote a book, my first, commissioned by the Soviet State

Publishing trust.[1] The opening part of it is a narrative of the Zeppelin expedition, as reflected in a mind by then thoroughly steeped in Marxist dialectics, and seen through eyes conditioned to filter-perception. In these memoirs I have made a number of embarrassing admissions; none of them, however intimate their nature, is more painful and humiliating than the experience of being confronted today with the grinning pages of that book, written eighteen years ago, in the state of cold intoxication typical of the Com-munist neophyte. I quote:

'Like a silver arrow we had whizzed in twelve hours over five countries and two seas; the huge globe down there turned like the little one in school when the teacher's finger set it spinning; forests, rivers, marshes and towns had emerged and vanished in sweeping, fleeting motion over the rim of the horizon; jubilant crowds and stampeding animals, the howling whistles of factories and steamers had followed us like a steady echo where our shadow trailed along the earth.

'Yet all these impressions paled and became extinct at the sight of a tiny viaduct, far down, which suddenly rose in open country over the railroad tracks from Reval to Leningrad: the arch of triumph of the Red Continent, the gate which separates the two worlds of this planet. It was as if an electric shock had traversed the ship, filling some with joy, others with hatred. What up to now had merely been landscape, lost its neutral character: the forests were no longer green fairy-tale woods but a given quantity of exportable timber. The fields no longer were mere green and yellow squares, but battlefields between

[1] *Von Weissen Nächten und Roten Tagen,* Ukdershnazmenwydaw, Charkov, Ukrainian S.S.R., 1933. It was printed in German, for the German-speaking national minorities in the U.S.S.R. Ukrdershnazmen-wydaw stands for the initials of 'Ukrainian State Publishing Company for National Minorities.'

tractor and hand-plough; the people down there were no longer little waving puppets, but friend or foe. The frontier—that invisible line which, more distinctly than the Equator, divides our planet into two halves, also divided our ship. . . .'

A few pages later, this *leit-motif,* the perception of a landscape through the dialectical filter, is further developed. For it is a basic tenet of Marxism that there is no such thing as a politically neutral attitude to nature, or art, or astronomy, or dentistry or pipe-smoking. As for the Freudian every object has its hidden symbol-value, so the disciple of the Marxist closed system soon learns to superimpose a 'class-conscious aspect' on every object and experience he encounters. This mode of perception soon becomes a conditioned reflex. To perceive a duck merely as a duck means to be guilty of *bourgeois* objectivism; a duck is a fowl destined to fatten the bellies of members of the ruling class and denied to the toiling masses. The passage which follows is an example of this acquired technique which, for years to come, was to haunt all my writings like a persistent virus in the blood.

We had passed Leningrad and were approaching the Arctic Circle across the primeval forests of the Karelian Soviet Republic:

'Lake Ladoga lay behind us, the Taiga opened its green arms and enclosed the whole horizon in its embrace. The virgin forest of firs moves past in majestic monotony. For hours on end we can detect no human being from horizon to horizon, no animal, no house, no sign that a living being has ever penetrated into the heart of this green darkness. Then a few small settlements, built of logs hewn out of whole trees on the banks of rivers that wind their way through the forest; then several small lakes, like drops of dew on the green forest-fur which covers the earth;

then the tundras, bottomless swamps like yellow, sup-
purating wounds.

In one of the settlements a wild panic breaks out at our
appearance—men and cattle flee headlong in all directions into the woods; in their eyes we are indeed the
Zeppelinosaurus, a flying giant lizard which will start
spouting flames at any moment. As we do nothing of the
sort and merely wave at them through the windows, they
gradually calm down, but they do not wave back—maybe
if our handkerchiefs were red, they would become faster
reconciled to our uncanny apparition.

For, though these citizens of the autonomous Karelian
Soviet Republic have never seen a Zeppelin before, in
their politics they are more advanced than we are, and
they could teach our Professors on board a lot. They
could tell us how General Miller's Army of Intervention
invaded their beautiful land of forests and lakes with
bloodshed and discord; how the Karelian hunters, fisher-
men, woodcutters and peasants turned into Red Partisans
—as Russians, Uzbeks, Jews and Tartars did elsewhere;
how they threw Miller out of their country as others
threw out Kolchak, Wrangel and Yudenitch; how, in
1920, they banded together in the "Karelian Kommune"
and, after another defensive war against their kinsfolk,
the Finns, were eventually admitted, as an autonomous
republic, into the Federation of Soviet Republics. The iron
laws of the class-struggle have proved just as valid in this
country of the midnight sun, as in the scorching steppes
between the Amu-Darya and the Syr-Darya. . . .'

This passage is followed by an imaginary conversation
between a member of the Zeppelin crew and the author:

' "Look," the author exclaims, pointing through the
window at the main street of Petrozavodsk, the Karelian
capital, "look, that is Karl Marx Street, and over there is

Engels Boulevard. In the factory whose belching chimneys
you see over there, there is a blackboard and a red board on
the wall of every workshop, and a bulletin-board with
friendly quips at the management. That new building is the
Workers' Club, where yesterday a meeting was held protest-
ing against the sentences passed on the seven Negro boys
from Scotsboro. That castle yonder is now a children's crèche,
and that former church a school. That little park on the
shore of Lake Onega . . ."

' "How do you know all that?" my partner in the imaginary conversation asked. "Have you been to Petrozavodsk?"

' "It's quite simple. Imagine for a moment that this town
is situated not in Karelia, but in Thuringia. Then what
would the main street be called?"

'The sailor grinned. "Kaiser Wilhelm Street, of course."

' "And what other details can you make out?"

'He grinned again. "In the factory, there is a list in every
workshop with the names of the workers who got fired
because of the crisis. The new building over there belongs to
the social-fascist Trade Unions, who yesterday decided in a
meeting not to go on strike but to go on negotiating with the
management. That former castle belongs to Herr Direktor
Meinecke, and the park on the shore of the lake . . ."

' "There you are. How can you see all that from a height
of 2,000 feet?" '

After this Socratic dialogue, I duly reported that the timber
production of Karelia was, according to official statistics,
rising at the rate of forty to sixty per cent per annum, and
that its population had, since the Revolution, increased from
220,000 to 360,000. What I did not know when I wrote that
book in 1933, was that the settlements on the river banks in
the perennial forest with their roughly hewn log-cabins were
concentration camps; that the increase in population and
productivity was almost entirely due to convict labour; and
that the stretch of Karelia over which we flew, roughly from

Petrozavodsk to the Solovetsky Islands, was one of the oldest and most notorious regions of slave labour in Soviet Russia, the cradle of the future slave-continent in the Arctic.

The Dialectic, as so many of us were to learn, has the deadly irony of a boomerang.

In Leningrad we were greeted with that overwhelming Russian hospitality which, however deliberate in intent, becomes spontaneous after the first few glasses of vodka, and is a natural, and well-nigh irresistible, ally of Soviet propaganda. At the frontier we had been met by five Russian military aeroplanes that escorted us all the way to Leningrad, looping and capering around us in the air like merry dolphins around a whale. In Leningrad itself, there was the usual sumptuous banquet at the airfield; it included half a dozen different sorts of caviar, eaten with wooden spoons as if it were pea soup; toasts by the German Ambassador, the chairman of the Leningrad Soviet, the President of the Russian Academy, and so on; songs by the Red Army chorus and, as a comic touch, a huge banner with 'WELCOME TO THE RECKLESS HEROES OF THE ARCTIC.' This distinction is mostly conferred posthumously; it was nice to receive it in advance.

Though not yet in the Party, I was at that time a member of the 'Society of Friends of the Soviet Union'—a barely disguised front organisation. I showed my membership card to my neighbour, a huge, jovial officer of the Red Army, who passed it on to others; it earned me several toasts, hugs, shoulder-slappings and embraces. The vodka, the Zeppelin, the consciousness of having set foot at last in the new land of promise—everything contributed to make that night as festive and memorable as only one occasion had been before : that first *Kneipe*-banquet at the quarters of 'Unitas' in Vienna. Once again I was being accepted into a friendly, fraternal community—but this time the experience of comradeship, the feeling of belonging, was not the cause, but the effect of my political evolution.

The banquet broke up in the small hours, when the celebrated white night of the Neva began to glow with the approach of day. As we made our way through the milky mist on the airfield, past the blinking torches of the sentries, to our ship, I felt that this had been the most wonderful experience of my life, one of those rare moments when intellectual conviction is in complete harmony with feeling, when your reason approves of your euphoria, and your emotion is as a lover to your thought. It was not drunkenness, but a sensation of complete fulfilment. Reflectors had been mounted near the ship bathing its floating hull in a violet, phosphorescent hue; attached to its mast, it seemed to swim through the drifting gusts of mist like a gentle prehistoric monster. We crept into our sleeping-bags, listening to the sound of the Russian songs through the fog.

The next morning, the Arctic flight proper began at last. We took off at 8 a.m. on July 26, and did not land again until July 30 at 6 p.m., after a continuous flight of four and a half days during which the sun never set for us. From the news reporter's point of view the expedition itself was an anticlimax, for all went smoothly and there was nothing spectacular to report. Arctic expeditions only get exciting when things go wrong, and the explorers, caught in the Polar blizzard, devour their last dog prior to devouring each other. To my half-conscious regret, nothing of the kind happened to us. Ensconced in the electrically-heated belly of our whale, where the temperature never sank below freezing point, the only discomfort we endured was lack of sleep; for every member of the expedition had his allotted research task, and what with photographing, and mapping unknown lands, meteorological observations, measurements of earth-magnetism, of cosmic radiation, and so on, everybody had more work on his hands than he could cope with.

As I have said before, it was this undramatic, outwardly uneventful, matter-of-fact character of the expedition which made it a significant turning point in Arctic exploration. The era of the dog-sledge and of the marathon ice marches had been succeeded by that of the flying laboratory. The last previous attempt at Polar exploration by airship—Nobile's *Italia*—had ended in disaster. Since the Zeppelin expedition, at least five hundred routine flights from Alaska over the Pole have been carried out by the 375th U.S. Weather Squadron. But these were made by high-speed aircraft which accomplish their missions, race-boat fashion, in a few hours. We, on the other hand, hovered in the Arctic air for several days, moving at a leisurely average of 60 miles per hour— slower than any self-respecting motorist—and often stopping in mid-air to complete a photographic survey, or to release small weather-balloons, with self-registering instruments, into the stratosphere. It all had a charm and a quiet excite-ment comparable to a journey on the last sailing ship in an era of speed-boats.

The first day took us across Lake Ladoga and the Karelian Republic, over Archangel and the Kola Peninsula, out into the Barents Sea. At 8 p.m. Central European time we crossed the Arctic Circle. I had to send a radio report every two hours—a task which became increasingly difficult, for we had run into fog and I could see nothing outside; as for life inside the ship, I had squeezed the last drop of local colour out of that during the preceding forty-eight hours. The following despatches may serve as samples of a reporter's predicament:

Radiogram Ullsteinhouse Berlin
18:45 centropatime stop flying along wintercoast approaching arctic circle preparing for ships arctic bap-tism which will solemnly celebrate stop its getting colder

this morning we had 74 degrees now only 50 stop weather ahead anyone's guess as bad radioreception from arctic stations whose reports partly couched in unknown cipher stop end

Radiogram Ullsteinhouse Berlin
20:00 centropatime stop sky overcast temperature still 50 stop gray mirror of Barents Sea 700 feet under us covered by mist stop this arctic twilight which wont deepen into night weighs like lead on us stop fog thickens rugged leaden puffs drift past gondola windows stop ship swims blind through this brooding mess like butterfly in a russian steambath stop bridge just reported $66\frac{1}{2}$ degrees latitude so this is it comma ham sausages biscuits and wine rolling into messroom comma earthmagnetism expert professor Ljungdahl sings gloomy swedish folksongs stop end

A reporter's dream assignment indeed! I was beginning to wish they had sent me to cover a football game. . . .

Radiogram Ullsteinhouse Berlin
midnight centropatime stop fog lifted for short while could just catch glimpse of lonely lighthouse on Cape Kanin comma where eight men hold this extreme outpost of civilisation under conditions of unimaginable hardship stop now the good earth is behind us comma are flying across open Barents Sea with course set on distant Franz Josef Land to keep our polar rendezvous with soviet icebreaker Malygin stop the local time is two a.m. time for bed but who wants bed comma arctic sea looks like infinite desert in milky shimmer of ghostly polar twilight stop strong northwesterly wind lashes gondola floating veils and rags and tatters of white mist give landscape absolutely fantastic character everybody wildly elated stop end.

The one dramatic event of the expedition was the meeting

with the *Malygin,* which took place on the afternoon of the next day. It was dramatic from a sporting point of view, for it represented the first landing of an airship on open sea, and also because we had a rather narrow escape from being crushed by drift-ice. But above all, it had a moving quality of all meetings between men in a hostile wilderness; in this case a stretch of the Arctic Ocean at eighty degrees latitude.

During the morning we had been slowly plodding north-ward against a headwind of thirty miles per hour, through more of that thin, milky Arctic fog which we had come to loathe. By noon we had passed the 75th parallel and Eckener took a calculated risk by climbing over the foggy strata into the clear upper air. Changes of altitude are risky for an airship in the Arctic because of the concomitant changes of temperature which may lead to the sudden for-mation of an ice-crust on the hull; in view of the enormous surface involved, the weight of the ice would be fatal—as the tragic example of the *Italia* proved. But our weather-balloons gave us reliable information about the temperature of the upper strata, and all went well; though we were often worried by the mirage-like tricks of the atmosphere which made one wonder whether some rugged white peak in front of the ship was an iceberg or just condensed mist. Another strange and beautiful phenomenon was our shadow, which faithfully trailed underneath us on the milky surface of the fog, suddenly developing a rainbow-coloured ring around its head, like a luminous halo.

At one point the strange milky shapes around us became so confusing that even Eckener was perturbed, suspecting that his altimeter was playing tricks on him. He came into the messroom and growled at Samoilowich: 'I wish some-body would tell me whether that thing ahead is made of cheesecloth or ice.' Luckily it proved to be cheese-cloth.

The two leaders of the expedition had, of course, devel-oped a hearty dislike for each other. Generally speaking, there was little friendly feeling on board. Partly this may have been due to the fact that German professors are never exactly a cosy lot; and as they were either Nazi, or reactionary to the marrow, they and the Russians displayed a mutual distrust veiled by stiff academic courtesy. But it may be that the well-known psychological influence of the Arctic landscape was also asserting itself, even during that short period of four days. Of all colours I found white the most depressing when exposed to it continuously and without relief.

At long last, around three in the afternoon, the fog dissolved, unveiling a leaden sea mottled with drift-ice. We had crossed the 78th parallel; for the last few hours we had been in radio contact with the *Malygin*. She was waiting for us off Hooker Island—one of several islands forming the group known as Franz Josef Land. An hour later, the drift-ice had become pack, with only a few narrow channels of water between the icefields, like black veins on the surface of grey marble. Another hour, and we sighted Cape Flora on the southernmost island of the archipelago. Then suddenly the whole landscape changed in a miraculous fashion.

Up till then, the world had consisted of various shades of greyish-white—mist, ice, twilight sky, had all looked like varieties of chalky whitewash. Now the midnight sun changed to red, and the glaciers of Cape Flora reflected this colour with the intensity of mirrors. Around the Cape there was a stretch of open sea, and the colour of the water was black. On to this black surface the red glacier poured its reflection like a burning flow of lava. It was all too spectacular to be beautiful, and the colours were too lurid; but it was certainly the most startling sight that I have seen. As we came nearer, the island, glaciers and rock constantly changed their colour, from red to violet to molten gold, and the sea from black to faint lavender. Yet this fantastic display caused no surge of elation—rather a feeling of awe and oppression; in the heavy silence which dated from the last

Ice Age, the faint hum of our engines swelled to a roaring blasphemy. The empty immensity indicated that we were trespassers, definitely not wanted here.

Snow-blindness is a physiological symptom; but there is also a psychic effect of the Arctic landscape, known as *Eiskoller*, the 'glacial tantrum'. It has been responsible for many Polar tragedies, and seems to stem from the unbearable feeling of solitude which befalls man when he is exposed to the influence of another pre-human geological age—an experience of cosmic rejection.

More islands came into sight—Prince George Land, McClintock Land—and were passed. They all had the same look of icy incandescence—debris of glacier and rock strewn upon the infinity of the Polar ocean, in a hostile, barbaric colour display. Then, with grateful relief, I saw live beings in that frozen world : a family of polar bears drifting on an ice-floe on open sea. They too seemed to disapprove of us; one of them, probably the male, rose on its hind legs, shaking its head—then the whole family took to the water and swam away. The ice-floe, now empty, drifted on. . . . Some people believe that Amundsen may have travelled on such a float from Bear Island, where his plane had crashed into the sea, the two thousand miles to Franz Josef Land. An American by name of Fiala had published this crazy hypothesis; and just before our start Eckener had received a letter from a clairvoyante, describing a certain bay off Franz Josef Land, where Amundsen's corpse was allegedly to be found. That bay did in fact exist, and corresponded fairly closely to the medium's description—maybe she had procured a good Arctic map. We searched with our telescopes every nook and cranny without discovering any human object, living or dead. The pointless search was carried out mainly as a friendly gesture towards Ellsworth, who had been Amundsen's friend. The two of them and Nobile had been the first to fly over the Pole in the *Norge,* in 1926. After that expedi-

tion, Amundsen and Nobile had quarrelled bitterly. Two
years later Nobile set out on his own, on the ill-prepared and
ill-fated *Italia* voyage, undertaken for Mussolini's greater
glory. The *Italia* crashed on the ice; Amundsen flew from
Spitzbergen to save his enemy's life and perished; but
Nobile was saved. Now Ellsworth was on board with us, and
Nobile was on board the *Malygin*—which gave this Arctic
rendezvous of the surviving members of the trio an added
intimate touch—the kind of tragic piquancy which the
public likes.

We sighted the *Malygin* shortly after 6 p.m. She was
riding at anchor in an open bay of Hooker Island, all jollied
up with flags and pennants, her whistles howling with joy.
We circled her for a while, then stopped the engines, opened
the gas escape valves and began to sink. Three hundred feet
above sea level two canvas buckets on ropes were thrown
into the water, to serve as anchors. When we got farther
down, a hose was lovered into the sea and through it water
pumped into the ship to make it heavier and thus avoid the
sacrifice of more precious gas. The pneumatic buffers on the
bottom of the nacelle touched down and the ship came to
rest on the calm sea.

We had to alight more than two hundred yards from the
icebreaker, lest sparks from its smoke-stack set us on fire. An
inflated rubber raft lay ready in the messroom, but before
we could get it out a boat from the *Malygin* had reached us
and made fast alongside the nacelle. Then general confusion
broke out and the remainder of this historic occasion is
merely a short, chaotic jumble in my memory. The door of
the nacelle was blocked by the accursed mail-bags which
Eckener had ordered to be unloaded first. So the men in the
boat, all very picturesque looking in their heavy fur coats,
had to content themselves with popping their grinning faces
in through the windows of the nacelle, clutching the outer
rails and yelling in Russian. One of them was shouting for

Ellsworth; this was Nobile. Ellsworth rushed to the window and shook hands with him, uttering the memorable words : 'Hallo, how do you do?' That was about as far as they had got when Eckener's voice rose in a roar and several members of the crew came racing from the bridge through the mess-room, to disappear aft through the little door leading into the belly of the ship. Before we knew what was happening, jets of water were spouting through the hoses, the canvas anchors came flying in, the fur-capped heads vanished from the windows and we had decamped into the air, leaving the startled occupants of the boat to crane their necks and gape after us. We had alighted on a current that was rapidly carrying the ship towards huge chunks of drift-ice; they would have crushed the fragile nacelle like matchboard on the first contact.

The whole adventurous rendezvous had lasted exactly thirteen minutes. As the bay began to veer out of sight, the *Malygin*'s whistle broke into a long, plaintive howl, like an abandoned bride.

We spent the remainder of the day making a geographical survey of Franz Josef Land.

This archipelago had been discovered in 1873, and been roughly mapped during the following years.

Our first objective was an island called Albert Edward Land. But that was easier said than done, for Albert Edward Land had the disadvantage of not existing. It could be found on every map of the Arctic, but not in the Arctic itself; we looked for it carefully but it just was not where it ought to have been, nor anywhere else.

Next objective : Harmsworth Land.

Funny as it sounds, Harmsworth Land didn't exist either. Where it ought to have been there was nothing but the black Polar sea, and the white reflection of the Zeppelin floating on it.

Heaven knows whether the explorer who put these islands

on the map (I believe it was Payer), had been the victim of a mirage, mistaking some icebergs for land, or whether they have since been swallowed by the sea, which is rather unlikely; at any rate, as of July 27, 1931, they have been officially erased from the face of our earth.

Until midnight we cruised over the scattered islands of the archipelago, re-mapping its contours. The ship with its slow motion, which could be brought to a complete standstill, was ideally suited for such work. Besides, we had some newly invented geo-photographic cameras on board; one of them a fascinating gadget that looked like an octopus with nine lenses pointing in nine different directions, and all taking simultaneous pictures which, fitted together, covered a large area of the horizon. But the real fun was to watch the phlegmatic Samoilowich feverishly mapping and re-mapping outlines in his sketch-book—like an artist trying to catch his model in an expressive movement—adding, erasing, taking a bulge off a coastline, adding a peninsula to another. Two islands vanished in the process, six new ones were discovered, a dozen others completely changed their shape on the map. But alas, none of the new islands could be annexed as a spa for Tel Aviv, and no bearded rabbi would be faced with the problem whether tufted puffins are kosher birds or not.

By midnight we had finished our job and reached Cape Fligely, northernmost point of Franz Josef Land on the fateful 82nd parallel. The weather was perfect, the pale sun spreading an even layer of frosted milk over the sea and the misty sky. Only a few hours ahead of us lay the Pole, with its icy, sphinxian smile. There was of course nothing there—but still, who knows ...

Sure enough, as soon as Cape Fligely was passed we veered round through ninety degrees, setting course due east. The insurance companies had asserted themselves over 'the reckless Heroes of the Arctic'. How right Karl Marx was after all!

The next morning at seven we were over Severnaya Zemlya—Northern Land—our second main objective. It had been discovered in 1913 by Wilkitsky, but only part of its eastern coast had been mapped; the remainder was still a blind spot on the chart.

It is a rare privilege to look at a blind spot and see it filled in by a panorama of startling beauty. I was beginning to appreciate differences in the Arctic landscape. Franz Josef Land, for all its colour display, had a forbidding, static quality about it; Northern Land seemed dynamic and alive in a rather awe-inspiring way, for its huge glaciers were capped by small puffs of mist, so that they looked like white volcanoes spouting iced lava into the air. Even among the Arctic veterans on board the consensus was that they had never seen a more grandiose view. I enjoyed it all the more, as since Cape Flora we no longer had any radio contact with the world; freed from the drudgery of filing a sensational despatch every two hours, I could at last watch and wonder and live through my eyes without verbalising what I saw.

For the next six hours we were busy filling in the details of the blind spot, hampered by occasional fog. Northern Land turned out to consist of two large islands, instead of one as had hitherto been thought; the so-called Sokalsky Bay was not a bay but a channel, dividing the land into halves. As a matter of fact, I couldn't have cared less; since our transmitter was off the air, I had become a tourist on a pleasure cruise. Not even the message reporting our meeting with the *Malygin* had gone through; I imagined with malicious pleasure how furious they would be at home, in the office. Ten thousand dollars for the news monopoly, and not a single word received during these sensational, climactic, map-shattering twenty-four hours! The chaste glaciers had taken their revenge on the merchants. We could hear on our receivers all stations as far as Japan—but we on our side, prisoners of the white silence, could not make ourselves audible anywhere.

Having finished with Northern Land, we paid a courtesy visit to Samoilowich Island which lies just off its eastern shore. 'A shabby piece of rock,' the Professor remarked with modest pride. I hope the island still bears the same name.

About noon we passed Cape Chelyuskin, the most northerly point of the Asiatic Continent, then flew in a southwesterly direction across the Taymyr Peninsula which is part of Siberia. Its gigantic forests, alternating with barren hills, have remained in my memory as a symbol of unfathomable loneliness—except for an occasional herd of reindeer in a clearing which, frightened by us, broke into panic flight. Curiously, they did not flee in a body after a leader, but stampeded from the centre outward in all directions; and as some of these herds seemed to consist of several hundred deer, their radial stampede formed the beautiful image of an exploding star. . . . There is also a mountain range in this God-forsaken wilderness called the Byrranga, which reaches up to five thousand feet, but neither its height nor contours were exactly known. So we mapped that range, and also an expanse of water called the Taymyr Lake which, if the mythical sea-monster exists, is the most likely habitation for it; and thus ended the third day.

On the fourth we 'did' Dickson Island, and then turned north again and 'did' Novaya Zemlya. The tourist expression is quite in order here, for we still had no radio contact with the outside world. On Dickson Island, which is in the Kara Sea at 73 degrees latitude, there was a notorious Russian weather station serviced by six lonely men—notorious because of the gruesome events which were said to have taken place there during the Polar night, when the men are cut off from every contact with the world. Once, so I was told by one of the Russians on board, when the relief crew arrived in spring, they found all six men dead. By some mishap their food supply had been damaged so that one by one they fell ill and died. The last survivor had buried four of his comrades and was carrying the fifth outside when he collapsed at the door of their shack; that is the position in which he was found, the body of the other man still pick-a-back on his shoulder.

The station consists of a radio mast and a couple of shacks, with nothing around for probably several hundred miles. We dropped three parcels, attached to parachutes, with fresh vegetables, newspapers and mail; then we watched the six men race and stumble to the parcels, dance, gesticulate and jump into the air, as if they had gone out of their minds. It made one shudder to think that a great event like this came to them perhaps two or three times a year. There is no woman on the island.

While we were plodding north-westward across the Kara Sea, one of our scholars introduced me to the science of Ice Observation which has its special jargon and all the niceties of other scientific pursuits. I learned the differences between inland ice, pack and drift; that glaciers were in the habit of 'calving' by giving birth to little icebergs; and that according to a theory by Professor Wiese, there was a causal connection between the changes in ice-coverage on the Barents Sea, and the variations of the water level on Lake Victoria in Central Africa. I also became acquainted with a gadget called 'Aitken's dust counter' which serves to assess the number of dust particles in a cubic centimetre of air. Since we had crossed the Arctic Circle, the counter had registered an average of 200 to 300 particles of dust, whereas in industrial towns the average for the same volume unit of air is 300,000 to 400,000.

To complete my education, I was allowed, for twenty glorious minutes, to take the helm of the ship. More precisely, the helm which governs the vertical rudder; for the Zeppelin is always steered by two men, standing side by side on the bridge, one manipulating altitude, the other direction. The helm is an electrically operated servo steering gear as used on ocean liners; it consists of two compressible handles; according to whether you press the right or left handle, the nose of the ship will veer right or left. To see the enormous whale obey a light pressure of your thumb is of course a very intoxicating feeling, and made my mental age instantly recede by ten years; if Eckener had offered me a job as helmsman of the Zeppelin I believe I would have accepted on the spot.

Novaya Zemlya—New Land—was the last of the Arctic landmasses on our programme. It is a long, narrow island which stretches in a roughly north-south direction from the 70th to the 77th meridian. About half-way it is divided in two by a waterway called Matochkin Shar. This channel is in fact a canyon, cut between two precipitous walls of mountains and glaciers, some of them over 3,000 feet high, and of a savage beauty which surpasses even that of Northern Land. Yet my memory of it is polluted by the later knowledge that Novaya Zemlya has since become another concentration camp. Its copper, lead and coal have been worked, since the middle 'thirties, exclusively by forced labour. There are stories circulating among the inmates of the other Russian labour camps about conditions in the Arctic mines during the Polar night more fantastically gruesome than the record of the gaschambers of Belsen.

While still over Novaya Zemlya, our radio transmitter established contact with a steamer off Spitzbergen, and shortly afterwards with Continental stations. The spell was broken, the adventure drawing to its close. I took a last long look at the sparkling glaciers, the icebergs floating on the tranquil sea; then said farewell to the Arctic nirvana and surrendered to my typewriter. Twenty-four hours later we landed in Berlin, welcomed by the blazing July sun, and a frenzied crowd which sang *'Deutschland, Deutschland über alles—Uber alles in der Welt.'*

XXXV. What's in a Name

I HAVE dwelt probably at tedious length on this expedition, partly because it occupies a prominent and luminous space in my memory, and partly because it became another turning point in my life.

On our return, I received the usual invitations for speeches and lectures from all over Europe. I obtained a six weeks' leave and, equipped with my log and a set of lantern slides, went on a lecture tour through Germany, Denmark, Sweden and Holland. When I got back in September, the Ullsteins offered me the job of foreign editor and assistant editor-in-chief of the *B.Z. am Mittag*—Germany's largest midday paper—in addition to retaining my post as science editor of the *Voss*. I accepted. It was an unusual combination of jobs which involved a considerable amount of work, a high salary, and much professional satisfaction. It lasted for about nine months; half-way through I formally joined the Communist Party.

The political evolution which led up to this decision I have discussed in previous chapters. The peculiar timing of the decisive step is more difficult to explain. It coincided with the most rewarding phase so far attained in my professional career. It seems logical that a person should enlist in a revolutionary movement when he is in despair, starving, frustrated, out of a job. But I was doing fine in this putrid *bourgeois*-capitalist world; in fact I had never done better. And this, precisely, explains the timing of the decision. Having proved to myself that I was perfectly capable of 'making good', I at last felt at liberty to 'turn bad'—without fear of it being suspected that the grapes of success were beyond my reach.

I have always wanted to write a sequel to La Fontaine's fable of the fox and the grapes. The poor fox is constantly mocked by his friends about the sour grapes, until he develops an inferiority complex. Night after night, while the other members of the pack divert themselves by stealing nice, fat hens, he is secretly engaged in taking climbing lessons. After several weeks of dogged effort, he finally succeeds in getting at the grapes—only to discover that they really *are* sour, as he had pretended from the beginning. But who will believe him? He does not even believe himself. The grapes become an obsession with him. He has to climb after them, panting and sweating, and eat the beastly fruit for the only purpose of proving to himself that they are sour. He gets more and more skinny on this diet and, after a nervous breakdown, dies of gastric ulcers.

The parable is meant to illustrate the tragedy of intelligent snobs and careerists. The sophisticated snob, *à la* Proust or Evelyn Waugh, knows quite well that duchesses are sour and boring, yet he has to feed on duchesses to prove to himself that they are within his reach. The same is true of successful executives, screen stars, and members of the liberal professions. After their first achievements in climbing, they find out that the coveted fruit is not at all what they imagined it to be. Yet they are under the compulsion to go on panting and straining and guzzling the acid fruit of success until the end.

After my return from the Arctic, I felt suddenly liberated from this compulsion. And as soon as I did feel free, the impulse to burn my bridges asserted itself once again. I had given up my studies and run away from home just before obtaining my degree. Now I took the plunge which sooner or later must lead to the loss of my job and make me again into a fugitive and a vagabond. It was the same recurrent pattern which had first appeared when I was a child of five, daydreaming of running away and buying a spade. It was to reappear on several later occasions. Each of these bridge-burnings gave a new turn to my life, and I have come to accept them as an inescapable part of my destiny.

These psychological considerations have no bearing on the validity or otherwise of my political evolution which I have sketched in before. The fact that a lot of psychological problem-cases turn to Marxism neither proves nor disproves the Marxist theory. But it is also true that it is not Marxism or any other ism which turns such individuals into rebels. It is an existing disposition in their character which makes them susceptible to revolutionary theories. The theory then serves as a rationalisation of their motive conflicts; but for all that, the rationalisation may still be correct. I am stressing this point once again, because of the prevailing tendency of our time to confuse the political and psychological levels of argument. The two levels interact; but logical cleanliness requires that each of them be analysed separately in its own terms of reference.

After I became convinced that Communism was the only possible solution for Europe—both as a lesser evil compared to Fascism and as a road to Utopia—I could have remained a discreet fellow-traveller of the Party, or even voted for it in elections, without going farther. It was in becoming an active member of the Party and of its intelligence apparatus, that the psychological bridge-burning tendency manifested itself.

Several years earlier, I had explained my sudden decision to throw up my studies as an enamouredness with unreason itself, as an urge to jump off the track on which my future seemed destined to run like a train with fixed stations and shunting points. The chaotic conditions created by the infla-tion years, which reduced common sense to absurdity, had served as an additional excuse and justification for embracing the course of unreason.

This time I had an even better alibi. The Weimar Republic was heading towards civil war; whether the Nazis or the Communists won in the end, in neither case could the Liberal Press survive. Thus once again the irrational impulse, which compelled me to throw away the fruit of years of labour, proved in the end eminently rational in a world of mass insanity. Had I behaved reasonably, I would in all likelihood have ended in the crematorium of Belsen. The tragic plane on which the world moves in times of upheaval has a logic different from the homely reasoning of the trivial plane. For the average citizen it is difficult if not impossible to make the transition; he suffers passively the unreason of floods, wars and revolutions, while apparently crazy adventurers, artists and other emotionally unbalanced people accustomed to living on the precarious edge where the tragic and the trivial planes intersect, jump with alacrity from one to the other. They seem to thrive on catastrophes; their folly is their guardian angel.

Though I had been steadily moving towards the Communist position for more than a year, the final decision to become an actual member of the Party was again a sudden one. I had burnt my Matriculation Book in a state of euphoria following the discussion about determinism and free will with that Dostoyevskian character, my friend Orochov. This time the event that clinched the issue was of a more profane nature. More precisely, it was a whole series of grotesque events, crowded into one December evening in 1931.

It was a Saturday; early in the afternoon I had gone to fetch my little car from a garage where it had been laid up for nearly three weeks. A leak in the oil-pipe had caused the pistons to stick, so that the cylinders had to be rebored and the whole engine done over. As I needed a car desperately for my job, I was very glad to get it back.

From the garage, I drove to a friend's flat, where a traditional poker party was held on Saturday afternoons. The friend was the late Dr. Alfred Apfel, a famous defence lawyer and a well-known social figure in Berlin. Apfel was also a Communist sympathiser who had defended in court various revolutionary leaders. A heavy and jovial Johnsonian character, he was renowned for his wit, and merciless at poker. Married to a beautiful and extravagant wife who kept a leftish intellectual salon of sorts, he had a knack of luring literary gents to the poker table where, amid much jolliness and the coining of brilliant aphorisms, he fleeced them to the hide. As I loved poker and was a hopeless duffer at it, I usually lost; but that afternoon I lost considerably more than I could afford—the equivalent of several months' salary.

Dejected, I drove to an after-dinner party of the radical bohemia, where I promptly got drunk, as under the circumstances was only to be expected. The party lasted until two or three in the morning, and I paid no attention to the fact that it had turned very cold, and that I had no anti-freeze in my radiator. When I left, the engine-block of the newly repaired car had burst, and a thick icicle was sticking out of one of the cylinder-heads—a sight to make any motorist weep, even if the car was not his own.

On seeing my dismay, a girl who had been at the party and who had always got on my nerves, offered me the hospitality of her nearby flat; this again leading to the consequences which were to be expected. I woke up in the morning with a super-hangover mixed with self-reproach, anxiety and guilt, next to a person whom I disliked, financially broke, and with a bust-up car.

Now I have always held a perhaps superstitious, but deep belief in the significance of events which come in series.

When major and minor calamities crowd together in a short span of time, they seem to express a symbolic warning, as if some mute power were tugging at your sleeve. It is then up to you to decipher the meaning of the inchoate message. If you ignore it, nothing at all will probably happen; but you may have missed a chance to remake your life, have passed a potential turning point without noticing it. It is not an altogether naïve superstition if one concedes that such series are often produced by unconscious arrangement; that the warning may have been issued by that 'he in me who is more me than myself'. Later on I discovered that André Malraux holds a similar superstition—or belief; he calls that tugging-at-the-sleeve by apparent coincidence *le langage du destin*.

In my experience, the 'language of destiny' is often couched in vulgar slang. The series of grotesque misadventures on that Saturday night looked as if they had been arranged by a crude jester; but the face of a clown, bending close against your own, can be very frightening. By the time I got back to my flat my decision was made, though I hardly felt it to be mine; it had made itself. Pacing up and down in my bedroom, I had the sudden impression that I was looking down from a height at the track along which I had been running. I saw myself with great clarity as a sham and a phoney, paying lip-service to the Revolution which was to lift the earth from its axis, and at the same time leading the existence of a *bourgeois* careerist, climbing the worm-eaten ladder of success, playing poker and landing in unsought beds. If a trifling calamity like the breakdown of my car could upset me to the extent which it did, it showed that I had become hopelessly enmeshed in the web of trivialities—and then farewell to the arrow in the blue. . . . Fortunately, the Baron had once more come to my rescue. Already I felt the jubilant exultation of being free, and of looking back, and seeing the burning bridge behind me.

As a tramp and lemonade vendor and editor of my one-man press agency in Haifa I had been my genuine self; as a brassy journalist I had not. True, the science part of it had been fun—but without something to regret, there would be no value in the sacrifice. The seven fat years were over; I was ready for the seven lean ones. I was impatient to reunite my life with my faith, as on that first occasion when I had embarked for the New Jerusalem; impatient to get back from the trivial plane to the tragic plane of existence, from journalism to the barricades of the Revolution—which, twelve months before Hitler's rise to power, appeared as a quite literal and imminent possibility. In short, my joining the ranks of the Communist Party was as much an act of faith as it was an expression of the yearning 'to become myself, and nothing else besides'.

I applied for membership on December 31, 1931; the new life was to start with the new calendar year. My application was addressed to the Central Committee of the Communist Party of Germany; it contained a short curriculum vitae, and expressed my readiness to serve the cause in whatever capacity the Party decided.

The Party decided that I could best serve the cause by remaining in my job, keeping my membership secret, and working under a cover-name for its intelligence service. At the end of our first meeting, my future boss asked me to choose a cover-name. As usual in such cases, my mind, for a moment, was a blank. Then a name occurred to me, and I said: 'Ivan Steinberg.'

'Ivan' was an obvious choice: it sounded Russian and nice. But what had made me think of 'Steinberg'—which, in German, means 'the stony mountain'? I knew no person by that name.

Or did I? As I was walking home from that crucial meeting whose shadow will accompany me all my days, I suddenly remembered my friend Har-Even, the psycho-analyst. I remembered how he had tried to persuade me to retrace my steps, to go back home and finish my abandoned studies. 'If you don't go back and graduate,' he had kept repeating, 'you will always remain a runaway and a fugitive on the earth.' Dear old Har-Even. 'Har' means mountain, and 'Even' stone; his name was a Hebraised version of Steinberg.

So the language of destiny could even be expressed in Hebrew. I thought it was a dirty trick of it to recall thus, crossword-puzzle fashion, the Biblical curse pronounced by my psychiatrist friend. On the other hand, if one was destined to remain a vagabond and a fugitive on the earth, it was just as well to know it, and to accept it.

Epilogue

AFTER I had finished this book, and it had gone dead on me, my publishers asked for an Epilogue 'to establish continuity with the forthcoming second volume'; so here it goes.

Guided by the two impulses which, as I believe, make people write autobiographies—the 'Chronicler's urge' and the *'Ecce homo* motif'—I have patiently tried to draw both figure and background, to unravel the crotchets of my mind within the larger pattern of which it is part. I am fully conscious that much of it sounds self-conscious; but where is the professional writer who, writing about himself, would not be self-conscious? What matters is that I have not consciously tried to make my self better or worse than I know it to be, as far as my knowledge of it goes.

It seems to be fitting to end this first volume at the decisive point of my joining the Communist Party—as those old-time film serials used to end with the hero suspended on a rope over a crocodile-infested river, followed by the promise : TO BE CONTINUED. But then the audience knew that the hero would not really fall among the crocodiles, whereas I did; which makes this tale, I hope, all the more improving.

Fontaine le Port, France; Island Farm, Pennsylvania January, 1951–February, 1952